THE SYMPHONY
OF SCRIPTURE

THE SYMPHONY OF SCRIPTURE

Making Sense of the Bible's Many Themes

MARK STROM

P&R PUBLISHING

P.O. BOX 817 • PHILLIPSBURG • NEW JERSEY 08865-0817

All Scripture quotations, unless otherwise indicated, are from the Holy
Bible, New International Version. Copyright © 1973, 1978, International
Bible Society. Used by permission of Zondervan.

Printed in the United States of America

Library of Congress Cataloging-in-Publication Data

Strom, Mark, 1956-
    The symphony of Scripture : making sense of the Bible's many
themes / Mark Strom.
        p. cm.
    Originally published: Downers Grove, Ill. : InterVarsity, c1990.
    Includes bibliographical references and indexes.
    ISBN 0-87552-192-4 (pbk.)
    1. Bible—Criticism, interpretation, etc. I. Title.

BS511.3 .S77 2001
220.6—dc21

                                                        2001036432

for
Susan

LIST OF DIAGRAMS

ACKNOWLEDGEMENTS

The author thanks the following for permission to quote from works for which they hold copyright.

Abingdon Press, *The Kingdom of God* by John Bright, Abingdon, 1953 © renewed 1981 John Bright; Anzea Bookhouse Ltd, *Paul's Idea of Community: The Early House Churches in their Historical Setting* by Robert Banks, Lancer, 1980, used with permission; Baker Book House, chart from *The Pauline Eschatology* by G. Vos (Princeton, Princeton University Press, 1930; reprint Grand Rapids, Baker Book House Company, 1979), p. 38; Cambridge University Press, *Paradise Now and Not Yet* by Andrew Lincoln, Cambridge University Press, 1983; InterVarsity Press, *Ezra and Nehemiah* (TOTC) by Derek Kidner, 1979; and *How to Read the Gospels and Acts* by Joel Green, 1937; Macmillan Company of Australia, *The End of Stupor? Australia toward the Third Millenium* by Ronald Conway, Sun Books, 1984; Paternoster Press, *Gospel and Kingdom* by Graeme Golsworthy, the Paternoster Press and Bookhouse Australia, 1981; *The Gospel in Revelation* by Graeme Golsworthy, the Paternoster Press and Bookhouse Australia, 1984; Scripture Union, *Bible Study Commentary: The Teaching of the Old Testament* by John Job, Scripture Union, 1984. Pub. in USA by CLO; Universities and Colleges Christian Fellowship of Evangelical Unions, *Themelios* 11:1, "The Hope of a New Age" by I. H. Marshall; and *Themelios* 7:3, Editorial by David Wenham; H. N. Wendt for Table (adapted) of the Kings of Judah and Israel from *Crossways: A Survey Course of the Narrative and Major Themes of the Old and New Testament*, 1984; The Zondervan Corporation, *Evangelism: Doing Justice and Preaching Grace* by Harvie M. Conn © 1982, The Zondervan Corporation. Used by permission.

*"The days are coming," declares the LORD,
"when I will raise up to David a righteous Branch,
a King who will reign wisely
and do what is just and right in the land.
In his days Judah will be saved
and Israel will live in safety.
This is the name by which he will be called:
The LORD Our Righteousness."*
(JEREMIAH 23:5-6)

*Jesus found a young donkey and sat
upon it, as it is written,
"Do not be afraid, O Daughter of Zion;
see, your king is coming, seated on a donkey's colt."
At first his disciples did not understand all this. Only after
Jesus was glorified did they realise that these things had
been written about him. . . .*
(JOHN 12:14-16)

*Surely you have heard about the administration of God's
grace that was given to me for you, that is, the mystery
made known to me by revelation, as I have already
written briefly . . . This mystery is that through the gospel
the Gentiles are heirs together with Israel, members
together of one body, and sharers together in the
promise in Christ Jesus.*
(EPHESIANS 3:2—3, 6)

INTRODUCTION

THE UNITY AND DIVERSITY OF THE BIBLE

Three presuppositions have shaped this book:
1 The Bible is essentially the record of God's dealings with his people over thousands of years and within several different cultures. A central story line and the constant interaction of themes such as sin, judgement and grace unify its diversity
2 Jesus Christ is the key to understanding this unity in diversity
3 The books of the Bible should be read with respect for their historical and cultural context and the literary conventions they reflect

The book works through the main events and features of the Bible story. My aim is to show how these events and insights contribute to the overall pattern, and to suggest some ways in which the coming of Jesus completes it.

At each point, I could have filled out the picture with more background details, relevant passages and a host of other things. But that was not my aim. Instead, I have concentrated on providing some key ideas about how each historical period, event, institution or book adds something and fits in to the Bible's overall story.

Occasionally, and particularly within the second half of the book, I have commented about why and how I read the Bible this way. I did this in order to suggest some ways forward for your own study. If you take the different chapters as ends in themselves, then their value will be greatly limited.

But if you push behind what I've said and probe *why* and *how* I arrived at my conclusions, then you can debate and sharpen your own approach to bible study.

HOW TO GET THE MOST OUT OF THE BOOK

Some intrepid souls will read the book straight through—but that's not what I intended. Each chapter is a self-contained section. For example, each of the Old Testament chapters begins by making links to the previous chapter, presents several key details of its topic, traces some of their subsequent development in Israel's history, and concludes with some suggestions about how the gospel completes or reshapes the topic.

That leads me to another point. When I say "gospel", I mean the life, death and resurrection of Jesus Christ—the events recorded in the four books known as the Gospels. Yet when we turn to consider *the gospel* we will proceed most often to the apostle Paul's writings rather than to Matthew, Mark, Luke or John's. The reason is simple enough. I am particularly concerned with the interpretation and significance of the person and events of Jesus. In this respect Paul stands apart. His guidelines for interpreting both the great themes of the Old Testament and the issues of everyday life in terms of the person and work of Christ are profound.

You will need to do the exercises and think about the questions to get the full benefit of each chapter. Many of the assignments show clearly how I would answer them. Rather than hide what I believe or pretend to be neutral, I preferred to give you something to interact with—I'd be delighted if your disagreement led to fruitful personal study and/or group discussion.

I have included references throughout. I suggest that you first read each chapter quickly *without* looking up the references. Use the references when you want to study the section in more detail.

My hope is that these studies will make it easier for you to pause at different sections throughout the Bible and—looking backwards and forwards—understand its place in the development of the whole story.

Mark Strom

BACKGROUND INFORMATION ABOUT ISRAEL

The following timeline (diag. 1) should help you to put the major events and features of the Old Testament into perspective. You might like to refer to it from time to time:[1]
Israel's culture and international relations were remarkable. Culturally, they were an oddity: none of the nations around them believed in one God, none banned idols and none insisted on social equality. Israel's political importance stemmed from their occupation of one of the most important thoroughfares in the ancient Near East. Whenever an Egyptian army moved north or north-east to fight the Hittites, Assyrians or Babylonians, or whenever one of the latter nations moved against Egypt, they had to pass through Israel. Thus whoever controlled Israel, or was on side with them, had obvious military and trading advantages.

AN OUTLINE OF ISRAEL'S GEOGRAPHY

Israel's geography was also remarkable. The land of Israel, sometimes called Canaan or Palestine, is a study of contrasts. Although the land only extends for approximately 600 kilometres from north to south and 120 kilometres from east to west, its height varies from 3000 metres above sea level on Mt Hermon in the far north to 600 metres below sea level on the surface of the Dead Sea in the south. Similarly, although Jericho and Jerusalem are only 30 kilometres apart,

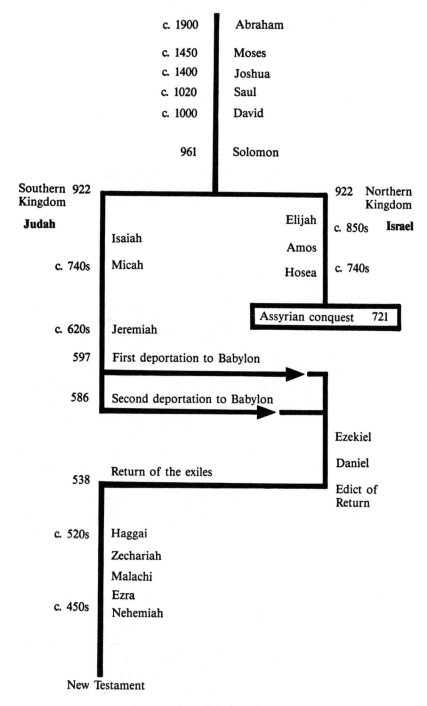

	c. 1900	Abraham		
	c. 1450	Moses		
	c. 1400	Joshua		
	c. 1020	Saul		
	c. 1000	David		
	961	Solomon		

Southern 922
Kingdom

Judah

922 Northern
Kingdom

Elijah   c. 850s   **Israel**

Isaiah

Amos

c. 740s   Micah

Hosea   c. 740s

Assyrian conquest   721

c. 620s   Jeremiah

597   First deportation to Babylon

586   Second deportation to Babylon

Ezekiel

Daniel

Return of the exiles

538

Edict of
Return

c. 520s   Haggai

Zechariah

Malachi

Ezra

c. 450s   Nehemiah

New Testament

Diagram 1: A time line of the history of the Israelites

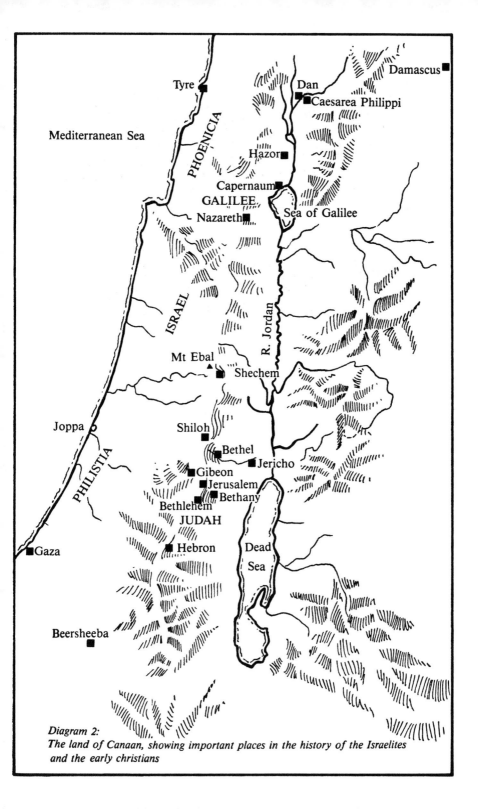

Diagram 2:
The land of Canaan, showing important places in the history of the Israelites and the early christians

it can be 20 degrees celsius in Jericho and 0 degrees celsius in Jerusalem. With such dramatic contrasts, competition has always shaped life in Israel; competition between the sea and the desert, the fertile moist lands and the harsh drylands.

You might find it helpful to refer to the map (diag. 2) as you go along. Keep in mind that the places and nations marked do not reflect any one period in Israel's history—I have included different details from across this history.[2]

Notes
1 This model is adapted from Graeme Goldsworthy (1981), *Gospel and Kingdom: A Christian Interpretation of the Old Testament*, Paternoster.
2 A good Bible atlas will not only provide maps of Israel's geography, it will also provide historical outlines and a variety of other useful information. I recommend J.J. Bimson and J.P. Kane (1985), *New Bible Atlas*, IVP-Lion/Tyndale.

1 THE BEGINNINGS: GENESIS 1—11

*Summary: **The key to this study***
The first eleven chapters of the Bible provide an account of the events and themes which shaped the entire course of its story. They introduce us to God's purpose for his creation, the devastating effects of sin¹ upon the creation and the first glimpses of God's plan to restore harmony and order to the world and people he had made.

GENESIS 1–11 AND THE IDENTITY OF THE ISRAELITES

Genesis 1-11 was *not* written at the creation of the world. Rather these chapters belong to the times of Moses and the Israelites' experience at Mt Sinai. We need to explore the significance of this.

When the Lord¹ rescued his people from Egypt, he led them through the desert to Mt Sinai. The Lord then gathered Israel around himself and explained where they had come from, who they now were and what their role would be from there on. In other words, the Lord clarified their history, identity and calling as his people (see e.g., Exodus 19:3-6). Regarding their history, the Lord explained to them that he had acted on their behalf to fulfil promises which he had made to their forefathers. Israel needed to remember and understand this heritage. So Moses told them the stories of Abraham, Isaac, Jacob and Joseph which are found in Genesis 12-50.²

Yet the Israelites' roots went back beyond Abraham and his children. In fact, the Lord's relationship with Abraham arose as a direct response to the events at the tower of Babel (see Genesis 11:1-9). And behind the Babel incident, a pattern of sin and judgement stretched back to Adam and Eve's rebellion in the garden. Thus the Israelites' roots went back to creation. Or, perhaps more precisely, the Israelites' ultimate roots lay in the Lord's plan to reverse the effects of mankind's sin and to create a new people who would live with him in a renewed earth. Ultimately, Jesus fulfilled this plan through his life, death and resurrection (and his future return). But until the time of Jesus, the Lord worked out his plan through the nation Israel.

Thus Genesis 1-11 narrated the Israelites' roots. It unfolded the story of how God's plan started. The record helped the Israelites to see that their recent experiences in Egypt and at Mt Sinai were founded on generations of promises. The Israelites' origins stretched back to a covenant as old as Abraham, and further to a promise and pattern as old as mankind's first sin.

THE PATTERN OF GENESIS 1-11

Genesis 1-11 records the story according to a recurring pattern. In these chapters there are five major cycles after the account of creation. Each cycle follows the same pattern of sin, judgement and grace. Here in brief are the five cycles:

Creation

Sin	Adam and Eve sin
Judgement	God curses them and drives them from Eden
Grace	God allows them to live (3:1-24)

Sin	Cain murders Abel
Judgement	God drives Cain away
Grace	Eve gives birth to Seth and many generations follow him (4:1-5:32)

Sin	Human wickedness increases greatly
Judgement	God sends the flood
Grace	God renews his purpose for creation through Noah (6:1–17)

Sin	Ham shames his father Noah
Judgement	God curses Ham and Canaan
Grace	Many generations follow (9:18–10:32)

Sin	Mankind opposes God at Babel
Judgement	God scatters mankind
Grace	God makes a bond with Abraham (11:1–12:3)

What are we to make of this?

It is as though the story of Genesis 3 is repeated over and over again. The pattern preserved a link between the successive sins of Cain, Noah's generation and son, the rebellion at Babel and the original fall into sin. And, on each occasion, God stepped into the chaos to ensure that his purposes were fulfilled. On a narrow scale, this purpose focused on a deliverer rising from the recurring warfare between the respective offspring of the woman and the serpent. On a wider scale, the Lord was keeping alive his purposes for the whole creation. The two greatest re-affirmations of this purpose came through God's dealings with Noah and Abraham.

The flood virtually took the earth back to its state before creation. Like the watery mass before the first day (Genesis 1:2), the earth showed no sign of life apart from the ark and its occupants. But the Lord had not finished with humanity or the earth. After the Lord dried up the land, he re-established his relationship with both the earth and Noah (9:1–17). He reestablished this relationship in precisely the same terms as in Moses' record of the events and significance of the original creation.[3]

Despite this new beginning, things looked hopeless by the time of Babel. The people tried to make a name for themselves, and to make their name great. In reply God scattered them across the earth. It looked as though the cycle had been broken so that judgement would be the final verdict. Yet the Lord dramatically restored the pattern through Abraham. Abraham would receive the very things for which the people at Babel had grasped: he would have a great name; he would father a great nation; and he would become a source of blessing throughout all the earth. In other words, the Lord would maintain his purposes for creation and humanity through Abraham and those who followed him.

THE WIDER SIGNIFICANCE OF GENESIS 1–11

As much as Genesis 1–11 gave the Israelites their starting place, it did the same for the whole story of the Bible. It began the story by introducing its central characters, themes, and hopes. Not that Genesis 1–11 actually mentions all these ideas. Rather it—in particular Genesis 1–2—provides the basic framework or model for all that follows.

Graeme Goldsworthy also focuses on Eden as the original pattern for the kingdom of God—God's people in God's place under God's rule (diag. 3).[4]

Genesis 1–11 presents creation and the origin of the struggle between the kingdom of God and the serpent's kingdom because of sin (3:15). This struggle was so intense that at Babel (11:1–9) it looked as though there was no people of God in God's place under God's rule. But in Abraham, we see the clear beginnings of a new people of God, a clear promise of land, and a very specific expression of God's rule, called a covenant (12:1–3; 15:1–6).[5]

THE THEME OF NEW CREATION

Genesis, the first book of the Bible, starts with creation and a garden. The book of Revelation (22:1–5) ends with an Eden-like scene. But this final picture goes beyond the original garden. For example, there is no longer the dangerous possibility of sin. Nor is there a sun or moon. This new garden reflects the accomplishments of the new man, Jesus.

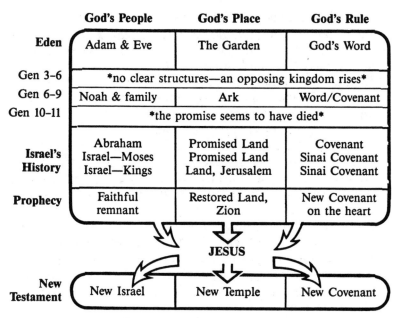

	God's People	God's Place	God's Rule
Eden	Adam & Eve	The Garden	God's Word
Gen 3–6	*no clear structures—an opposing kingdom rises*		
Gen 6–9	Noah & family	Ark	Word/Covenant
Gen 10–11	*the promise seems to have died*		
Israel's History	Abraham Israel—Moses Israel—Kings	Promised Land Promised Land Land, Jerusalem	Covenant Sinai Covenant Sinai Covenant
Prophecy	Faithful remnant	Restored Land, Zion	New Covenant on the heart
		JESUS	
New Testament	New Israel	New Temple	New Covenant

Diagram 3: A model of the story of the Bible seen through the pattern of "God's people in God's place under God's rule"

The nations receive healing and forgiveness, sin is no longer their experience or memory, and they gather intimately around God and the Lamb. We might say that this garden is as much greater than the first garden as Jesus is greater than the first Adam.

But how did we get this final vision? And why is it so appropriate?[6]

We have already noted briefly that the themes and events of Genesis 1–3 provide a pattern for the whole story of the Bible. We have also noted that this implies that the Lord regarded his plan to save his people as a part of his bigger plan to fulfil his original intentions for the whole creation. Graeme Goldsworthy's model captures the essential point of how this plan worked itself out through the pattern of Genesis 1–3. Each stage of the story drew on different aspects of the pattern to keep the original vision alive.

At first, the vision seemed hazy and incomplete, and was built mainly around analogies like Canaan as a bigger but imperfect Eden. This is certainly how the Israelites understood what God had done for them in the Exodus from Egypt. They believed that the Lord had created them as his new people and that he was leading them into a new land which would be a sanctuary like Eden had been for Adam and Eve (see e.g., Deuteronomy 8:6-9).[7]

Prophets like Isaiah and Ezekiel clarified this vision many centuries later. Their ministry was essentially twofold: they exposed the sins of Israel and the nations and pronounced doom over them; and they announced the Lord's plans to redeem his people. On the one hand, the prophets stressed that the Lord would remain faithful to the promises associated with Abraham, Mt Sinai and David and maintain the traditional features of his relationship to Israel. On the other hand, they believed that Israel had sinned to such an extent that the Lord must initiate an entirely new beginning for his people.

The prophets referred to the theme of creation and the Lord's purpose for creation as grounds for their belief. In other words, they probed beneath the Israelites' traditions to the foundation on which they stood. Thus the prophets looked to a time of total restoration and re-creation (see e.g., Isaiah 36:6-10; 41:18; 44:3-5; 65:17-25; Ezekiel 47:1-12; Joel 3:18).

THE BEGINNINGS AND THE GOSPEL

The new creation dawned in the miracles, death and resurrection of Jesus. Sin perverts life, creating unnecessary confusion, frustration and chaos; salvation restores things to what they should be. This is what we see in Jesus' ministry. Jesus showed what total restoration would be like in his miracles over sickness, death, the demonic realm and the unruly forces of nature (Luke 4:16-19). He also submitted himself to death, seen as the ultimate curse and undoing of creation. But he overcame death and became the source of new life for his people (2 Corinthians 5:17; Colossians 1:15-20; 3:1-4).

We could now look more closely at the gospel from the perspective of new creation, and we will in later studies. But for the moment we will focus our attention on how Paul used this perspective pastorally with the Colossian church in the middle of the first century A.D.

Some people at Colossae were threatening the believers' faith, security and confidence by pushing their own bizarre, but seemingly "spiritual", set of ideas and practices as the norm for every christian (Colossians 2:16-23 outlines these wrong emphases). Paul's method of dealing with error in every context was to take his friends back to the gospel. On this occasion, he used the perspective of creation to remind his readers of Christ.

Paul's appeal to creation in Colossians is brilliantly simple. Since Jesus is the creator, the restorer of creation, and the new Adam, Paul argues, then being a christian is all about returning to "normal" life. In other words, we experience the gospel's power through the Lord remaking us in his image (Colossians 3:10). The Lord wishes us to live the way he originally intended for his creatures. Therefore, we reject any thought of material things being evil (2:21-23), and we concentrate on changing in the nitty-gritty areas of life, like personal relationships (see 3:18-4:6).

Paul's emphasis on creation helped him to build a picture of the christian's life free of artificial rules and practices of troublemakers like those at Colossae. Instead of involving ourselves in weird teachings and activities in search of a "deeper walk with God", we are to discern life intelligently and sanely through focusing on who Jesus is and what he has done for us (see Colossians 2:2-8; 1:15-20).

DISCUSSION QUESTIONS

1 Do you think that the creation/evolution debate can distract christians from the central importance of the gospel? How?

2 Where do you think an emphasis on salvation as re-creation would be practically helpful today? Can you see how the idea could be pushed to unnecessary and even damaging conclusions?

EXERCISES

1 Read God's covenant with creation and Noah in Genesis 9:1-17 and make a list of its similarities to Genesis 1:1-2:24. What is the point of these parallels?
2 Prepare a bible study on Genesis 3:1-15. Include Romans 1:18-25 and Philippians 2:5-11 in your thinking. Don't try to pick up every detail of the passage. Instead, focus on:
   a) The nature of sin; and
   b) The way the gospel destroys the effects of sin.

Notes

1 I will use the title "Lord" and the general description "God" interchangeably throughout these studies. I am not trying to follow consistently the convention of using "Lord" for the Hebrew word *Yahweh* which the New International Version renders as "LORD".
2 The authorship of Genesis (and Exodus-Deuteronomy) is one of those issues which, though important, tend to distract us from wrestling with the message and structure of the book. I consider that Moses played the most formative role in the long history of tradition and writing which gave us these books. For some helpful discussions of the role of tradition in scripture, see A.R. Millard and D.J. Wiseman (1983), *Essays on the Patriarchal Narratives*, Eisenbrauns/IVP.
3 If you would like to explore the significance of the covenant with Noah, see William Dumbrell (1984), *Covenant and Creation: An Old Testament Covenantal Theology*, Lancer/Paternoster, pages 11-46.
4 The above model is a modified version of the one in Goldsworthy, *Gospel and Kingdom*, page 100.
5 We will look at the idea of a covenant in the next chapter.
6 If the Bible is new to you, you might like to take a few moments to familiarise yourself with its basic layout before reading any further. Consult the contents page of your Bible. The Old Testament records the 2000 year history of God's dealings with Israel, descendants of Abraham. The first few books (Genesis-Deuteronomy) outline the foundations of this nation. In particular, they describe Israel's miraculous escape from Egypt through Moses, and the establishing of their constitution at Mt Sinai a few weeks later. The history books (Joshua-Chronicles) outline what happened between Mt Sinai and the nation's ruin almost 900 years later. After their ruin, Israel attempted to rebuild their former glory (Ezra-Nehemiah, Haggai-Malachi). During both the decline and rebuilding, numerous writers and preachers (prophets) expressed their heart responses to God and his dealings with them (Esther-Zephaniah). And then Jesus came, and the books we call the New Testament. Matthew-Acts record Jesus' life and the first few years of the new christians. Several writers wrote Romans-Revelation to help their friends reflect on the significance of Jesus for their own lives.
7 We will return to this belief in chapter 3.

2 THE FATHERS: ABRAHAM, ISAAC AND JACOB

Summary: The key to this study
The story of Abraham and his children introduces us to the beginnings of the nation of Israel. The note of hope found in Genesis 1-11 now focuses on a specific family and a particular type of relationship between God and this family—a covenant relationship. The promises which God made to Abraham through this covenant shaped the history of Israel and the manner in which Jesus fulfilled his Father's plan for the creation.

THE PROMISES TO ABRAHAM AND GENESIS 1-11

It is possible that God's scattering of the people at Babel (Genesis 11:6-9) was more than an act of judgement. It may well have included a note of grace for, if staying together meant that mankind would rebel against God more and more, then their sins against each other would increase too. Thus the Lord's decision to scatter the people may have prevented them from working out the full extent of their sin against each other. Yet, despite that glimmer of hope, the overwhelming tone at the end of the Babel incident is despair.

Whatever the full implications may be of the scattering at Babel, the note of grace came through most powerfully in the story of Abraham. When we looked at the five cycles in Genesis 1-11 in our last study, we saw that each cycle ended on a note of grace. However, apart from the covenant with

Noah, this note of grace either remained shrouded in mystery (Genesis 3:15) or else was limited to the fact that God continued to allow people to live and populate the earth. In no case do we see a developed picture of how God would fulfil his creation purposes. But this changes with the story of Abraham.

The story of Abraham introduced the new idea of God working out his creation purposes through a *particular people*. It introduced the fundamental way in which God would deal with his people from then on. God would now establish covenants with his people.[1]

THE COVENANT WITH ABRAHAM

We normally speak of one covenant with Abraham, yet it unfolded in three stages: Genesis 12:1-3; 15:1-21; 17:1-22. We will look at each of these.

In Genesis 12:1-3, the Lord outlined the basic framework of the coming covenant, and listed its blessings. This passage makes it clear that God chose Abraham purely because of his (God's) grace.

Then in Genesis 15:1-21 the Lord actually made the covenant and sealed it by giving Abraham a vision (verses 17-18). In ancient times, two parties would sometimes seal a covenant by cutting animals in half and walking between them. The idea was brutally simple: "If you or I don't live up to our side of the covenant, may we end up like these carcasses!" In the vision, God (symbolised by the smoking pot and blazing torch) performs the ceremony alone. Abraham could not have been given a more powerful statement of God's initiative and grace, nor a stronger confirmation that God would always be faithful to his promises.

Finally, in Genesis 17:1-22 the Lord reaffirmed his covenant when it seemed an impossible hope. Abraham and Sarah were old people way beyond childbearing, yet the covenant still depended on them producing a son. The Lord confirmed that they would have a son, and then he required Abraham and his children to circumcise themselves as a sign of this eternal covenant.

Together these passages correspond with Graeme Goldsworthy's model of the kingdom of God:

God's people—Genesis 12:1; 15:5; 17:2,7–8; 18:19

In God's place—Genesis 12:1,7; 13:14–15; 15:18–21; 17:8

Under God's rule—Genesis 12:1,4; 15:6,7–18; 17:1–21

As well as becoming a distinct people, Abraham's descendants would also become a great nation (see Genesis 12:2; 13:16; 15:5; 16:10; 18:18). Moreover, their history would determine the history of the world (12:3; 17:4–6), because their God was the Lord of all the earth and he intended to channel his plans for all nations through them.

The promises to Abraham also destroyed any thought of mankind, either as individuals or nations, being able to earn a relationship with God through what they do. Abraham did not deserve this covenant relationship (Genesis 12:1; Joshua 24:2,14,15); he could not lay claim to God's love as though it were his right. The reason why God chose Abraham and not someone else remains a mystery of his love and grace. The only appropriate response for Abraham was gratitude and trust (Genesis 15:6); accordingly he became the model of faith for all who followed him (Romans 4:16–18; Galations 3:6–4:7).

THE IMPORTANCE OF THE STORY OF ABRAHAM AND HIS SONS

After the obvious importance of Genesis 12, 15 and 17, the rest of Genesis seems miserably insignificant. Apart from some revealing episodes of human nature, it all seems like so many trivial family squabbles. At least it seems that way until we put those squabbles into the context of the covenant with Abraham.

The fulfilment of God's promises to Abraham depended on a continuous line of direct descendants from him. This makes the intrigue in Abraham's family anything but trivial. Each of the dramas surrounding Abraham and Sarah, Ishmael and Isaac, Rachael and Leah, Jacob and Esau, and Joseph and his brothers, centred on a question: "Can the Lord make sure there will always be an heir, and therefore that the promises will one day lead to the expected great nation?"

Through miracles, spectacular appearances to individuals (known as theophanies), and the day to day seemingly trivial and at times even foolish decisions of ordinary people, the Lord kept his promises alive. Without these stories we wouldn't have a bridge between the covenant with Abraham and the exodus.

These stories also gave the Israelites the origins of many of the nations around them, and an explanation for the hostility they showed towards Israel.

THE IDEA OF A COVENANT

A covenant is a solemn bond between two parties. There are two kinds of covenant in the Bible: a covenant between equals (e.g., 1 Samuel 18:3-4 and Amos 1:9); and a covenant between a greater and a lesser (e.g., Joshua 9-10). The covenants between God and the Israelites were obviously of the greater-lesser kind. There were also two types of greater-lesser covenant:

God bound himself to his people—the commitment was all on his side (e.g., Genesis 15:1-21; 2 Samuel 7; see also 9:8-17)

God bound his people to obey him—there was a two-way commitment (e.g., Mt Sinai)

In both of the last two types of covenant God clearly took all the initiative—they were built on grace from first to last. So although the Israelites could break the second kind (Sinai) and did, they could never create the covenant relationship or deserve it, only respond to it. In the story of Abraham and Sarah, God's people could not guarantee that the covenant would continue (Genesis 15:1-6; 21:1-7). Similarly, the exodus had nothing to do with the Israelites' ability to get out of bondage, but everything to do with God's faithfulness to his word (Exodus 2:23-25; 20:2).

THE COVENANTS IN ISRAEL'S HISTORY

There were several major covenants in the Old Testament. In this short section, I want to provide a brief sketch of how the covenants contributed to the developing story of God's dealings with his people. We have already discussed the covenant with Abraham, so we will commence with the covenant God made with the Israelites at Mt Sinai after he brought them out of Egypt.

The archaeologists have been a great help in understanding the covenant made at Mt Sinai. We now know that covenants between a greater (called a suzerain) and a lesser (a vassal) were common before the time of the exodus. We also know that these covenants were made and recorded in a standard way:

Introduction—"this is who I am"

A short history—"this is what I have done"

Requirements—"this is what I expect from you"

Storage—"write, keep, read and obey the covenant"

Witness—"your words have been heard; take them seriously"

Blessings and curses—"your well-being depends on what you do"

This is the way the Lord chose to make his covenant with the Israelites at Mt Sinai (the covenant with Abraham also includes these features but not in the exact order). The point which the Lord was making is simple yet profound. The Lord was Israel's king (see Exodus 15:18, 1 Samuel 8:7-8), and he bound them to obey him. Moreover, they could count on him to keep his promises, including both his promises of blessing and his threats of judgement.[2]

The covenant with Abraham looked forward to a time when God would settle his people in their own land and make them into a great nation which brought blessing to the nations around it. The covenant made at Mt Sinai laid down the blueprint for what life would look like for a nation inhabiting its inheritance. Neither of these blessings occurred in Israel's life until the Lord secured the land and Jerusalem through his servant, king David.

That day came when David brought the ark of the covenant (the key symbol of the Lord's kingship) to its permanent home in Jerusalem, the place where God would establish his throne and name (2 Samuel 5-6). David then moved to build a palace (temple) for the Lord. But the Lord replied through a play on the word "house": David would not build a house for God, but God would build a "house" for David, a house for kings forever ruling over God's people. This promise to David was a covenant (2 Samuel 7:5-16; see Jeremiah 33:21).

The covenants with Abraham, at Sinai, and with David, promised a great future for Israel. Yet Israel's history brought a certain tension to these covenants. On the one hand, God promised to maintain his covenants with Abraham and David throughout all generations. On the other hand, the covenant made at Sinai contained the provision for God to cancel the covenant if Israel was unfaithful. And Israel was. Therefore, a tension arose: What should and would the Lord do to the Israelites when they consistently disobeyed him? Should he keep the promise to Abraham alive and forgive them? Should he stick to the letter of Sinai and destroy them? Could the promise to David survive in such turmoil?

The prophets felt this tension more than anyone else because they were the watchdogs of the covenant. They stood before the Israelites, and especially the kings (as Israel's representatives), and either called them back to the Lord or announced the coming of the covenant curses. So what were the prophets to say?

Each of the prophets contributed to the answer to this dilemma. But it was Isaiah (42:1-7; 49:1-26; 52:13-53:12), Jeremiah (31:31-34) and Ezekiel (36-37) who painted it clearly. Firstly, God would keep his promise to Abraham. Secondly, he would continue the hope of a messiah-king first given in the covenant with David. Thirdly, he would create a new covenant with the Israelites which would replace the Sinai covenant. And through this covenant, he would solve the problem of the Israelites' unfaithfulness by giving new heart to all his people.[3]

THE COVENANTS AND THE GOSPEL

Jesus fulfilled all the covenants of the Old Testament through his life, death and resurrection. He took on our side of the covenant, the full demands of perfect obedience to God's law, and kept it all on our behalf (see Romans 3:21-22; Galatians 4:4-5; Hebrews 10).

In fact, Jesus himself is the new covenant; that is, God made it with him (Isaiah 42:6; Luke 22:20; Romans 5:12-21). We enter this covenant through being brought under his name, through becoming *in Christ* (Galatians 3:26-4:7). After all it only takes one act of disobedience to break a covenant, so where would we be if it was made directly with us?

In several later studies, we will fill out this picture of the different covenants and of how Jesus fulfils each one. At this stage, a summary of the ways Jesus fulfilled the individual covenants will help us to appreciate the breadth of the significance of Jesus' ministry, and how closely the New Testament related it to the Old Testament:

The covenant with Abraham
Jesus is the son of Abraham (Matthew 1:1)
Jesus chose a new people for himself (John 15:16)
Jesus guarantees our inheritance (Ephesians 1:14)
Jesus brought blessing to all nations (Revelation 7:9-10)
Believing in Jesus makes us children of Abraham (Romans 4:1-25; Galatians 3:29)
Jesus "circumcised" us (Colossians 2:11-12)

The covenant made with the Israelites at Mt Sinai
Jesus kept the whole law for us (Galatians 4:4-5), including the sacrificial laws (Hebrews 10)
Jesus took the covenant curses for us (Galatians 3:13-14)
Jesus is our law, temple, priest, prophet etc.

The covenant with David
Jesus is the Son of David (Matthew 1:1)
Jesus is the Son of God (Hebrews 1)
Jesus is the eternal King (Philippians 2:6-11)

The New Covenant
Jesus body and blood are the basis of the new covenant (Luke 22:20)
Jesus gives us a new heart (2 Corinthians 3:3-18)
Jesus began the new covenant (Hebrews 8:7-13)

DISCUSSION QUESTIONS
1 It is often suggested that, in the Old Testament, people
were saved through what they did. Some even talk as though
there were different ways of becoming God's people in the
Old Testament. What do you think? (Hint: read Romans
4:1–8).
2 How would you harmonise Ephesians 2:8–10 and James
2:14–26?

EXERCISES
1 Read Genesis 12:1–3, 15:1–21 and 17:1–8 and link up the
ideas in those passages with my outline above of how Jesus
fulfilled the covenant with Abraham. Spend some time
thinking over the connections, then write one page on how
Jesus fulfils this covenant.
2 Create a bible study outline from the work you did in
exercise 1.

Notes
1 Strictly speaking, God began to deal with his people through covenants with
Noah. It is even possible that Genesis 1–2 presumes that God had a covenant with
Adam and Eve. But the Bible consistently looks back to God's covenant with
Abraham as the starting point of the Israelites' history.
2 Many people have explored the nature of the suzerain/vassal covenant formula
and its significance for understanding God's dealings with his people. See Meredith
Kline (1978), *The Structure of Biblical Authority*; Eerdmans, pages 27–38 and
William Dumbrell (1984), *Covenant and Creation: An Old Testament Covenantal
Theology*; Lancer/Paternoster, pages 94–99.
3 We will look more carefully at the Sinai covenant, the covenant with David and
the new covenant in chapters 4, 7 and 11 respectively.

3 THE EXODUS

Summary: The key to this study
Through the covenants with Abraham and his children,
God created a new people who would become the
nation of Israel and his channel for bringing blessing
to the whole creation. But these people found them-
selves in slavery in Egypt. God rescued them in the great
event which we call the exodus. This event profoundly
influenced Israel and it became one of the most
important patterns in the Bible for understanding who
Israel was, what was happening in their history and
what would happen through Jesus.

THE EXODUS AND THE PROMISES TO ABRAHAM

The story of Joseph links the exodus to the promises God made to his forefather Abraham; through Joseph we know why the Israelites found themselves in Egypt. At the same time, Israel's stay in Egypt introduced a new element of drama to the ancient promises.

A number of the promises to Abraham had come true by the time of the exodus. For example, the seed had not died out and Israel was a great nation (Genesis 12:2; 15:5; Exodus 1:7). Yet their bondage in Egypt (which Abraham knew would happen, Genesis 15:13-16) threatened the covenant in several ways. Firstly, Israel had not entered the promised land and had no immediate prospect of doing so. Secondly, Pharoah tried to destroy the promised line (Exodus

1:15–22). Thirdly, Pharoah's claim to own Israel questioned the Lord's faithfulness and credibility.

Not surprisingly, the exodus is explained in terms of the Lord's promises to Abraham. For example, he was still the God of their fathers (Exodus 3:6) and he was keeping his word (6:2–8). In fact, he was so committed to his word that he would fulfil it to the letter. He had promised to curse those who cursed Abraham and his descendants. Thus when Pharoah killed the Israelite children, the Lord responded by killing Pharoah's (Genesis 12:3; Exodus 1:22, 11:1–10).

Later, the Israelites realised that the Lord had brought them out of Egypt to lead them into the inheritance which he had promised to Abraham (Exodus 15:13–18).

THE SIGNIFICANCE OF THE EXODUS

The Lord revealed his name

The exodus began with the call of Moses. At the burning bush (Exodus 3), the Lord made it clear that he was still working to the agenda he had outlined to Abraham. Then he announced his intentions and commissioned Moses to lead his people.

Moses' encounter with God introduced something new to the people's understanding of the Lord's identity. While the Lord emphasised that he was acting out of faithfulness to his word to Abraham, he added that he was now revealing himself in a new way through the name *Yahweh*, the word which most Bibles write as the LORD (e.g., Exodus 3:13–15; 6:2–3). We need to get behind the importance of this name and event.

Following the custom of his day, Moses wanted to know the Lord's precise name because he needed to know the character of the God who stood behind the name. Only then could Moses be confident about the stability of this new stage in Israel's relationship with God, and only then would he feel confident to worship and follow the Lord. The name the Lord used to reveal himself wasn't new to Moses or his forefathers. But Moses sensed that something new was about to happen. He sensed that God was initiating some new development in his relationship to his people. So hearing the name wasn't new, but its significance was.

What did the name reveal? No one knows exactly how to translate the word, except that it is most likely a form of the verb *to be*. It could mean "I am who I am", "I will be who I will be", "I create (i.e., cause to be) what I create", or "I will bring into being what I will bring into being". Perhaps it is deliberately vague. But what is clear enough is that the Lord staked the meaning of his name, and therefore his reputation, on what he was about to do. So forever after the name suggested the idea of the Lord who brought Israel out of Egypt, the Lord who is totally different to every other god (Exodus 20:2-3).

The Lord demonstrated his universal kingship

After Moses' encounters with the Lord, Moses and Aaron confronted Pharoah through the plagues. What we have seen about the significance of the Lord giving his name to Moses clarifies the issues behind these encounters with Pharoah.

The dispute centred on Pharoah's claim of ownership over Israel. In other words, who was the God and king of Israel— Pharoah or Yahweh? Yet there was also a bigger dimension to the question: Was the Lord king over *all* the earth? These two dimensions came together in two phrases that Moses and Aaron quoted repeatedly: "let *my* people go", and "that you may know that I am the Lord" (e.g., Exodus 7:16-17). The plagues and the crossing of the Red Sea demonstrated both realities. Israel, Pharoah, Egypt, and the whole earth, learned that Yahweh was the universal king and that he ordered history around his concern for his people and his own name.

At the same time, Moses and Aaron established a pattern for the role of the prophet. They had heard the Lord reveal his true name and they had seen its significance. Moreover, they knew that the Lord called them to be his servants. In particular, their role meant calling Israel and the nations to acknowledge the true name and identity of the Lord. Thus

they were messengers of the universal king to all who disputed
his rule. Prophets like Elijah reinforced this pattern later on.
The pattern probably also influenced the prophecies against
the nations in books like Amos, Zephaniah, Jeremiah and
Ezekiel.

The Lord revealed Israel's need for forgiveness

The events on the eve of Israel's departure from Egypt
returned curse for curse on Pharoah's head (as we noted
above). At the same time they clarified the Lord's character
to Israel, and spoke about their own need.

The events celebrated in the passover demonstrated the
sort of purity which the Lord demanded through his
covenant. If the Israelites were to reflect the character of their
great king, then he had to purify them. Israel had to learn
that the covenant was about grace in the sense that they
needed the Lord's protection from their enemies. But they
also had to see the need for personal forgiveness and purity.
Without this cleansing, they too stood under the threat of
judgement (The passover account is recorded in Exodus 11:1
to 13:16).

Israel saw the exodus as an act of creation

Moses and the Israelites used themes from the promises to
Abraham and the religions and cultures of their time to
celebrate the exodus and to look forward to the coming
settlement of Canaan (Exodus 15:1-18). We need to look at
how they blended these older ideas and events with the new
thing which had happened to explain the significance of the
exodus for God's overall plan for his people.

What did Israel draw from their sources? Firstly, Israel
drew ideas from the promises to Abraham. For example, the
Lord had remained faithful to his covenant (Exodus 15:13),
Canaan was the promised inheritance (verses 13,15,17), and
the Lord would live with his people (verses 13,17). Secondly,
Israel adopted a number of ideas from the creation myths

of the ancient Near East. In particular, Israel took the ideas of their God as a warrior and king (verses 1, 3–4, 6–12), the sea as the representative of chaos and evil (verses 5, 8, 10, 12), and the enthronement of God the king in a palace/sanctuary on a great mountain (verses 17–18).[1]

So what did all this add up to?

Israel saw the exodus and its goal in Canaan as an act of new creation. We have noted before how the promises to Abraham served to develop and continue God's plan for creation. Israel took the creation overtones of the blessings to Abraham (Genesis 12:1–3) and married these to familiar images of creation and divine kingship from their own time. From this perspective, the exodus and the conquest of Canaan was one long coronation procession for Yahweh, the king of all the earth; first he passed through the walls of water (Exodus 15:8), then through walls of nations (verses 14–16) into Canaan the centre of the earth (verse 17), the garden sanctuary in which he would place the people he had just created.

This sets the covenant made on Mt Sinai into perspective. The Lord, the king of all the earth, had created Israel as his special possession. At Sinai he would bind the people to himself in a covenant as his servants. Then he would work out his will for all the earth through this new nation (see Exodus 19:3–6).

THE EXODUS AND ISRAEL'S HISTORY

It is most accurate to speak of Israel as beginning with Abraham. He was the people's forefather, and the promises he received shaped their identity and destiny. Yet the exodus shaped Israel's identity, national life and hopes more than any other event. Ask any question about Israel and the answer leads you back to the exodus:

Who is Israel? The people God brought out of Egypt

How should Israel live? As redeemed people reflecting the character of the one who brought them out of Egypt

What will God do in the future? Lead them into "Egypt" and the "desert" for judgement; then cleanse them and lead them back into a renewed promised land.

To get a better idea of how the exodus shaped Israel's life, we'll look briefly at the conquest of Canaan, Israel's later history and the message of the prophets.

The conquest of Canaan was like a second exodus

The conquest of Canaan under Joshua was the next major event in Israel's life after the exodus and the gathering at Mt Sinai. In many respects this event (more like a period of time) was part and parcel of the exodus (see Exodus 15:13-17). Yet, interestingly, the conquest happened like a second exodus:

1 Joshua was a second Moses figure (Joshua 1:1-9)
2 Israel sent out spies (Deuteronomy 1:19-25; Joshua 2)
3 The Lord went before Israel (Exodus 13:21-22; Joshua 3:1-4:18)
4 The Lord divided the waters (Exodus 14:13-31; Joshua 4:14, 23-24)
5 Israel set up a memorial (Exodus 24:3-7; Joshua 4:1-7)
6 Israel renewed their covenant vows (Deuteronomy 5-34; Joshua 24)

The exodus generation as a model of sin

A number of passages in the Old Testament which look back to the exodus stress the sins of the generation which first came out of Egypt and wandered in the desert. In particular, these texts stress the *irony* of Israel's sin by repeatedly contrasting the hard-heartedness and rebellion of Israel with the remarkable benefits God gave to his people. For example, Psalms 78 and 106 recounted the saga of Israel's disobedience in the light of the privileges the Lord gave to them.

Similarly, when the Lord appeared to Solomon after the king had built and dedicated the temple, he finished his challenge to Solomon to remain faithful with a reminder of the exodus. The Lord stressed that if the present generation acted as those in the desert had acted, then he would destroy the temple and reject the land (2 Chronicles 7:22). Likewise,

Nehemiah 9:29 viewed the sins of the exodus generation as the model of Israel's later history of rebellion. "The catalogue of sins described there shaped the situation in which, after the return from exile, the people were still unable to attain to the freedom implied by the original promises to Abraham."[2]

The prophets used the exodus as a model for the future

Part of seeing the Bible as one book is realising that the different books and authors never really pulled anything out of the hat; nothing was totally unexpected or without a precedent. The prophets are particularly good examples of this tradition of building on the past to explain the present and future. Consistently, they drew on Israel's origins and traditions and recast them as the shape of the future. They built their hope on God's ability to remember the past and to make it all happen again, even if it happened differently the second time around.

The exodus is probably the picture which the prophets used the most in this way. Sometimes, they obviously referred to the exodus. At other times, they were more subtle. Sometimes, they spoke of a complete new exodus. While at other times, they only picked up one feature like the plagues or wilderness wanderings. And, on yet other occasions, they combined strong exodus features with other major themes like a new creation, a second David, or the restoration of Zion (a shorthand phrase for identifying Jerusalem as the Lord's present and future throne).

Whichever of these they focused on, the idea of a second exodus never moved from the heart of their hopes for Israel. Here are some of their ideas:

1 A new return from Egypt (Hosea 11:1)
2 Passing through the sea (Zechariah 10:11)
3 The desert as a place of:
   a) judgement before deliverance (Jeremiah 2:5-9; Ezekiel 20:32-36)
   b) betrothal (Jeremiah 2:1-3)
   c) cleansing (Ezekiel 20:37-38)

    d) reorganisation before reentering the promised land
       (Isaiah 40:1–11; 43:14–21)
  4 A new covenant with connections to the one made at
      Mt Sinai (Jeremiah 31:31–34)

Some of the prophets before the exile (especially Isaiah
and Jeremiah) looked at the experience of exile as similar
to a return to Egypt. Therefore, they also saw the return from
exile as a new exodus (e.g., Isaiah 40:1–11). In particular,
Ezekiel, the prophet of the exile, structured most of what
he said around ideas and phrases from the original exodus.

Several of Ezekiel's most famous prophecies looked back
to the exodus as the basis for both the people's present guilt
and future hope (e.g., Ezekiel 16, 20 and 23). Ezekiel also
used the exodus saying, "that you may know that I am the
Lord" in the same way as Moses. In other words, Ezekiel
called Israel and the nations to acknowledge that Yahweh
is the universal king. Ezekiel even structured the last half
of his book (chapters 25–48) so that it reads like a new
exodus; the prophecies move from Israel in captivity, to
judgement against the nations, to a perfect symbolic picture
of all that Mt Sinai, Jerusalem and Canaan meant to Israel.[3]

THE EXODUS AND THE GOSPEL

The way the New Testament uses the exodus to show what
happened in Jesus is rich and varied. Here are some
examples.

The Gospel of Matthew presents the early events of Jesus'
life around a new exodus theme. Here are the highlights:
  1 Jesus escaped Herod's attempt to kill all the male
     children (Matthew 2:13–15). Pharoah had tried to kill
     Moses and the other Israelite children
  2 Jesus returned from Egypt to fulfil a prophecy of a new
     exodus (1:15, see Hosea 11:1)
  3 John the Baptist saw his ministry in the light of one
     of the greatest new exodus passages of the prophets
     (Matthew 3:3; see Isaiah 40:1–11)
  4 Jesus passed through the Jordan (Mathew 3:15–16)
  5 Jesus was named God's Son (Matthew 3:17). This was

the title God gave Israel before the exodus (see Exodus 4:22)

6 Jesus went into the desert to be tempted for forty days (Matthew 4:1-11). He faced similar temptations to those Israel faced in the wilderness, and he quoted the scriptures which belonged to those original temptations

7 Jesus gathered together his new people (Matthew 4:18-22) as the Lord had gathered Israel to himself

8 Jesus went up on the mountain to give the new law (Matthew 5:1-7:29). He made direct comparisons to Moses on Mt Sinai.

Jesus understood his life, death and resurrection in the light of the exodus. When Jesus fed the multitude, he explained the significance of his actions in terms of Moses and the manna in the wilderness (John 6:22-51). Jesus even spoke about his coming death as an "exodus" (Luke 9:31). He also placed his arrest and death in the context of the passover. Jesus knew the story of the original passover and what it suggested about his coming ordeal. Jesus saw himself as the new passover lamb sacrificed to protect his people. He also understood that God strictly warned the Israelites to stay inside their homes on the night of the original passover. Yet he went outdoors immediately after the passover meal to be arrested and placed under the death sentence (Matthew 26:27-30; Exodus 12:21-30).

The New Testament letters also used the exodus to expound the significance of Jesus' death and resurrection. For example, Paul had this basic picture in mind when he wrote that Jesus "has delivered us from the dominion of darkness and transferred us into the kingdom of his beloved Son, in whom we have redemption, the forgiveness of sins" (Colossians 1:13-14). The writer of Hebrews saw Jesus' death and resurrection as fulfilling Moses and Joshua's hope of establishing rest for God's people (Hebrews 2:10-4:10).

DISCUSSION QUESTIONS

1 Miriam's song (Exodus 15:1-18) seems bloodthirsty—is that the point?

2 The original passover was a fearful time for the Israelites

as the Lord passed over the cities of Egypt. Yet afterwards Israel celebrated the event. Similarly, the last supper in the upper room was a difficult time since the disciples did not know what was happening. But since then the Lord's supper has been a time to remember and celebrate Jesus' completed ministry. So what about the way we act and feel during the Lord's supper: should we sit sad, solemn and silent; or gladly share, pray and sing together?

EXERCISES

1 Read Psalm 106. In what ways does it refer to the exodus? How did that event help the writer to face his own time and situation?

2 Isaiah 40–55 is a long prophecy of restoration and renewal. Read through 42:1–17 carefully, noting wherever Isaiah seemed to have in mind the events of creation and the exodus. How did he use these exodus memories to get across his own message?

Notes

1 I am not suggesting that Israel accepted these myths as historically true. Rather they took familiar concepts and reworked them to express truths about the Lord, the one and only true God. For a fuller discussion on Old Testament contacts with other religions and cultures, see Peter Craigie (1983), *Ugarit and the Old Testament*, Eerdmans, pages 67–90.

2 John Job (1984), *The Teaching of the Old Testament*, Scripture Union/Christian Literature Crusade, page 34. I have written the last two paragraphs around his discussion of the same passages.

3 This picture of Ezekiel and the exodus is filled out in chapter 11.

4 ISRAEL AT MT SINAI

Summary: The key to this study
The Lord had established the covenants with Abraham
and his children, and had rescued them from slavery
in Egypt. Why? Because he had chosen to love the new
nation of Israel and to use this people to accomplish
his plans for the whole earth. At Mt Sinai, the Lord
explained to his new people who they were and what
he required from them. But the Israelites repeatedly
misunderstood the purpose of these requirements.
When Jesus came to earth he reshaped these laws,
pointed to their true meaning, and did what no one had
ever done before or since—he obeyed the laws perfectly.

THE COVENANT ESTABLISHED, BROKEN, RENEWED AND
EXPANDED

Israel's Sinai experience is a major key to the story of the
whole Bible. If we misunderstand what happened there we
will misunderstand both the later history of the Israelites
and the significance of the gospel. In this chapter and the
next we will outline the key points of the drama which
unfolds from Exodus 19 to the end of Deuteronomy. The
sections in brackets will be discussed in chapter 5:

Exodus 19-24	The covenant established
(Exodus 25-31	Worship as true covenant response)
Exodus 32-34	The covenant broken and renewed
(Exodus 35-40	The ongoing problem of sin within the covenant relationship)

(Leviticus	A fuller description of covenant worship and the problem of sin in the covenant)
Numbers	A story of covenant failure and grace
Deuteronomy	The covenant renewed and expanded

Exodus 19-24: The covenant established

Israel's identity and calling Exodus 19:3-6 provided a foundation for everything which happened and was said at Mt Sinai. There are several expressions in verses 5-6 which relate to all that followed at Mt Sinai:
1 "The whole earth is mine" (verse 5d)
2 "My own (or treasured) possession" (verse 5c)
3 "Out of all the nations" (verse 5b)
4 "A kingdom of priests" (verse 6a)
5 "A holy nation" (verse 6a)
The first expression ("the whole earth is mine") recalled what we saw in our last study about the Lord's kingship over all the earth. Moses' call at the burning bush, the conflict with Pharoah, and the ancient hymn in Exodus 15:1-18 each stressed this truth. Whereas the promises to Abraham presupposed that God ruled over all the earth (e.g., Genesis 12:1-3), the exodus established the meaning of God's name and demonstrated its truth for all the world to see (Exodus 19:4).

The second and third expressions ("my own possession... out of all the nations") built naturally on the first. In other words, the Lord can choose whoever he wants because he is king of the whole earth. This particular expression, "own possession", occurred in the suzerain-vassal covenants of the same period as a description of the vassal.[1] Although all the nations were under his authority, only the Israelites would enjoy this covenant relationship with the Lord. And given the strong tones of grace and mercy running throughout the entire exodus-Sinai drama, there is a deliberate note of intimacy in this unique privilege: Israel is Yahweh's treasured possession.

The fourth and fifth expressions belong together: They

parallel each other and together fill out the picture implied by "my own possession...out of all the nations". "Kingdom of priests" (or "priestly royalty") perhaps alluded to God's promise to bless the earth (Genesis 12:3b) since it was the priests' role to bless people, while "holy nation" stresses Israel's separation from the rest of the nations.

The last expression ("holy nation") also implied something else about Israel's role as priests in the world. Normally the Lord called the Israelites a "people" and everyone else a "nation". In fact, the Lord usually only called the Israelites a "nation" when he was handing down judgement (i.e., when they had become a nation just like everyone else—e.g., Zephaniah 2:1). But here he used the word favourably. Why?

It seems that the Lord was saying that the Israelites would become the model society for the world. They would demonstrate life under God's kingship as a picture of what God intended for all the earth. This is the key to Israel's priestly role. There is no missionary idea here. But like a priest's role in an ancient society, "Israel serves her world by maintaining her distance and her difference from it", by being the "vehicle through whom the divine will is displayed".[2]

The role of law in Israel's life The covenant at Mt Sinai gave a political form to the theological idea of Israel as God's people. In other words, the covenant now meant that Israel was to express their relationship with the Lord through structures which were appropriate to their identity and role *as a nation*. This is the key concept behind the giving of the law in Exodus 21-23. The Lord gave the Israelites the law to guide them as they sought to express their status and calling as a "kingdom of priests" and a "holy nation".

The Lord never made keeping the law a condition of his love. The Lord did not give the law to establish his relationship with the Israelites. He gave it because he already had a relationship with his people and he wanted them now to learn how to express this relationship faithfully. So God's commitment to his people would never change. Nevertheless, their enjoyment of this relationship would depend on how well they translated their faith into action. This was the function of the law.

Sadly, we often think of law as a set of rules which establishes a relationship. God's law, however, provided direction for living in relationship with him. The law was the Lord saying, "I love you, I have redeemed you and I will bless you; so live as loved, redeemed and blessed people". Likewise, Israel could respond, "We love you and appreciate that you brought us out of bondage. We know that you are our great king, and we will serve you from our hearts".

After giving the Israelites their guidelines for life in the covenant (Exodus 20:1-17), the Lord explained how these would apply in specific social contexts (chapters 21-23). Finally, the Lord confirmed the covenant through a sacrifice (Exodus 24). The meaning of sprinkling the people with blood (verse 8) isn't altogether clear. If Leviticus 8 provides any clues, then it seems that God was ceremonially enforcing what he had previously said in Exodus 19:5-6. In other words, the Lord dramatically symbolised that Israel was now separate from all the other nations and consecrated for his special use. The meal (24:9-11) was another common way of sealing and celebrating a covenant. It occurs in a similar way later on in the Bible's story (Isaiah 25:6-8; Revelation 19:7-9).

Exodus 32-34: the covenant broken and renewed

It is easy to gloss over the importance of these chapters. On the surface they read like this:

1 The Israelites broke the covenant through their worship of the golden calf (Exodus 32:1-6)
2 The Lord threatened to end the covenant (32:7-10)
3 Moses interceded for Israel (32:11-35)
4 The Lord maintained his covenant with the Israelites and reaffirmed this through new stone tablets, his appearance over Mt Sinai and his promise to go with them into Canaan (33:1-34:28)

But the fourth step wasn't as simple as it sounds above. The Lord didn't renew the covenant with Israel in the sense that everything would continue as it was before. Instead, he transferred many of the privileges and blessings of the covenant from the people as a whole to Moses their leader. In particular, Moses would now be the only one to experience personally the Lord's glory and presence.

We read the first hints of this transfer in Exodus 32:10. There the Lord said he would destroy the Israelites and fulfil his promises to Abraham through Moses alone. Moses interceded for the Israelites. In particular, he built his case on God's love and faithfulness shown in his promises and the exodus. How could the Lord reject the people he had delivered from Egypt? Moses also reminded the Lord that the nations would hear of his rejection of Israel and dishonour the name which he had established and proclaimed through the exodus (verses 11-14). The Lord relented, but the matter was obviously unresolved (verses 34-35).

Then, in Exodus 33:1-17, God spelt out a new shape for his relationship to Israel. The Lord would be only with Moses. God would allow the Isralites to enter their inheritance, but God would not go with them. Moses and the people both knew that spelt disaster for all the Israelites except Moses. They knew the nation was doomed if the Lord did not go with them. So once again Moses interceded, and again the Lord relented. But in doing so, the Lord made it clear that he only did so because of Moses.

Two things emerged in the following account of the Lord's appearance to Moses and his continuing presence with him (Exodus 33:18-34:35):

Moses enjoyed a unique experience of God's presence which Israel couldn't survive, let alone enjoy

Moses "wore" this glory whenever he acted "officially" on behalf of the Lord, probably both as a sign of his authority and a continual reminder of what the Israelites as a whole had forfeited.

So in the overall history of Israel, Moses stood both as a picture of what the Israelites should have experienced under the covenant and as a rebuke for their sin. From here on Israel's experience was veiled (2 Corinthians 3:7-18).

Numbers: a story of covenant failure and grace

It is all too easy to skip from Israel's first encounter at Mt Sinai, straight to the conquest of Canaan. But there are forty years between the two events. Numbers fills in this important gap in the Bible's story.

At the end of Exodus everything seemed ready for God to add the finishing touches to his promises to Abraham. But Israel's murmurings (Exodus 15:22–17:7) and rebellion (32:1–6) had shown their true colours. Numbers is a tapestry woven from these two threads—Israel's stubbornness and God's determination to finish what he started. Despite their sin, the Lord still lived with his people and a new generation emerged to enter the promised land.

Deuteronomy: the covenant renewed and expanded

After wandering in the desert for forty years watching the generation who made the golden calf die out, the Israelites came to the plains of Moab, east of the Jordan. There the Lord renewed his covenant to remind this new generation of their history, their relationship to him, and their responsibilities to each other.

Deuteronomy 30 records God's final summary of the covenant and his plea with Israel to understand and keep it properly. The passage emphasises four themes: love, land, blessing and cursing, and life. This is how the Lord summarised their relationship: the Lord's love was the foundation of Israel's relationship with him, and love was the only appropriate response. The love to which God called his people went beyond a mere emotion. Such love was an active commitment consciously built on God's choice of them and expressed through obedience. If they expressed their faith in this way, then God would stay with them and protect them in the land. He would give them the blessing of life.

So God placed a choice before them—life or death. Ironically, Israel's history shows that they chose death.

THE COVENANT AT MT SINAI AND ISRAEL'S HISTORY

At Sinai the Lord rephrased his promises to Abraham in terms which were appropriate to Israel's new existence as a nation. From there on, God meant his people to express his character in every aspect of their cultural, national and international life. The ideas of God's kingship, covenant and separateness were meant to challenge and direct every aspect of their experience. Here are a few examples of how this would work in practice.

The way they treated each other had to reflect the way the Lord had treated them. They were to love and respect each other, and protect each other's inheritance (Deuteronomy 15:12-18). This is the framework within which the special officers of Israel were intended to operate: e.g., the priests, sacrificial system and tabernacle/temple provided a way to focus Israel's service to the Lord as worship; the king was to ensure that Israel's lifestyle followed the prescribed pattern (17:18-20); and the prophets were Israel's "covenant watchdogs", monitoring the people's (and particularly the king's) faithfulness and calling them to turn their hearts to the Lord.

But Israel *wasn't* faithful to the covenant. Time and again the people either abandoned the Lord altogether, or blended their faith with the gods of other nations, or made the covenant a matter of purely external rituals (Amos 4:4-5). Frequently, the kings clashed with the prophets because the kings carried a special responsibility to uphold the covenant, yet they almost always failed to do so.

Two hundred and fifty years after Solomon a common verdict began to rise among the prophets: Israel and Judah would lose their covenant status and inheritance. Their only hope was for Yahweh to act again as he had done in the past. By the time of the exile in Babylon, this would mean a whole new covenant (Jeremiah 31:31-34).[3]

SINAI AND THE GOSPEL

The most obvious connection between the covenant made at Mt Sinai and the gospel is that Jesus kept the law for us.

But, as important as that is, we've come to see that Sinai revealed far more than the law. Sinai was about Israel's identity, role and framework for life. It revealed Israel's unique relationship with the king of all the earth (Exodus 19:3–6). This gives an even better understanding of how Jesus fulfilled the covenant at Mt Sinai.

In Isaiah 40–55, there are four great prophecies known as the Servant Songs (Isaiah 42:1–4; 49:1–6; 50:4–9; 52:13–53:12). In these songs, sometimes the servant seems to be an individual, and sometimes a renewed Israel. But ultimately the two possibilities came together through Jesus acting on behalf of the people he was creating. Jesus was the servant, the true Israelite, the only Jew who ever kept the covenant with perfect faithfulness (Matthew 3:17), the only son of Abraham who loved the Lord with all his heart, all his mind and all his strength (Deuteronomy 6:5). Jesus lived as the true people of God—Jesus was Israel (see how the vine(yard) image is transferred from the Israelites in Isaiah 5:1–7 to Jesus in John 15:1–7).

Because Jesus took Israel's identity, and kept the covenant, he passed on the full extent of the Lord's Sinai promises to his new people. That's why Paul used Moses' experience (as described in Exodus 32–34) as a picture of our own experience (see 2 Corinthians 3:7–18). Israel could not survive the Lord's glory or even understand their relationship properly (verses 7, 14–15). Even Moses' experience of God's presence and glory was limited, although dramatic (verses 7, 10–11, 13). Now we see and experience God's glory through the Spirit as a permanent life-changing blessing (verses 17–18).

Now, Peter and John tell us, the calling and status of the Israelites as recorded in Exodus 19:3–6 belongs to us (1 Peter 2:4–10; Revelation 1:6).

DISCUSSION QUESTIONS

1 Israel often lifted the law out of its true context. They saw it as a way of gaining a relationship with God, rather than as a means of expressing that relationship. Is this still a problem for us today? Do we structure our lifestyles as individuals and churches around laws instead of the gospel?

2 Paul said that the Israelites did not experience God as intimately as Moses did. He also said that *all* christians experience something even better. Do we often act as though some christians are closer to God, or have more of his Spirit? How does the gospel show us that this is wrong and foolish?

EXERCISES

1 Try tracing the theme of the Holy Spirit in the Bible from these passages:
Numbers 11:26-29; Judges 11:29; Psalm 51:11; Isaiah 11:1-3; 44:1-5; Joel 2:28-32; Ezekiel 36:26-27; Luke 3:22; 4:1; Matthew 12:28; John 7:37-39; Acts 2:14-41; Galatians 3:14; Ephesians 1:13-14; Romans 8:14-27

Don't try to make it an exhaustive study. Instead, pick out the key ideas and pay particular attention to the way the theme developed throughout the Bible's story. We are after an *overview* of the story from one perspective.

2 There are numerous parallels between Israel's experience at Mt Sinai and what happened on the day of Pentecost (Acts 2). Explore these connections. The list below outlines the events associated with Sinai, the Old Testament reference, and a New Testament reference which may suggest parallels between the events of Sinai, the gospel and Pentecost:

a) God gathered his people around himself at Sinai after he led them out of bondage (Exodus 15:1-18; John 7:39; Philippians 2:6-11)

b) Israel celebrated the Feast of Weeks to show that God owned the entire harvest (Leviticus 23:9-16; Numbers 28:26; Acts 2:1; Ephesians 1:13-14; Romans 8:23)

c) The Lord appeared to the Israelites in spectacular circumstances (Exodus 19:16-19; Acts 2:1-4)

d) The Lord commissioned the Israelites (Exodus 19:5-6; Acts 1:1-11)

e) The Lord promised to be with the Israelites (Exodus 33:1-6, 14-17; John 14:12-23; Acts 1:1-11)

f) The gathering at Sinai partly fulfilled God's promises to Abraham (Genesis 12:1-3; Exodus 19:6; Acts 2:17, 39; 1 Peter 2:9-10)

So what happened at Pentecost?

Notes

1 We discussed these covenants in chapter 2.

2 William Dumbrell (1984), *Covenant and Creation: An Old Testament Covenantal Theology*; Lancer/Paternoster, page 90.

3 We will return to the new covenant in chapter 11.

5 PRIEST, SACRIFICE AND TEMPLE

Summary: The key to this study

The story of redemption is about God using his authority as the universal king to renew and fulfil his original purposes for creation. A special part of those purposes was an intimate relationship with his people. These themes help us to see the importance of Israel's worship which began at Mt Sinai. The sacrificial system presupposed that the Israelite worshipper was already enjoying a covenant relationship with the Lord. The elaborate cult of priests, sacrifices and temple was meant to enrich Israel's intimate relationship with the Lord. But the Israelites perverted the sacrificial system by regarding it as a mechanical process—a guaranteed formula for forgiveness. The book of Hebrews carefully shows how Jesus' ministry as priest, sacrifice and temple has replaced the Old Testament cult. Jesus has provided perfect and free salvation for his people forever through his life, death and reign in heaven.

WORSHIP, COVENANT, CREATION AND KINGSHIP

God intended the Israelites to represent his character as their king, to carry out his purposes and to express their love and faith in him through their national institutions and experiences. The relationship still rested on God's love and choice of them, but God's words at Mt Sinai introduced a highly organised, political way of expressing this relationship.

This perspective also helps us to understand the elaborate details of the tabernacle, priests and sacrifices (these three things are known as Israel's *cult*).[1] Through this ritual, the Israelites recognised the Lord as their king and they demonstrated how he had made them holy to himself by choosing them (Exodus 19:5-6). In other words, worship was their way of acknowledging the true nature of the covenant; that the Lord was king, and that they were his subjects (see Psalm 95:1-7).

Sin made the cult critically important. As we noted in our last study about the golden calf incident (Exodus 32-34), sin amounted to a breach of the covenant. The hardness of the Israelites' hearts always threatened their covenant relationship. But the cult provided a way for them to continue to live under grace—within the covenant—through the experience of forgiveness.

THE SIGNIFICANCE OF THE SACRIFICIAL SYSTEM

Did Old Testament sacrifices really work? Did Israelites really experience forgiveness? Most of us probably answer "No" to the first and "Yes" to the second question since Hebrews 10:4 says, "it is impossible for the blood of bulls and goats to take away sins". After all, the prophets condemned Israel's sacrifices (e.g., Isaiah 1:11-14). But if we take Leviticus 4:35 seriously, we'll have to answer "Yes" to both questions: "In this way the priest will make atonement for him for the sin he has committed, and he will be forgiven".

Perhaps we can get a better understanding of forgiveness and sacrifice in the Old Testament through some more questions and answers:

1 Did the sacrifices offer automatic forgiveness? No!
2 Did the sacrifices depend on the broader covenant relationship, including both God's love for the Israelites and their need to have faith? Yes!
3 So is God's grace the ultimate reason why he accepted the sacrifice? Yes!
4 Did the Old Testament sacrifices point towards Jesus' sacrifice? Yes!

5 Were the Old Testament sacrifices obsolete by the time of Hebrews 10:4? Yes!

6 So the Old Testament sacrifices were a real but temporary means of forgiveness? Yes!

The whole sacrificial system presupposed that the worshipper was in relationship with the Lord. As Bill Dumbrell puts it, "The aim of the covenant sacrifices was to preserve what had been established, not to initiate new relationships".[2] There was nothing abstract about sin. It was a personal offence against the Lord (and usually another Israelite). This is why the worshipper had to lay his or her hands on the animal—he had to identify with its fate (Leviticus 1:4). Even the order of sacrifices conveyed the idea that the covenant relationship was the key to the system. The following order comes from Leviticus 9:

1 The priest offered a sin offering for his own sin (Leviticus 9:8–11)

2 He offered a burnt offering for himself (verses 12–14)

3 He offered a sin offering for the people (verse 15)

4 He offered a burnt offering for them (verse 16–17)

5 He offered a fellowship offering for all of them (verses 18–21)

6 He blessed the people (verses 22–23)

There is a clear rationale behind all this. The priest represented God's people. In order for him to represent them, he first had to deal with his own sin. Moreover, the sacrifices symbolised a movement from forgiveness to rededication to fellowship: God's anger was turned away from the worshipper (the sin or guilt offering); then they were rededicated or consecrated to the Lord (the [whole] burnt offering); and, finally, the Lord and his people renewed fellowship (the fellowship or peace offering).

We can restate all this in explicitly covenantal terms. The covenant breach was healed, then the worshipper's covenant identity was restated and the Lord and his people renewed their happy relationship. Last of all, the Lord's representative, the priest, would officially declare that the covenant would continue (Numbers 6:22–27).

THE SIGNIFICANCE OF THE PRIESTS

The Old Testament priests were both like and unlike everybody else. They had to be like them in order to stand in for the people as their mediators. They had to be unlike the people in that they had to maintain a rigorous purity. The priests were responsible for offering sacrifices, praying for the people, teaching them, and even occasionally finding out God's will for them.[3]

We now understand a little more about what the priests did. We also need to see what they represented. When we understand their significance in this way, we will see how they fit into the bigger picture of what was happening at Mt Sinai. We can gain this insight by concentrating on the themes of creation, covenant and kingship, and by focusing on the instructions for Aaron (and his sons) in Exodus 28:

1 The priest was a *real* man (Exodus 28:1; also Hebrews 5:1–2). Leviticus 21 went further and required that he must be a perfect man—without defect, including being able to have children

2 The priest was a *righteous* man (Exodus 28:2, 36; also Psalm 132). His identity came from the Lord and he enjoyed a right relationship with him

3 The priest was a *glorified* man (Exodus 28:2, 40; also Psalm 8). His shame was covered, and he wore the Lord's righteousness. More than that, he was magnificent to look at

4 The priest was a *representative* man (Exodus 28:9; also Leviticus 4:3). Whenever the priest entered the Lord's sanctuary, he represented every man, woman and child in Israel. Whatever he did, they did through him

So what did all this add up to?

The priests represented what the covenant relationship was all about. They represented life under the Lord their king. They symbolised God's creation purpose for his people. Their qualifications, garments and activities symbolised the blessings and glory which God had intended for all humanity, and which he would restore to his people. In other words, they symbolised mankind restored to their created glory—blessed, fruitful and whole. They visualised the hope of man enjoying a right and intimate relationship with their Lord.[4]

THE SIGNIFICANCE OF THE TABERNACLE

Moses began to meet with the Lord at the edge of the camp in a tent known as the tent of meeting sometime after the Israelites crossed the Red Sea (see Exodus 33:7-11). The Lord would come to Moses there in the cloud and the pillar of fire, the symbols of his king-warrior glory and presence (see 13:21-22; 14:19-25). Even after the great scene of God's appearance on Mt Sinai, the Lord still localised his glory in this tent. So when the tent of meeting became the tabernacle (though some argue that the two stayed separate), the tabernacle was bound to inherit the significance of the Lord's appearances at the sea and the mountain.

This move from the edge of the camp to its centre also highlighted a great truth about the Lord and about Israel's new identity (in Exodus 19:5-6 terms). The Lord lived among his people as their king. (For the basic structure of the camp and tabernacle see diag. 4.)

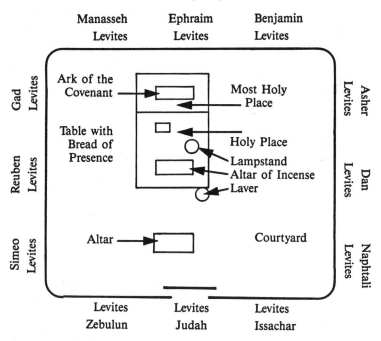

Diagram 4: The floorplan of the tabernacle and the positions in which the Israelite tribes camped around it (not to scale)

The tabernacle inherited and symbolised the traditions of the Lord's glory in battle and his status as their king. Since his glory now dwelt in the tabernacle, and since he lived there as king, then it was a natural progression to see the tabernacle as the Lord's throneroom and the ark of the covenant as his throne (Numbers 7:89; 1 Samuel 4:4; Psalm 99:1). That's why the ark was the centre piece of the tabernacle. It is also why the Israelite camp was arranged equally around it (this arrangement is recorded in Numbers 2). Israel's camp site illustrated their theology: the king of the covenant stood at the centre of Israel's life and his presence established their purity, unity and equality.

THE CULT IN ISRAEL'S HISTORY

Israel repeatedly lost sight of the true role of the cult and perverted its practice. For example, Israel and Judah mingled their cult with pagan worship, including cultic prostitution (Amos 2:7); the priests were corrupt (Micah 3:11); and they set up idols (Micah 1:7; 5:13). The prophets unanimously attacked this abuse. Several passages are particularly pointed in their denunciations of the cult and we will pause to consider a few of these briefly (the main passages are Amos 4:4; 5:5, 21-26; 8:14; Hosea 6:6; Isaiah 1:11-18; Micah 6:6-8; Jeremiah 7:21-23).

In Amos 5:25, the prophet denounced Israel's false trust in the cult. In the words of Geerhardus Vos, "God hates, despises their feasts, because these things cannot avail to stem the judgement, as the foolish people believe they are able to do. Not sacrifices but retribution will satisfy Jehovah: 'Let judgement roll down as waters, and righteousness as a mighty stream.' "[5] Similarly, Isaiah would never have condemned prayer and visiting the temple in Jerusalem. Yet when the people of Judah did these things unrepentantly, with hands and hearts putrified by injustice, extortion and oppression, the prophet demanded that they end their hypocrisy (Isaiah 1:10-17).

The different prophetic condemnations originated in a central insight: the cult should serve the covenant relationship, rather than be used to establish or prop it up. It was a simple matter of first things first. Thus Hosea (6:6) and Micah (6:6-9) called for mercy rather than sacrifice because God always required repentance and faith as the necessary prerequisites to sacrifice. On an even larger scale, Jeremiah reminded the people that God rescued their ancestors from Egypt *before* the cult existed and that this act of salvation and God's gracious choice of the Israelites were the foundation for the cult's existence and meaning (Jeremiah 7:21-23).

Despite the severity of their indictments of the cult, the prophets did not oppose it—only Israel and Judah's abuse of it. It was not prayer they opposed, but the heartless prayers of the unjust and cruel; not sacrifice, but sacrifices by people who refused to acknowledge the Lord; not temple worship, but the foolish and historically ignorant idea that such things could create a relationship with God.

But if we leave our survey here we risk painting a misleading image of the cult in Israel's experience. The perversion of the cult was only one side of the story. Some Israelites experienced the joy and liberation which it brought to those who worshipped in faith (see Psalms 51 and 116). Such worshippers knew and trusted the bigger picture of the covenant; they confidently sought mercy and forgiveness on the basis of God's character, his covenant promises and the history of his gracious dealings with them as individuals and as a nation.

It was this kind of faith which led Isaiah and Zechariah to a vision of sacrifice and forgiveness on a higher level. Having experienced the marvel of forgiveness for himself (Isaiah 6:1-7), Isaiah saw a time when the servant of Israel would bear the guilt of his people as a sacrifice for their sins (52:13-53:12). Zechariah, too, glimpsed a sacrificial act of another order (Zechariah 3:1-10). Although this passage does not elaborate on how God would atone for his people, the prophet saw God cleanse the high priest, Joshua, in a most extraordinary way and then heard the word of the Lord: "The Lord Almighty. . .will remove the sin of this land in a single day" (verse 9b).

We who live on this side of Jesus' death miss the drama

of this promise. But consider its impact on people who experienced the on-going spectacle of ritual preparations and thousands upon thousands of sacrifices! No wonder the early Jewish christians were so fascinated and intimidated by the cult of the Jerusalem temple, and that they found it so hard to accept that perfect freedom and forgiveness came through the death of a carpenter's son.[6]

THE CULT AND THE GOSPEL

The Jewish christians who first read Hebrews lived in the shadow of the elaborate rituals of the Jerusalem temple. Like us, they longed for a settled conscience—the calm confidence of forgiveness and acceptance. But to what should they appeal for a clean conscience?

The answer many of them gave, or were tempted to give, was the cult. After all, *it* was tangible and immediate and shrouded by an aura of grandeur and holiness. In contrast to this, Jesus did something once (which most of them probably never saw), was now invisible and left no impressive symbolism or ritual for his followers. The cult seemed so strong, while Jesus seemed so weak.

But the epistle overturned this perception. Slowly, the writer moved through Israel's history and traditions showing that they were both temporary and incomplete. Against this backdrop, the writer presented Jesus as the great High Priest who went beyond the holy place of Jerusalem into the throneroom/temple of heaven bearing the blood of his own self-sacrifice; now he has made his people perfect for all time and he has earnt the right to sit at his Father's side and mediate for these people (see especially Hebrews 7-10).

Can you see the difficulty of those early Jewish christians? They underestimated Jesus. The cult drew them with its impressive priesthood and rituals; they could see it, participate in it, and run back to it whenever their consciences accused them. But the writer saw through this.

Firstly, the cult brought no true freedom (Hebrews 10:1-3). Secondly, it couldn't because its time had passed (10:4-18; 7:17-22). Thirdly, God had completed his great act of redemption in his Son—the great turning point of history had come. The only stage left now in God's programme for history was the day of judgement, and this was the only prospect for those who rejected the finished sacrifice of Jesus in favour of the Jewish cult (6:4–6; 9:24–28).

THE LAW, THE GOSPEL AND LIVING AS A CHRISTIAN

Summary: *The key to this section*
God's people of every age face the temptation to live by law rather than by grace—to base their hope and conduct on rules, confessions and traditions rather than on the finished work of Jesus Christ. Our faith matures as we discern how this temptation faces us and refuse to give in to it.

It is all too easy for us to peer condescendingly down the corridors of history at the foolishness and blindness of our forebears. But the same issue has plagued God's people of all ages: Will they live by grace or by the law? In other words, will they base their perceptions of themselves and others, their treatment of others, their hope for a clean conscience and a right standing with God on the finished work of Christ, or on rules, confessions, constitutions and traditions?

Consider how the New Testament writers tackled the many forms of this struggle between grace and law. Consider, too, our own folly today.

New Testament pictures of the tension between law and grace

Hebrews: Jesus, not the cult The readers of Hebrews underestimated Jesus. They could not come to grips with the startling reality that the death of Jesus offered full and final forgiveness, both now and forever. They could not grasp that Jesus had opened up perfect access to the Father. They could not grasp that they needed no other priest.

This scenario is remarkably contemporary. Many christians today directly associate their forgiveness with the

Lord's Supper, the prayers of the clergy, prayers of rededication, the laying on of hands, a feeling of elation in various experiences, and sundry other things. The theology of other teachers is not so crude; they understand that forgiveness comes through the work of Christ, yet they perpetuate traditions and perceptions which condemn people to anxiety and a self-destructive conscience. Browbeaten by the teaching and traditions of their leaders, such folk carry the load of their guilt from one service or experience to the next. If only they could hear the message of Hebrews, they might be set free.

Galatians: Jesus, not law   The book of Hebrews responded to one side of the temptation to turn back from Christ to Jewish tradition—the temptation to regard the temple cult as more effective than Jesus's death and resurrection. But more often (especially for those Jews and their non-Jewish converts who lived away from Jerusalem and could not witness or participate in the temple activities) the temptation took the form of insisting that for a right standing with God it was still necessary to keep the Old Testament law.

The Jewish followers of Jesus always struggled to appreciate the radical shift from Judaism to the gospel of Jesus Christ; though that is not to say that many of them outrightly rejected the uniqueness of Christ—they didn't. The main threat was more subtle and therefore more dangerous.

The problem was that Jewish christians added the law to Christ. They insisted that a person could only be right with God (justified) if they submitted to the Old Testament law and made it their guide for life. In particular, they insisted on circumcision, special religious observances (like the sabbath) and on various ceremonial and food laws (Acts 15:1–5; Colossians 2:16–17, 20–21; Galatians 2:11–16, 3:1–5, 4:8–11).

Paul, the ex-Pharisee, the man who had once zealously guarded and upheld the law, exposed the folly of the Judaisers. He had experienced the pinnacle of Jewish religious success and honour, yet he had rejected its privileges for the sake of knowing Christ (see Philippians 3:1–9). In Galatians, Paul tore apart the false hopes of salvation through the law and presented clearly the mystery of Jesus fulfilling the law on our behalf (Galatians 3:10-14; 26-4:7). The Father, Paul argued, had pronounced that his people are right with him (righteous) because of the life, death and resurrection of his Son. Moreover, we have entered this privilege through faith not works, and no act in heaven, earth or hell can cancel our inheritance.

But once again we must ask what this means to *us*. Like the Judaisers, few of us would ever deny the centrality of Christ's work. Yet when it comes to our definitions and expectations of a christian lifestyle we defer frequently to laws as the true test of the genuineness of someone's faith (including our own). Instead of circumcision, we might read tithing; instead of food laws, perhaps we read abstinence from tobacco and alcohol; instead of Jewish religious prestige, we judge a person's theology, personal experiences or position within the church; instead of facing conflict with a spirit of integrity and compassion, we use rules to sidestep our relationships and the responsibility of love.

Colossians: Jesus, not mysteries and experiences   No book of the Bible has influenced my own pilgrimage to comprehend the wonder of the gospel as profoundly as Paul's letter to the Colossians.

Some years ago I belonged to a particularly zealous group of christians; we desired to follow the Lord closely and for him to use us significantly. But despite our motives, aspects of the group's teaching led us into murky waters. The "unusual" increasingly fascinated us; e.g., the demonic and angelic, tales of unusual experiences and visions, and a deep commitment to immediate messages from God as being more authoritative than the Bible. Like other similar groups, we articulated *obedience* as the foundation of any true "deeper" or "higher" christian life. These emphases combined to reinforce other beliefs such as that a christian may lose salvation and/or become demon-possessed through disobedience.

This teaching produced mixed results. While some were mature enough to take what was good and leave the rest, most of the group experienced the increasing influence of three false attitudes: (1) a sense of one-up-manship—of having "arrived" as a christian—and a corresponding disdain or pity for others who did not share our ideas; (2) a thirst for new revelation which took us further and further away from the gospel onto the thin ice of curious commands about each individual's future and rules concerning abstinence from various people, activities and substances; and (3) a (sometimes fearful) conviction that a christian is protected from evil and mishap only through praying certain prayers regularly and maintaining a high level of obedience.

Colossians was a personal letter for me. The names and details had changed, but the troublemakers at Colossae entertained the same superior and fearful commitment to revelations, visions, mysteries and laws as I had (see Colossians 2:16–23). Paul's answer for his friends (and for me and mine) was startlingly simple; the mystery of all mysteries was the (now public) good news of what Jesus did on the cross for his people (1:28–2:5). Moreover, Paul made it plain that maturity came through understanding this gospel better and better, not through laws, experiences and revelations. According to Paul, such rules always sound spiritual but they are totally ineffective and even anti-gospel since they lead people away from the central importance of Christ (2:19, 22–23).

2 Corinthians: Jesus, not strength and success   Christians throughout the western world have accepted the spirit of industrialization. We believe, along with the rest of our society, that bigger is better, that progress is the highest good for mankind, and that power, riches and success must always be preferred and honoured over frailty and vulnerability. Sadly, we reflect this spirit in our christian sub-cultures in such things as our commitment to denominations, church buildings, tyrannical and bureaucratic leadership, high profile and pressured evangelistic systems, and tertiary education as a prerequisite for ministry.

Some christians go so far as to identify unbelief and disobedience as the root cause of all poverty, ill-health and failure. Consequently, many christians who are sick, poor, depressed, emotionally disturbed or lacking in social skills feel that they must be "second rate", "ineffectual" and "unspiritual" because of their difficulties.

The apostle Paul faced similar attitudes. His critics most likely gloated over his failures and sufferings and tried to undermine the value of his ministry to his friends (2 Corinthians 2:17–3:2; 5:12; 10:1–11:15). Like Job's acquaintances, these "false apostles" probably believed that weakness and suffering were the evidence of inferiority and even unbelief. Paul's response went to the heart; he rejoiced in his weakness for he chose to follow the way of Jesus, which is the way of the cross, and its apparent weakness and foolishness (4:7–18; 6:3–10; 11:21b–29; 12:7–10).

Live by grace, not by law

Why say all this? Why pause for so long to consider these misunderstandings and the various New Testament responses?

I do so because I am convinced that the same mistakes pervade the christian scene today. Like the people of God through all ages we misunderstand and distort the relationship between what *God has done* (the "is") and what *we should do* (the "ought"). In particular, this departure from the gospel shows its ugly head in the politics of church and denominational structures and activities, and the search for a deeper, higher, more powerful and prosperous christian life.

We should know better. The gospel shows us that God accepts us fully on the basis of Christ's finished work. If we understand this, then we begin to experience a wonderfully realistic and other-centred way of life: We worship Christ through our jobs, recreation and relationships, our good times and bad, and we use our new freedom to serve others. Life is no longer about our egos, security or comfort. Free in the knowledge of what Christ has done, we fear no longer to confess our weaknesses, nor do we grasp at glib answers to remove the paradox and sting of failure and suffering.

But is this what we see? In my experience, church life often seems more concerned with political lobbying (and even deception) than with service. Whether the agenda is theological or financial, church members divide into factions and manoeuvre for a win rather than seek to prefer and serve each other and speak and act with integrity. All of this is anti-gospel, for God calls us to treat each other as he has treated us in Christ (see Philippians 2:1–11).

And what of the search for a greater christian experience? Such teachings always confuse the "ought" with the "is". For example, rather than remind people of the security we have in Christ's death and resurrection, some teach that victory is only ours through certain prayers and acts; rather than point to our full forgiveness in Christ, some urge us to calm our troubled consciences by embracing esoteric ideas about repentance and obedience; rather than remind us that the Spirit of God has come fully to point us to Christ, some teach that we must fill our minds with "deeper truths" and experience more of him. In every case, we pervert the gospel; we turn what Christ did for us into something that we must do for ourselves.

Finally, one group of people trouble me deeply—those who struggle under the rules and expectations of their christian friends and leaders. Among these are the divorced, the depressed, the socially inept, the unsuccessful, the sick, the average, the separated, the poorly educated, the lonely, the doubting, the intimidated, the hurt and the shy. They cannot appreciate their acceptance and worth in Christ because of the stumbling blocks placed before them by preachers of rules and experiences who spiritually rob them and leave them under the burden of false guilt.

What a difference the gospel would make.

DISCUSSION QUESTIONS
1 Read Colossians 2:16–17. Christians shouldn't observe a weekly sabbath. Do you agree? Why?
2 Many churches do not consistently reflect the fact that all christians are priests. Do you agree? Why or why not? Does your church need to change in this area?

EXERCISES

1 In the section above on "The Cult in Israel's History" I focused on sacrifice. But that is only part of the story about the cult. Use the following passages to build a picture of how the idea of priest developed:
   1 Samuel 2:12-36; 16:1-3; 2 Chronicles 5:2-14; Isaiah 28:7-13; Hosea 4:4-11; Jeremiah 2:26-27; Isaiah 61:4-7; Ezekiel 44:10-28; Zechariah 3:1-10; 6:9-13; Mark 10:45; Hebrews 2:10-18; 4:14-5:10; 8:1-6; 10:19-23; 1 Peter 2:4-7.
2 Earlier in this chapter there is a list of four priestly characteristics from Exodus 28. Use these as headings to build a picture of Jesus' priesthood. Finally, compare your findings with the picture of Jesus' priesthood in Hebrews 5-7.

Notes

1 The word *cult* is used this way throughout this chapter. The word does not suggest anything negative in this context. It is merely a convenient shorthand for "priests, sacrifices and temple".

2 William Dumbrell (1984), *Covenant and Creation: An Old Testament Covenantal Theology*, Lancer/Paternoster, page 111.

3 The priests at times would discern the Lord's mind through the Urim and Thummim (Exodus 28:30). Although many people have speculated about the meaning of these stones, no one really knows what they were or how they worked.

4 Much of the above material on priests comes from a series of bible studies on the biblical theme of priesthood by John Davies, principal of the Presbyterian Theological Hall, Sydney, Australia.

5 Geerhardus Vos (1975), *Biblical Theology: Old and New Testament*, Banner of Truth, page 268.

6 Although the cult also includes priest and temple, this section focuses on sacrifice. Regarding the history of Israel's priests and the development of the idea of priesthood you should work through these issues for yourself in the exercises at the end of this chapter. The temple theme will be developed in chapters 8 and 21. See also William Dumbrell (1985), *The End of the Beginning*, Lancer/Baker, chapter 2.

6 THE CONQUEST OF CANAAN

Summary: *The key to this study*
The covenant with Abraham, the Exodus from Egypt, and the gathering at Mt Sinai had called the nation of Israel into existence and established its place within God's plan to undo the effects of sin on creation. Like Eden of old, the land of Canaan symbolised the paradise and sanctuary in which God desired to live with his people. But as Joshua and the following generations discovered, entering and securing the inheritance was not easy both because of the ferocity of the Canaanites and the hard-heartedness of the Israelites. The prophets and Psalm writers linked these early experiences to the story of the Exodus and developed ways of using the theme of warfare to describe the Lord and the salvation he brought to his people. The New Testament writers followed this tradition at times to explain the gospel.

JOSHUA CONQUERS THE LAND OF CANAAN

After the Israelites received the law for the second time—this time on the plains of Moab (recorded in Deuteronomy)—they were ready to take possession of their inheritance. And as we noted in our study of the exodus, Joshua led the people through the Jordan and into Canaan like a second Moses performing a second exodus.

The Book of Joshua divides into three sections:

1 Securing the land (chapters 1-12)
2 Dividing up the land between the tribes (13-22)
3 A theological reflection on how far they'd come and how far there was to go (22-24)

After the whole nation crossed the Jordan, Joshua set up camp at Gilgal, circumcised the men, and celebrated a passover (Joshua 5). Gilgal was Joshua's headquarters throughout his campaigns into southern Canaan (9:6; 10:6-9). Jericho was Joshua's first battle and victory (chapter 6). After this he secured the central highlands then swung north as far as Mt Ebal (near Shechem) where he renewed the covenant (8:30-35). At this time Joshua was tricked into an alliance with the Gibeonites (9:1-27) which in the end led to a miraculous victory over five Canaanite kingdoms (10:1-39). With most of the centre and south secure, Joshua turned north again and defeated another Canaanite coalition at Hazor, the largest Canaanite city of the day (11:10-11).

Despite the almost flawless run of victories (see however Joshua 7), the Israelites never occupied every part of the land (13:1-7). They avoided a large area of Philistine territory in the south-western coastal area and parts of the far north. And because they didn't finish the task, in many places they resigned themselves to having the Canaanites as neighbours (Judges 1:27-36). Yet the overall verdict was that the old promises were now fulfilled (21:43-44).

When Joshua had completed his battles, he initiated a covenant renewal ceremony to call the Israelites back to their heritage. This is recorded in Joshua 24. After recounting the history of the Lord's faithfulness to them (verses 1-13), Joshua drove home the challenge of the covenant. The Israelites were to serve the Lord their covenant king with a whole heart (verses 14-21, especially verses 14-15, and 23). Joshua concluded by reminding the people that both the stone which he had set up and their own words would serve as of witnesses against them. Thus the Lord used this ceremony to remind the Israelites to maintain their distinctive identity and calling as he had spelt these out at Mt Sinai (Exodus 19:5-6).

A side point. The archaeologists' might be able to throw some light on the Israelites' relationship to the cultures around them at this time. At a place called Tell El Amarna they found some correspondence between Egypt and Palestine which dates to around the time of Joshua and the Judges. The letters occasionally refer to a group of people called the Hapitu (Habiru). These people seem to have been a bunch of troublesome nomads and social misfits: not so much a distinct ethnic group, as a social class remarkable (for that time) for their practice of equality. The word Hapitu is most likely related to the Hebrew word *Hebrew* and, although no one is sure of the connection, it is interesting to note this as a possible foreigners' view of the Israelites.

THE PERIOD OF THE JUDGES

Sadly, the Israelites never changed: their forefathers Abraham, Isaac and Jacob frequently had taken matters into their own hands; those who had come out of Egypt complained in the desert and rebelled at Mt Sinai; and the generation which entered Canaan never followed consistently the Lord's requirements during the conquest (e.g., the sin of Achan in Joshua 7). The Israelites as a nation, it seems, repeatedly forgot their covenant promises and obligations.

The book of Judges recounts Israel's history as a series of cycles based around the theme of forgetting the covenant. Here are the stages of each cycle:

1 Israel forgets the covenant and sins
2 A foreign power dominates them
3 Israel is called to repent and cries to the Lord
4 The Lord appoints a deliverer hero (judge)
5 The deliverer fights and defeats their enemies
6 And the cycle starts all over again!

The judges probably focused their ministries on their own localities. Yet because Palestine is so small, any threat to their own locality could quickly become a national threat. For this reason it is most likely that the judges exercised authority throughout all the tribes.

The clearest picture of a judge's ministry is in Samuel. If we can take him as a pattern for the other judges, then they seem to have been men and women chosen and appointed by the Lord "to maintain Israel's covenant relationship by calling for inward reformation and by providing for defence against external aggression".[1] Like the kings later on (1 Samuel 8:7), the judges' ministry mirrored God's rule over the Israelites (Judges 11:27).[2]

The book of Judges finishes on a notoriously depressing note: "in those days Israel had no king; everyone did as he saw fit" (Judges 21:25). Yet this verse might well contain a glimmer of hope. The most obvious things about the verse are its negative assessment of Israel and an implied longing for a king. But the verse begs a deeper appreciation. On the one hand, Israel is in a mess; yet, on the other hand, the Lord has preserved his covenant through the judges. The Israelites still existed at this point in time, even though the Lord could have applied the curses of Deuteronomy 28 to the fullest extent by wiping them out.

Once again, the nature of the Israelites' covenant relationship to the Lord is clear. Their identity and existence never depended on their political constitutions or their ability to maintain the covenant. They could depend only on the faithfulness of their covenant partner.

THE CONQUEST IN ISRAEL'S HISTORY: THE THEME OF HOLY WAR

In our study of Genesis 1–11 we saw that the struggle between God's kingdom and Satan's is as old as the Fall, and that Genesis 3:15 had anticipated an on-going struggle before a final defeat of the serpent (Revelation 20:2). So the Fall set the scene for the conflict which followed; man challenging God's right to rule the earth for the sake of his people.

The exodus obviously fitted this pattern, and the Israelites came to understand the plagues, the crossing of the sea, and their entrance into Canaan as warfare (Exodus 14:13–14; 15:1–18). God's revelation at Sinai built on this and a "theology of holy war" emerged. The four essential features of this theology were that God was the real Warrior, the battle was his, Israel's enemies were God's enemies, and Israel only had to be faithful to the Lord in order to win (Deuteronomy 20).

This theology included such features as the war leader enquiring from the Lord as to whether or not he or she should attack (e.g., 1 Samuel 23:1-6; Joshua 5:13-6:5). Israel also had to keep the army pure (Deuteronomy 23:13-15), and offer praise to the Lord after the battle (Judges 5). Working from that basis, Joshua and Gideon successfully raided and occupied a considerable amount of the promised land.

But the most important element in this theology was that the Lord was the warrior who led the Israelites into the battle and who won the victory for them. This was the key to their escape from Egypt (Exodus 15:1-18), Joshua's victory at Jericho (Joshua 6) and Gideon's success over the Midianites with his band of three hundred (Judges 7). In fact, their survival was determined by how well they remembered and trusted that God was their true king and warrior.

As Israel grew as a nation and the kings increasingly controlled its domestic and international policies, the prophets' role as watchdogs of the covenant frequently focused on the theme of warfare. Sometimes this meant guiding and encouraging the king to battle (1 Kings 20:13-30); sometimes it meant announcing his doom (22:1-38).

In chapter three, we noted how the Israelites used ideas from the cultures around them when describing the Lord as their warrior and the exodus as a creation-warfare drama (Exodus 15:1-11). The Psalm writers did something similar when they applied to the Lord the image of the divine warrior riding on a cloud-chariot (e.g., Psalms 18:9-15; 104:1-4; also see Deuteronomy 33:26). This is the Lord mighty in battle; his saints cry to him for help and he answers by doing battle against their enemies.

The same image was used by the prophets (e.g., Isaiah 19:1; Nahum 1:2-3). It also forms part of the picture behind Daniel 7:13-14. In his vision, Daniel saw the Son of Man ascending to the Ancient of Days after conquering the beasts (verses 11-12). Related to this idea of the Lord as the cloud-riding warrior, but much broader in scope, is the idea of the day of the Lord (e.g., Ezekiel 30:3; Isaiah 13:6,9; Joel 1:15; 2:1,11; Amos 5:8-20; Zephaniah 1:7-8, and many other references). As one writer put it, "the Day of Yahweh encompasses a pure event of war".[3]

In their writings, the prophets used warfare to explain and describe God's judgement on Israel and Judah. When God fought against his people it was like "reverse holy war" (e.g., Amos 9:1–10). The prophets also used the theme to dramatise their oracles of judgement on the nations (e.g., Isaiah 13). Finally, the prophets used the theme to describe a final battle in which the Lord would deliver his people from all their enemies (e.g., Isaiah 24–27; Ezekiel 38–39).

THE CONQUEST AND THE GOSPEL

The New Testament writers used the holy war theme and other connected ideas like the day of the Lord to explain the gospel. For example, Jesus' birth was anticipated in language similar to the war talk of the Old Testament prophets (Luke 1:51–52; 68–71). Paul spoke about the "sudden destruction" waiting for unbelievers on the day of the Lord (1 Thessalonians 5:1–10). Peter also drew on the related Old Testament idea of the Lord destroying the earth (see Isaiah 24:1–13) when he spoke of this day (2 Peter 3:10). In other places, New Testament writers transformed this day into the day of Christ (1 Corinthians 1:8, 2 Corinthians 1:14; Philippians 1:6,10; 2:16).

The Psalmists' picture of the Lord as the cloud-riding warrior also came over into the New Testament via Daniel 7:13–14. In each of the so-called "little apocalypses" (Matthew 24; Mark 13; Luke 21) Jesus used Daniel 7:13 and the cloud imagery to describe his imminent coming in glory to the Father. In each case, the same Old Testament association of war and destruction of the earth is present (e.g., Joel 3:14–16). This association might also explain why Caiaphas was so shocked by Jesus' reply (Matthew 26:63b–65).

All of this provided a framework for understanding the gospel in terms of warfare. So for Paul, Jesus triumphed over death (1 Corinthians 15:54–57) and the principalities and powers (Colossians 2:15) through his death and resurrection. Finally, John saw Jesus establishing his rule over history for his people, we see Jesus as the Great Warrior—the Lamb who is also the Lion (Revelation 1:13–18; 5:1,13; 12:7–11; 19:11–21).

DISCUSSION QUESTIONS

1 Many preachers like to use Old Testament stories to illustrate morals and general principles for the christian life. In particular, some point to the conquest as a pattern for our christian experience. In other words, they see our experience from conversion until we die as being like the Israelites crossing the Jordan and experiencing numerous battles and setbacks on the journey towards Jerusalem. What do you see as the pros and cons of such an approach?

2 The Bible often talks about God in war-like and judgement language. How do you reconcile this picture of God with the fact of his love and mercy?

EXERCISES

1 Read Joel 2:1-11. How did this prophet use the warfare theme?

2 Outline a bible study on Ephesians 6:10-18. Be sure to draw on some of the broader biblical ideas about warfare and the gospel.

Notes
1 William Dumbrell (1984), *Covenant and Creation*, Lancer/Paternoster, page 130.
2 We will return to the theme of kingship in chapter 7.
3 We will return to the theme of the day of the Lord in chapter 10.

7 THE KINGS

Summary: The key to this study
The period of the kings in Israel's history included both
its highest and lowest moments. Although the Israelites'
request for a king stemmed from perverse motives and
their first king proved a failure, the reigns of David and
Solomon marked the golden era of the nation. After
this time, the nation split into Judah (the southern
kingdom) and Israel (the northern kingdom) and the
majority of their respective kings led them into a
downward spiral of injustice, idolatry and foolish
international alliances. Despite the attempts of the
prophets to halt this decline, both nations were
destroyed and carried into exile. Yet the prophets never
gave up their hopes of a renewed people led by an ideal
king and, though none of them lived to see his day,
the king, Jesus, did come.

THE KINGS, THE CONQUEST AND THE SINAI COVENANT

The first book of Samuel records a time of great political
and social change in Israel's history. At this time the Lord
altered the shape of Israel's life by allowing them to have
a king. The covenant framework which he had given at Mt
Sinai had included the role of the king (see Deuteronomy
17:14–20), but until the time of Samuel, Israel had not had
one.

In our studies on Israel's experiences at Mt Sinai and in

the conquest of the land of Canaan, we noted how the ideas of worship and God's kingship belonged together in the covenant. We saw how that worship involved acknowledging the Lord as the true king, and how the ark of the covenant, the symbol of his rule, occupied a prominent place in this worship. This same relationship of ideas lies behind the central point of the books of Samuel.

The two books begin with the corrupt worship at Shiloh (1 Samuel 2:12–36) and the "exile" of the ark (4:1–22), and move towards the return of the ark (2 Samuel 6:1–23) and the purchase of the temple site (24:18–25; see 1 Chronicles 21:18–22:1). In other words, the books move from Israel rejecting the Lord's kingship, and seemingly being rejected, to the Lord re-establishing his kingship and preparing the way for the temple, the most elaborate of all symbols of his rule. Thus the central issue of the books concerns how well human kingship will fit within the framework of God's kingship.

Within this overall structure of 1 and 2 Samuel, the books direct our attention to three major features which shaped the rise of human kingship within Israel:

1 The way Israel requested a king
2 God gave the prophets the role of holding the kings in check
3 The drama surrounding the houses of Saul and David led to God establishing a pattern for kingship in general, and David's dynasty in particular.

Israel's request for a king

There was nothing wrong with the idea of Israel having a king. In fact, as we noted above, Deuteronomy 17:14 had anticipated the request. Yet there were considerable problems with the circumstances and motives behind Israel's plea.

The Israelites' plea for a king at this time was symptomatic of their desire to be "like the other nations" (1 Samuel 8:5). Therefore, the request amounted to a denial of their separate identity and calling as a "holy nation" who were different from the peoples around them (e.g., Exodus 19:3–6)—they were dangerously close to rejecting their distinct identity and role as the Lord had given it to them at Mt Sinai. The nations around them all had kings. In particular, Israel knew the Canaanite city-state model of a dynastic, centralised, absolute style of kingship. If they welcomed such a model, then they would leave themselves open to the danger of directing Israel's internal and external affairs through political alliances.

Most importantly, their request amounted to a denial of the Lord's kingship (1 Samuel 8:7). This seems to be underlined by the fact that Israel made their request when they thought the Lord was far away in Philistia, where the ark was exiled.

So did Israel's two denials mean that kingship could never work? Did they mean that kingship could never find a legitimate place and expression within the covenant? Surprisingly, the books of Samuel did not draw this conclusion. Instead, they set out to provide a framework for how kingship should operate. There are two ways the books do this.

Firstly, the Lord had not rejected Israel. This is the point of 1 Samuel 12 which reads like a covenant renewal ceremony:

1 Samuel defended his own ministry (verses 1-5). The Lord had appointed him and Israel was wrong for regarding his ministry as inadequate

2 Samuel outlined Israel's history (verses 6-11). He emphasised the Lord's faithfulness during the period of the judges when Israel had no king

3 Samuel repeated that Israel's request for a king was foolish (verses 12-13, 19)

4 Samuel announced a sign from God to verify his counsel (verses 16-18)

5 Samuel called Israel to serve the Lord loyally in their new situation of having a king (verses 20-21, 25)

6 Samuel reassured Israel that the Lord had not rejected them (verses 22-24)

Samuel spoke as the messenger of the Lord of the covenant, both exposing the Israelites' sin and reassuring them that the covenant would continue. The Lord was saying that he would not allow this sad new state of affairs to destroy the covenant which he had made at Mt Sinai. In other words, the Lord was renewing his promises with Israel even though the way they had requested a king had torn at the heart of the covenant.

Secondly, the books developed a picture of ideal kingship —kingship that upheld the Sinai covenant—through the drama of Saul and David's families. In this drama, Saul represented the folly of Israel's request, while David represented God's choice and pattern for kingship. For example, when David fought Goliath, he demonstrated that he would uphold the covenant made at Mt Sinai when Saul would not do so. The particular issue involved the theology of holy war. The Sinai covenant stressed that the Lord was Israel's warrior and that Israel only needed to trust him to secure victory. David fought in the strength of this knowledge, while Saul (like the rest of Israel) cowered in his tent.[2]

The prophets received the role of checking the kings

Samuel's speech in 1 Samuel 12 followed a pattern set by Moses (Deuteronomy 32–33) and Joshua (Joshua 24). On all three occasions, the Lord secured Israel as they stood on the threshold of another political advance.

But there was always the threat that kingship might in practice undermine the covenant relationship (Deuteronomy 17:16–20; 1 Samuel 8:11–18; 12:13–15, 25). Against this backdrop, prophecy emerged as Israel's and particularly the king's "covenant conscience". The prophets carried the word of the Lord to the king and nation, calling them back to the faith and framework of the covenant of Mt Sinai.

Of course, prophecy existed prior to this time (we noticed this in Moses' and Aaron's role in the exodus). And, like kingship, the covenant at Mt Sinai had anticipated how prophecy would function (Deuteronomy 8 and 13). But when kingship actually commenced in Israel, it split the roles of king and prophet. In particular, the clashes between Saul and Samuel over policy matters (e.g., 1 Samuel 13:7b–14) seemed to establish the respective responsibilities of the two roles. For the rest of Israel's history, the king was expected to lead in war and general political decisions, while the prophet shaped the final spiritual direction of the nation. However, the prophets frequently had to act as conscience for the kings and call them back to their moral responsibilities. Elijah's confrontation with Ahab is the classic example. There was no doubt about their comparative authority; the prophet would always have the last word.

The pattern of ideal Israelite kingship

Kingship had to find its place within the framework of the covenant. This was especially the case given the models of kingship in the surrounding nations. In other words, how would the Israelites see *their* kings? Would they expect them to be like the kings of the other nations? Or would they welcome a new style of kingship—a kingship based on God's rule over them and which upheld the covenant?

Rather than wait for Israel's answers to such hypothetical questions, the Lord initiated the new pattern of kingship through Samuel. Four distinct features of ideal Israelite kingship emerged through the appointing of Saul and David:

1 God chose the king through his prophet (1 Samuel 9:16; 16:12)

2 The prophet anointed the king to confer authority on him to fulfil his role. The anointing spoke first of all to the Israelites, but it probably also spoke to the king, since he was anointed privately (1 Samuel 10:1; 16:2). It did not establish a relationship with the Lord. Rather, it confirmed his election

3 The king received the Spirit to empower him for his role. When God anointed a new king, the Spirit left the old king (1 Samuel 10:6 and 16:13)

4 God commended the new king to the Israelites by a public display of his abilities (1 Samuel 11 and 17)[3]

This amounted to the pattern for an ideal Israelite. We have noted before how Exodus 19:3-6 outlined Israel's identity and calling. We have also noted how the high priest symbolised the true Israelite and true man. Something similar happened with this ideal pattern of kingship. In particular, David showed that he was separate from the nations and that he would faithfully represent the Lord before them.

This was taken further in 2 Samuel 6-7. We have noted before that the ark was the supreme symbol of the covenant since it represented the Lord's throne. We have also noted how the books of Samuel show a movement from the Israelites disregarding and losing the ark to David regaining it and bringing it to its rightful resting place. David was the true and ideal Israelite because he responded appropriately to the Lord, the king of the covenant, and to the supreme symbol of the covenant, the ark. Thus the title *son*, which the Lord had given to the Israelites at the Exodus, passed to the king (Exodus 4:22; 2 Samuel 7:14).

DAVID AND THE KINGDOM OF GOD

We have alluded to the way in which the events of 2 Samuel 5-7 demonstrated that Israel's kingship could fit into the framework of the covenant made at Mt Sinai. We need to explore the significance of these events a little more closely. Note their order:

1 David secured Jerusalem as the temple site (2 Samuel 5:6-10; see 2 Samuel 24:18-25)
2 David brought rest to the land (2 Samuel 5:17-25; 7:1)
3 David (God?) brought the ark to Jerusalem (2 Samuel 6:1-15)
4 Saul's dynasty ended (2 Samuel 6:16-23)
5 God secured David's dynasty (2 Samuel 7:8-16)
6 Solomon built the temple (2 Samuel 7:1-7; 1 Kings 6)

What does this order suggest? David's actions reaffirmed the Lord's kingship before the Lord announced his promises to David. Why? Simply because David's rule could only work if he put the Lord's rule first.

But why did the Lord appoint Solomon and not David to build the temple, that supreme symbol of God's rule? Perhaps it was because the Lord had to initiate this new move even as he had initiated David's bringing of the ark into

Jerusalem. The Lord also had to choose the timing and builder of the temple. David was preoccupied with securing a state of rest for the land and people (2 Samuel 7:1) though he wasn't totally successful (verse 11; 1 Chronicles 22:8; 1 Kings 5:3). The promises outlined in 2 Samuel 7 suggest memories of God's promises to Abraham (Genesis 12:1-3). The Lord would make David's name great, then secure the land as Israel's inheritance and bless David with children (2 Samuel 7:9-12). Moreover, the Lord would bless the nations through David. This last point relates to verse 19. This verse contains the puzzling phrase, "this is the law for mankind". Recently, it has been suggested that the phrase should be translated as "this is the charter for mankind". If this is a reasonable suggestion, then the phrase would imply that David saw that God's creation purposes would continue through the covenant with David.[4]

KINGSHIP IN ISRAEL'S HISTORY

David and Solomon

The Israelite kingdom reached its highpoint under David and Solomon. At this time, their numbers and inheritance actually reflected the promises to Abraham (1 Kings 4:20-21; Genesis 15:5, 18-19; 17:2). Moreover, the themes and traditions which were associated with the Exodus and the covenant at Mt Sinai were now shifting to David and Jerusalem (1 Kings 5:4; 8:10-21). Yet, sadly, Israel's history from this point on shows the failure of the kings. Nonetheless, at the same time, the prophets kept alive the hope of the Israelites living under a just king.[5]

The prophets before the exile

Amos began his prophecy against the present and former member nations of the Davidic empire (Amos 1:3-2:16) from the standpoint that the Lord still ruled from Zion (1:2). Amos concluded his message by strongly affirming the future fulfilment of the covenant with David (9:11). So Amos kept the hopes of 2 Samuel 7 alive by interpreting them as part of the promises surrounding a great future act of deliverance by the Lord for Israel. He believed that the Lord was still enthroned as king in Zion, and that it was still possible for God to raise up a king who would rule in a manner which honoured the Lord's kingship.

A moment ago, we saw how the Lord intended Israel's kingship to serve his plan to bless the whole earth through Abraham (2 Samuel 7:19; Genesis 12:3). An example of this occurred when the "world" came in the person of the Queen of Sheba to listen to Solomon's wisdom (1 Kings 10, especially verse 24). Perhaps Isaiah had this in mind when he combined the themes of David and Jerusalem to speak of a great day when the Lord would make Zion the centre of the world. At that time, the nations would come to Zion to acknowledge the Lord's kingship, and from Zion the Lord would send out his word into all the earth (especially Isaiah 2:2–4; 4:2–6; 9:2–7; 11:1–16; 24:23; 42:1–9; 55:3–5; 65:17–19).[6]

So the prophets looked to the future as they developed the theme of kingship. But what about the writers of the history books of Kings and Chronicles; how did they assess the period of Israel's kings?

The Books of Kings

The books of Kings were probably written during Israel and Judah's exile in Babylon to explain why it had happened. The books of Kings did this by using Deuteronomy 12 as a test for each of the kings of southern Judah and northern Israel. The writer judged every king according to how well he had acknowledged the Lord's kingship through worship and had encouraged the rest of the Israelites to do likewise. And the acid test of this was how well he maintained the purity and centrality of Jerusalem and its temple. Every northern king failed and, out of twenty southern kings, only two got a clear vote of approval (Josiah and Hezekiah) with another six getting a so-so vote. As if to push the point, the books closed on the ambiguous note of Jehoiachin released from exile and enjoying the Babylonians' favour, but dining on defiled food in a pagan's palace!

The Books of Chronicles

Chronicles was written after the exile to encourage those who returned to persevere with their program and hopes for rebuilding Jerusalem, the temple, and the old empire. The Chronicler tried to do this by presenting David and Solomon as the ideal kings, and their reigns as the highpoint of Israel's history. He hoped they might serve as models for the leaders of those who returned, and for their hopes of a future king. The Chronicler used three parallels to show this.

Firstly, he saw Solomon as a second David. We see this emphasis in the way he included Solomon's name in the promises to David (1 Chronicles 22:7-10; 28:6). Solomon was the only king other than David who was specifically said to have been chosen by the Lord (28:5-6,10; 29:1).

Secondly, the Chronicler saw David and Solomon as though they were a new Moses and Joshua:

1 Both Moses and David were disqualified from achieving their goals, and their goals passed on to their successors (Deuteronomy 1:37-38; 31:2-8; 1 Chronicles 22:5-13; 28:2-8)

2 There were many parallels between the way Joshua and Solomon were appointed (Deuteronomy 31:5-8, 23; Joshua 1:5-9; 1 Chronicles 22:11-16; 28:7-9,20)

3 Both Moses and David made private (Deuteronomy 31:23; 1 Chronicles 22:6) and public (Deuteronomy 31:2; 1 Chronicles 28:8) announcements about their successors

4 Joshua and Solomon enjoyed the immediate wholehearted support of the people (Deuteronomy 34:9; Joshua 1:16-20; 1 Chronicles 29:23-24)

5 It is reported twice of Joshua and Solomon that God magnified each (Joshua 3:7; 4:14; 1 Chronicles 29:25; 2 Chronicles 1:1)

6 Both Joshua and Solomon led the Israelites into rest (Joshua 11:23; 21:44; 1 Chronicles 22:8–9)

Thirdly, the Chronicler drew numerous parallels between the building of the tabernacle and the temple. In particular, he presented Solomon and Huramabi (his chief builder) as the new Bezalel and Oholiab (the builders of the tabernacle).[7]

So what was the Chronicler trying to say through these comparisons?

He wanted to idealise Solomon's reign as king and the temple as the hallmarks of Israel's golden era. He wanted to show that this era had all the significance of Israel's experience at Mt Sinai, the events of the conquest of Canaan, and the promises made to David. In this way, the Chronicler made Solomon's era the model for Israel's hopes for a future king and kingdom. Through this model, he sought to encourage the rebuilding programme of those who had returned from Babylon.

The prophets after the exile

Although the Jews failed to rebuild the empire after the exile, the older prophetic hopes of a new and greater David continued (e.g., Amos 9:11). Perhaps they did continue as a result of the sort of idealism which had inspired the Chronicler. For example, Zechariah drew on the ancient promises and themes associated with David to paint a panoramic vision of restoration and hope (see Zechariah 9:9–13; 10:3–4; 12:1–13; 13:7–9). Each of these visions prepared the way for his final vision of a restoration brought about through the new David. At this time, the nations would acknowledge that Yahweh ruled the world from Zion, the centre of the earth (14:1–21).

KINGSHIP AND THE GOSPEL

Kingship is one of the richest sources of our understanding of who Jesus is and what he has done. The prophecies just before and after Jesus' birth are full of reminders of Old

Testament kingship hopes. For example, when Zechariah spoke of the coming ministry of his son, John, he put this in the context of Jesus as the deliverer from "the house of David" (Luke 1:68–69). And, when Simeon took Jesus in his arms in the temple, he believed that the day of the Lord had come; Isaiah's servant king had arrived (Luke 2:29–32; see Isaiah 42:6). Thus Jesus prefaced his ministry by saying that the kingdom of God had arrived (Mark 1:14–15).

When Jesus began his ministry, he demonstrated the four features of kingship which had characterised Saul, David, and the ideal king of Isaiah 11. Jesus was chosen by his Father to be king. This was confirmed by the prophet baptising ("anointing") him; by the Spirit coming upon him (Luke 3:21–22); and by Jesus demonstrating his authority in his victory over Satan and in the miracles he performed. On this last point, we should note that Jesus understood his miracles as the fulfilment of Isaiah 61:1–3, a prophecy in the spirit of Isaiah 11.

Jesus' sense of kingship also lay behind his use of the curious phrase "the Son of Man". This phrase drew its meaning from Old Testament sources like Daniel 7:13–14, Psalms 2 and 8, and Isaiah 52:13–53:12.[8] It seems that Jesus used the title to say that he was a king, but not the sort of king that the Jews had anticipated (see John 6:15). In many of the things he did, Jesus seemed to be the king they wanted (such as when he rode into Jerusalem, John 12:12–19). Nevertheless, he consistently refused to proclaim his kingship on their terms (John 19:1–22). Jesus' somewhat mysterious kingship gradually became clear in the picture of the servant king. Jesus was the one who held all authority but who displayed it by washing his disciples' feet (John 13:1–5).

Finally, Jesus clearly expressed this servant kingship in his death and resurrection (Philippians 2:6–11). Jesus was the ideal king, the ideal representative Israelite who stood in the place of his guilty subjects. He established his rule over his people's hearts by conquering them with his love. And because he humbled himself to submit to death, his Father exalted him to the throne at his right hand (Hebrews 1:1–13) and set a day when all the earth would acknowledge that Jesus is king.

DISCUSSION QUESTIONS

1 Peter described leaders as shepherds in 1 Peter 5:1–4. What do the pictures of Jesus as the Good Shepherd (see John 10) and the one who washed feet suggest about the way church leaders should function? Do you see many leaders acting this way? Does our system of selecting and training leaders encourage them to be shepherds in the way that Jesus shepherded his people?

2 Some christians speak about their leaders or themselves as being anointed in some special way that makes them different to most other christians. Usually, to support their claims, they appeal to the way Old Testament kings and prophets were anointed. What do you make of these claims? How are 2 Corinthians 1:21–22 and Ephesians 1:11–14 relevant here?

EXERCISES

1 Try putting a seemingly trivial detail in context. Given what we saw earlier about the order and importance of 2 Samuel 5–7, what is the significance of 6:16–23? Hint: who was Michal's father?

2 Prepare a bible study outline of Isaiah 11:1–16. Try to include something about where Isaiah got his ideas from, how the various themes go together in the chapter, and how the gospel connects with it all.

Notes

1 For a fuller discussion of the identity and significance of this ceremony, see William Dumbrell (1984), *Covenant and Creation: An Old Testament Covenantal Theology*, Lancer/Paternoster, pages 134–136 and J. Robert Vannoy (1978), *Covenant Renewal at Gilgal: A Study of 1 Samuel 11:14–12:25*, Mack, pages 61–91.

2 This theology of warfare is covered in chapter 6.

3 This pattern recurred roughly with Solomon, but with no one after that until Jesus. It did however shape Isaiah's picture of the future messiah-king (e.g., Isaiah 11:1–9).

4 As far as I know, Walter Kaiser first suggested this translation. See Walter Kaiser (1974), "The Blessing of David, the Charter of Humanity", in *The Law and the Prophets*, edited by John Skilton, Presbyterian and Reformed, page 311. My thoughts on the way the phrase may create a link with creation and Abraham come from Dumbrell's discussion of it, see *Covenant and Creation*, pages 151–152.

5 At this point we must introduce an important distinction in the way we use the word "Israel". The people of God existed as two related but distinct nations from shortly after the end of Solomon's reign (922BC) until the Babylonian invasion

of Jerusalem in 587 BC. The northern nation was known as Israel. It ceased to exist in 721 BC. The southern nation was known as Judah (named after one of the tribes of the older *combined nation* of Israel). It went into exile in Babylon in 587 BC. Although both nations were exiled, we usually refer to the time after 587 BC as *the exile.*

6 This theme of the nations gathering around Zion is developed in chapter 21.

7 Compare Exodus 31:1-11, 35:30-36:2 and 38:22-23 with Chronicles 22:9-10; 28:6-29:2 and 2 Chronicles 1-2. These parallels come from an article by Ray Dillard (1981), "The Chronicler's Solomon", *Westminster Theological Journal*, 43, pages 289-300.

8 There were also instances of this phrase in some Jewish writings. We will return to the title Son of Man in chapter 17.

8 THE PSALMS

Summary: The key to this study
The Psalms provide us with a chance to pause and catch our breath as we follow the history of the Israelites. They do not add any new events to the story, nor do they offer us an alternative school of Israelite thought. Rather they offer us the reflections of various poets on what has happened throughout the story thus far and its significance for the singers' own time and circumstances. Thus they show us how some Israelites translated their history into expressions of faith. And they drew together the themes of their past into a new appreciation of the city of Jerusalem, Zion, and developed a sense of the greater realities which it represented. The New Testament writers used the Psalms to portray Jesus as the ideal Israelite and the one who established on earth the heavenly significance of Zion.

THE PSALMS, THE COVENANTS AND KINGSHIP

The Psalms made two great contributions to the Old Testament. Firstly, they showed how an Old Testament person could and should respond to the Lord. They demonstrated faith expressed as prayer and praise. Secondly, they drew together and reflected on all the events, institutions and themes of Israel's history from Abraham to David, sometimes even going back as far as creation, and forward as far as the exile.

Faith as the true covenant response

The covenants were always about personal relationships. They were not mechanical, legalistic strategies for keeping the Israelites in line. Rather, they were God's way of establishing and continuing the intimacy which he had intended for his people since the creation. In other words, the covenants were about faith, love, and the heart. They were about people experiencing God personally.

Singing was a special way of expressing this experience. For example, after the exodus, Israel's greatest experience of salvation, the people broke into perhaps their finest hymn (Exodus 15:1-18). Similarly, in his final days, Moses sang his faith and joy over Israel's covenant relationship with the Lord and his hopes for their future (Deuteronomy 32:1-43). Many other Israelites also sang to express their experience of and confidence in the Lord's covenant faithfulness (e.g., Judges 5; 1 Samuel 2:1-10).

The arrangement of the Book of Psalms and the different types of psalms also reflect this focus on experiencing God within the framework of the covenant.

The Book of Psalms combines five smaller books: Psalms 1-41, 42-72, 73-89, 90-106, and 107-150. Like our modern hymn books, it is made up of songs collected together from different periods of time for use in formal worship. It was probably compiled by those who returned from exile in Babylon as the hymn book of the second temple.

Although it is hard to see any clear structure behind the order of the five smaller books, the position of Psalms 1, 2 and 150 is appropriate and significant. Psalms 1 and 2 introduce the entire collection by emphasising some of its most important features:

1 The intimacy of faith
2 The role of the covenant (law) in the individual's life
3 The covenant theme of blessings and curses
4 The Lord's personal care of his people—he is their refuge
5 The Lord's kingship over the Israelites and the nations
6 The king's role of representing God's kingship and portraying true faith

7 The significance of Jerusalem as Zion—the throne of
  God

Almost every psalm ends on some note of praise or
recognition of the Lord's greatness. So it is most appropriate
for the colection to finish with Psalm 150, where the poet
calls on the creation to join him enthusiastically in praising
the Lord.

There are three main types of psalm: lament (e.g., Psalms
3–7, 9–10, 22, 32, 42–44, 51, 60, 94, 102, 137); thanksgiving
(e.g., 18, 30, 32, 34, 56, 75, 107, 118, 138); and hymn of praise
(e.g., 19, 47, 92, 96, 103, 105, 111, 113–114, 117, 146–150).
These categories overlap a fair bit, and together they express
faith in a wide range of circumstances; the plea for help,
confidence that the Lord can rescue, thanks for help received,
and praise to the Lord for his greatness in creation, salvation
and kingship.[1]

The Psalms, the hymn book of the temple, show us the
nature of faith, the meaning of the cult,[2] and the focus of
worship as the recognition and experience of the Lord's
universal kingship. The psalms made it abundantly clear that
the ideal of the covenant was always that the people would
personally experience God and know him from the heart.[3]

The king as the ideal Israelite

A moment ago we mentioned that Psalm 2 probably belongs
with Psalm 1 as an introduction to the collection. I think
it belongs there for two obvious reasons and one not so
obvious reason.

The obvious reasons are that it introduces the themes of
God's kingship (Psalm 2:4–5) and human kingship (verses
2, 6–12) which are both extremely important in the psalms
(see e.g., Psalms 18, 21, 24, 29, 45, 47, 72, 93, 96–97, 99,
101, 110, 132, 144). The *less* obvious reason is the king's
relationship to the righteous man of Psalm 1. This righteous
man is obviously an ideal figure representing the faithful
Israelite, the true covenant son, the one who fulfils the
description of the Israelites in Exodus 19:5–6.

The psalm writers looked to their king as a flesh-and-blood example or representative of this ideal figure. The relationship is similar to the way in which the title *son* belonged to every Israelite (Exodus 4:22), yet it became especially appropriate as a title for the king (2 Samuel 7:14; Psalm 2:7; 89:26-27). Furthermore, the king was responsible for ordering Israel's life so that it conformed to the covenant. Therefore, he had to exemplify this covenant himself.

Perhaps the strongest evidence for seeing the king as the ideal Israelite is in the simple fact that *David* wrote so many of the psalms. In other words, at the highpoint of Israel's history, the one who led the Israelites to rest is also the one who most clearly demonstrated what being an Israelite really meant. In every experience David responded to the Lord's kingship from his heart, even in his sin (e.g., Psalm 51).

THE PSALMS IN ISRAEL'S HISTORY: THE THEME OF ZION

David's role in developing the theme

Although the book of Psalms as we know it today was probably compiled around the time of the second temple (after the exile in Babylon), many psalms come from and reflect a much earlier time in Israel's history. The fact that many come from the time of David reflects the significant impact which that period had on Israel's history and traditions. We need now to consider something of how David's life led to Jerusalem acquiring its new name of Zion.

David's conquest of Jerusalem (recorded in 2 Samuel 5-6) heralded the dawn of a new era for the Israelites, their golden years as a nation. As we've often noted before, the Israelites understood the ark as God's throne. Therefore, it symbolised God's kingship. Now consider what David did: he secured the land; rescued the ark; and made Jerusalem his capital and Mt Zion the ark's permanent location. Through these actions, Jerusalem took on the meaning associated with the ark. Jerusalem, therefore, became the throne of God, the place from which he ruled the Israelites and all the earth. One word became a shorthand description for speaking of Jerusalem as God's throne—Zion.

Psalms 9, 24 and 68 show that David was well aware of this new development. In fact, reflections like the ones in these psalms drew the attention of the prophets and later psalmists to the significance of Zion. However, the Israelites as a whole probably only realised the new significance of Jerusalem/Zion after the temple was built.

So David's conquest of Jerusalem, and his reflections on this event in his psalms, opened up a new way for the Israelites to understand their history and identity.

The contribution of the period of the kings

The highpoint of Israel's history under David was shortlived as the kings following him led the Israelites into decline. Not surprisingly, prophets like Isaiah responded to this decline by shifting the focus of Judah's and Israel's hopes away from the kings and Jerusalem as they knew them (e.g., Isaiah 1:1-23; 3:1-26; 39:1-8) to a future Jerusalem, restored and glorious as the Lord's throne in the centre of the earth (2:1-4; 4:2-6; 40:1-11; 51:1-16; 54:1-14).

Isaiah moved beyond the purely geographical or architectural importance of Jerusalem, whether past, present or future. He looked behind the physical Jerusalem and Zion to their eternal significance to the people of God. The essential reality was not the security and glory of the city, but the identity and privileges of the Lord's people. Zion became a symbol for the true covenant people of the Lord living obediently and securely under his kingship (e.g., Isaiah 51:1-16; 52:1-12; 54:1-14; 60:1-22; 62:1-12).[4]

The influence of the exile in Babylon on the theme

The destruction of Jerusalem and the exile of the people and their king raised enormous questions for the people. Despite the preaching of prophets like Jeremiah, Judah had continued to place its trust and hopes in the bricks and stones of Jerusalem (e.g., Jeremiah 7:1-8). But now the city was rubble, and the people wondered whether the Lord had finally rejected them and Zion, and removed all hope for the future.[5]

Ezekiel set the record straight. The Lord had not rejected his people or Zion, nor had he revoked his promises for their future. Like Isaiah and Jeremiah before him, Ezekiel pushed behind the symbols to the realities which they expressed. In fact, Ezekiel went even further. Although he used Zion categories to outline his magnificent and idealistic vision of the city and temple (recorded in Ezekiel 40–48), he never identified this glorious future city with Jerusalem. Instead, he named the place "the Lord is there" (48:35b).

The influence of the period after the exile

The rebuilding of the city and temple after the exile was a bitter disappointment. Those who returned may well have had Ezekiel's vision in mind, but their efforts proved Ezekiel's point that the vision could not come about through political or national effort. Indeed, no amount of human effort could fulfil it. This was the clear message of the obscure prophet Zechariah; only the Lord could restore Zion by coming personally as the great warrior and king to redeem his people (Zechariah 9:9–17; 14:1–9).

THE PSALMS AND THE GOSPEL

The New Testament writers quoted frequently from the Psalms to explain both various details in Jesus' life (e.g., Psalm 22:1; Mark 15:34) and the overall significance of his death and resurrection (e.g., Psalm 110:1; Acts 2:31–36). The writer of the book of Hebrews built a great deal of his or her teaching around Psalms 2, 8, 22, 40, 45 and 110. We will concentrate on what we have seen so far about how the Psalms relate to Jesus.

Jesus as the true covenant son

It is easy for us to overlook or even to play down Jesus' humanness. But his humanity is as important as the fact that he was and is God. It is equally important to remember his nationality. Jesus was an Israelite born and raised under the old covenant (Luke 2:41-42; Galatians 4:4).

Earlier, I mentioned that the writer of Hebrews used the Psalms to support his or her argument. The heart of this argument is that Jesus is superior to everything in the old covenant. Part of the reason why Jesus was able to establish a better covenant, Hebrews argues, is that he was the perfect covenant son (Hebrews 2:10-18 and 4:14-5:10). And, once again, Hebrews used the Psalms to demonstrate this (e.g., Psalm 2:7; 8:4-6; 22:22). In particular, Jesus was the perfect king and he identified fully with his people in praising his Father.

Jesus was a perfectly faithful Israelite, a true covenant son. Except for sin, he identified totally with the faith and experiences of his brothers as we read them in the Psalms. He was the righteous man waiting on the Lord, the suffering despised one, the seeker of justice, the king, and the one who praised his Father. Thus, wherever we turn in the Gospels, we see Jesus staking his identity, security and purpose on his intimate relationship with his Father. He even did so in his death (Luke 23:46).

Jesus and Jerusalem

Jesus maintained a split attitude towards Jerusalem throughout his ministry. On the one hand, he took up its symbolism and applied it to himself. For example, he saw himself as the new temple (John 2:12-22), and called himself the light of the world, a symbol which the prophets had applied to Jerusalem (John 8:12; Isaiah 60:1-3). On the other hand, he rejected the city and pronounced woes over it (Matthew 23:37-24:2; Luke 21:20-28).

Jesus reinforced his rejection of Jerusalem by centring his ministry around Galilee, the land and people which the Jews despised as Gentile. Consider the number of major events in his ministry which occurred in that region: Jesus grew up in Nazareth of Galilee (Luke 2:23); he began his ministry there (Mark 1:14); he performed his first and many of his other miracles there (John 2:1-11); he revealed his identity there (Luke 4:18-21; Mark 8:27-29); he gave the sermon on the mount there (Matthew 4:23–5:1); and he went there after his resurrection to commission his disciples (Matthew 28:6–8, 16–20). In contrast to this, Jerusalem was always the scene of his rejection and ultimately of his death, even though the city momentarily welcomed him as its long awaited king (John 12:12–19).

So what do we make of Jesus' split attitude towards Jerusalem?

Like the prophets before him, Jesus looked beyond Jerusalem, the symbol, to the eternal reality to which it pointed. But this time the reality had arrived. Jesus was now the throne of God. In other words, he was the focus of God's rule over all the earth; he was the light to which all the nations would come. Thus Hebrews could say that we have come to Zion because we have come to Jesus (Hebrews 12:18–24). And, by coming to Jesus, he has made us the new Jerusalem (Matthew 5:14; Galatians 4:24–28).

Yet the New Testament still leaves us with a sense of the unfinished, with the feeling that there is more to come. Indeed, we *have* come to Zion; yet, in some sense, we are *still* moving towards it (Hebrews 13:14). We still look to the day when we will fully experience our status and inheritance as the New Jerusalem (Revelation 21:1–4).[6]

DISCUSSION QUESTIONS

1 Read Psalm 55 and notice how bold and frank David was in prayer. Does the gospel encourage us to be less or more bold? Why do you think we use the word *just* so often when we pray (as in "Lord, we *just* ask you to. . .?"). How can the gospel help us to overcome our awkwardness and embarrassment when we pray?

2 What about our other emotions? The Psalms seem to reveal a wide range of emotions without apologising for any of them. Are we too coy about ours? Where do you think the gospel leads on this issue?

EXERCISES

1 The hardest psalms to understand and accept are probably ones like Psalm 58. (They're known as imprecatory psalms.) Outline a bible study on Psalm 58 giving some idea of how

102 *The Symphony of Scripture*

it fits into the rest of the Old Testament, and how you would connect it with the gospel. Start by identifying the key issues in the psalm and ask how the gospel resolves each of them. 2 Read some of your favourite psalms, also Luke 1:46-55, 11:1-13 and Philippians 1:3-11. Build up a big picture of prayer in the Bible. What did people pray and why? What are the common features in the prayers? You might like to finish by comparing your picture with how you see your own praying and that of your church.

Notes
1 For a fuller discussion of the different ways of categorising and reading the Psalms, see Tremper Longman (1988), *How to Read the Psalms*, IVP.
2 The word *cult* is used here as shorthand for "priests, sacrifices and temple". This is covered in chapter 5.
3 Tremper Longman includes a helpful discussion of the emotional power of the Psalms in *Psalms,* pages 75-85.
4 For a fuller discussion of this shift towards Jerusalem and Zion being symbols for God's people, see William Dumbrell (1985), *The End of the Beginning: Revelation 21-22 and the Old Testament*, Lancer/Baker, pages 1-34.
5 The book of Lamentations records the miseries of Jerusalem and Judah at the start of the exile in Babylon.
6 Again see Dumbrell, *Beginning*, for a more developed discussion of this theme.

9 THE WISDOM BOOKS

Summary: *The key to this study*
The wisdom writers of the Old Testament built their reflections of life upon the foundation of their understanding of creation. A wise person recognised the essential distinction between herself and God— between the Creator and the creature—and that a right understanding of life began in a right relationship with the Lord. From this perspective the wise person could begin to perceive the patterns, themes and subtleties of life, and recognise why so much remained hidden and mysterious. Without this starting point, one could only see the contradictions of a futile existence. The New Testament writers developed this wisdom perspective in three directions: Jesus as the wise person par excellence; Jesus' death and resurrection as the greatest expression of God's wisdom; and Jesus himself as the wisdom of God.

WISDOM, CREATION AND THE COVENANTS

So far in our studies we have seen how the themes of covenant and kingship have structured each stage of the unfolding story of God's plan to renew his creation. But the wisdom books are different.[1] Covenant and kingship are relevant to this part of Israel's heritage, but in a less obvious way than we have seen so far.

Unlike many of the biblical highlights—such as Abraham

and his sons, the exodus, the making of the covenant at Mt Sinai, the conquest and the kings—the wisdom books do not add any new events to the story. And, unlike the Psalms, the wisdom books do not reflect on those earlier events to draw implications for Israel's present and future. So how do these books relate to the overall pattern of creation, covenant and kingship? And what do they add to Israel's story? The answer lies in their emphasis on the theme of creation.

Whereas in other writings creation is kept somewhat in the background with the focus on the covenants and kingship, the wisdom books work the other way around. Wisdom was about creation. In particular, it concentrated on the order, patterns and harmony that God wove into the fabric of life (see e.g., Proverbs 8:22–36). In other words, to be wise was to be able to read life as it really was.

To be wise an Israelite had to be (re)oriented to the most basic distinction in life—the distinction which gives meaning to all of life's relationships and patterns. This distinction is the one between God and us, between the Creator and the creature. That's why the fear of the Lord was the starting point for becoming wise (Proverbs 1:7; 9:10; 15:33). An Israelite began to be wise only after facing up to who the Lord was.

So the wise Israelite was the one who understood life through her relationship to the Lord. It was about understanding and responding to the Lord. From this perspective, she could read the patterns of life that God made all around her, and her place in this relationship and these patterns. Wisdom knew nothing about our false splits between high and low IQs, or between academics and labourers, or between intelligence and wisdom, or even between thinking and doing. The wise Israelite glorified God and enjoyed him for ever in all of life.

At this point we have returned to the theme of covenant. Wisdom emphasised the fear of the Lord and the idea of living under God's kingship. This, of course, is the same thing as faithfully living under the covenant. In other words, wisdom and the covenants provided two different, yet complementary, perspectives of life in relationship to the Lord.[2]

THE EMPHASES OF THE WISDOM BOOKS

The wisdom books provide a deeper appreciation of the overall framework of wisdom. They show us some major signposts to life by giving us a working definition of and encouraging an intuitive feeling for wisdom.

Ecclesiastes: advice from a father to a son

Ecclesiastes was about a dad telling his son how to become wise, even though neither of them did much of the talking (only in Ecclesiastes 1:1, 7:27, 12:9-14). Dad wanted his son to know what the Teacher said because the Teacher was a wise man. The Teacher spoke of his experiences as a young man and reflected on those experiences from the (often cynical) perspective of old age. Finally, dad gave a split verdict; the Teacher was wise, yet his interpretations and life were not to be followed too closely (12:9-14).

So how should we understand the famous cry "Vanity, vanity"? Because the creation was subjected to sin (see Romans 8:19-23), life *is* futile in many respects. But futility is not the final destiny of the creation. God's plan of salvation has always been part of a larger plan to totally renew creation. Ultimately, in Jesus, we see what God intended us to be. Through his death and resurrection, Jesus had begun to recreate the world. And since we share in this re-creation (2 Corinthians 5:17), our labour is never futile (1 Corinthians 15:58b).

Job: the hiddenness of wisdom

If the Teacher of Ecclesiastes *thought* about the seeming futility and injustice of a corrupt world, Job *experienced* it. One of the questions people often ask about Job concerns the relationship between the answers given by Job and those given by his friends: who was right and why? But if we dwell on this we miss much of the power of the book. We can also miss out if we only look at the question of suffering.

It is more helpful to see that the book wrestles with a variety of interrelated issues: the righteous sufferer; the meaning of faith and wisdom; and the justification of God. The key issue in Job is perhaps the gap between divine and human wisdom.

The wisdom books built a clear framework for wisdom. God created the universe and wrote his wisdom into it; to be wise, a person learnt how to read the order and patterns of life starting from a right relationship with God. It seemed simple enough. But Job highlighted the exceptions to the rule. Because of sin, and even because of how great God is, we can't always see the order and patterns of life. In other words, there is a hiddenness, an inherent mystery about life.

This hiddenness came through the cycles of speeches found in Job 2:11–37:24. His friends had a clear framework of conventional wisdom. They believed that the Lord always prospered the righteous. Therefore, they were convinced that prosperity was a sign of righteousness, and calamity a sign of sin.[3] This theology was right *some* of the time. But it was all too abstract and predictable. Life wasn't as simple as they made it out to be. Job came much closer to the truth by recognising the complexities and seeming inconsistencies in life. Yet, in the end, even he was silenced by God's mind on the matter. So the book of Job left its readers with a more radical view of the sort of faith that is the fear of the Lord.

Proverbs: wise reflections on the day to day life

So the fear of the Lord is the beginning of wisdom. But that still leaves many questions unanswered. For example, just how do we learn to act wisely? Proverbs answered this by addressing the complexities of practical life. Proverbs recorded reflections on the subtleties of thinking and acting in every situation in the light of a relationship with the Lord.

Wise sayings, even the ones in the Bible weren't, and aren't, lucky charms or morals or laws. In other words, stacking up a great pile of proverbs as memory verses wasn't the way Israel was meant to learn from biblical wisdom. Instead, the people had to build a framework of biblical wisdom and then add to it from their own experiences as they interpreted them in the light of that framework.

Colossians makes a helpful transition here to our situation. The christians at Colossae were hindered by various misunderstandings of the gospel (e.g., relying on visions and imposing laws on others). Paul wanted his friends to become fully wise (Colossians 1:9-10, 28; 2:2-5; 3:16), yet it seems that the misinformed zeal of some led them to make a rule for everything. Paul's answer was to point them to Jesus, the creator and the restorer of creation. The Colossians could only know and do the will of God by growing in their understanding of Jesus. The fear of the Lord is faith in Christ.

Song of Songs: the mystery of sexuality

Apart from God's friendship, and life itself, the most precious gift God gave to man and woman in the garden was each other. The Song of Songs deliberately used garden imagery to return us to this original experience of that most puzzling and wonderful of all human situations, the intimacy of marriage. In many respects, the Song of Songs is a commentary on Proverbs 30:18-19: "There are three things that are too amazing for me, four that I do not understand: ...the way of a man with a maiden".

In this confused world of broken relationships, bitterness, selfishness and strife, the gospel makes it possible for men and women to return to the intimacy, harmony and joy of the early stages of that first marriage relationship in Eden (Ephesians 4:24; Colossians 3:10, 18-19).

WISDOM IN ISRAEL'S HISTORY

The connection between wisdom and creation went all the way back to the creation story. Adam and Eve were originally wise because they could read life through their perfect relationship with the Lord. But by rejecting the starting point of wisdom—the fear of the Lord—they became fools

(Genesis 3:1-13; see Paul's commentary on this in Romans 1:18-25).

The wisdom books probably originate in the folk wisdom of Israel's earliest generations. Popular folk wisdom expresses what a community has learnt through generations of experience. This form of wisdom probably developed in Israel as their identity and the purpose of the early events and covenants of their history became clearer.

Wisdom finally flowered when Israel reached its highpoint under David, and particularly Solomon. In his prayer of dedication of the temple, Solomon expressed the wisdom theme that the temple was meant to promote the fear of the Lord among Israel and the nations (2 Chronicles 8:38-43; see 10:1-13). Many psalms also followed wisdom themes (e.g., Psalm 1, 25, 34, 37, 49, 73, 78, 111-112, 119, 127-128, 133-139).

The prophets included wisdom in their visions of the future, probably because they built their hopes on the idea of a new creation (see Isaiah 29:13-14; 33:5-6). Isaiah 11 is a good example of this. Starting from a picture of the ideal future king as a wise man the prophet moved on to say that this king's rule would result in the total restoration of peace and harmony throughout the earth.[4]

WISDOM AND THE GOSPEL

Like everything else in the Old Testament, wisdom found its fulfilment and clearest expression in Jesus. We'll look at three ways that Jesus fulfilled the theme of wisdom:

Jesus as the wise man par excellence

Jesus' teaching was full of wisdom themes and allusions to Old Testament wisdom sayings. He even used wisdom literary forms like the parables. Moreover, Jesus constantly described his ministry in terms of God's wisdom confronting the foolishness of the proud (Matthew 11:25-30; Luke 11:39-41, 52).

Throughout his life Jesus displayed the characteristics of

wisdom found in Proverbs 1-9. In addition to his frequent use of parables, Jesus commended himself, promised life, claimed a full intimacy with God, invited guests to a banquet, sent messengers, saved and protected, and was scorned by sinners—all of which are attributed to wisdom in Proverbs.

Jesus' death and resurrection as the wisdom of God

In 1 Corinthians 1:18-2:16, Paul redirected the schismatic Corinthians to the gospel. His main point comes in 1:31. If the gospel is all of grace, Paul argued, then there is no place for boasting. Paul showed this by speaking of the gospel in terms of wisdom and foolishness.

The world looks at the gospel and scoffs. They think it is foolishness. But God's wisdom took what looks weak and foolish and made it the greatest expression of his strength and wisdom. This "foolish wisdom" of Christ crucified has silenced all the pretended wisdom of the ages. And now, because we have the mind of Christ through the Holy Spirit, the whole wisdom, mystery and power of the gospel is opened up to our hearts.

Jesus is all the wisdom of God

Jesus exercised the role of wisdom described in Proverbs 8: he established and upholds the order of life; he is the key to understanding everything in right perspective; and faith in him is what fearing the Lord is all about. That's why Paul used the theme of wisdom to tie the themes of creation and salvation together to finish his description of Jesus in Colossians 1:15-2:8. John built on a similar foundation when he called Jesus the Word of God, the perfect expression of God (John 1:1-4).

Now do you see why Paul urged the Colossians to grow in their knowledge of who Jesus was and what he had done for them? Because Jesus was all the wisdom of God he provided the ultimate key to understanding what was happening around them (Colossians 2:2-9). Like the Colossians, we need to look at how the gospel converts our

heads and allows and encourages us—no, more than that—
how it hounds us to think about life afresh.

WISDOM, THE GOSPEL AND LIVING AS A CHRISTIAN

Summary: The key to this section
Too often teachings on the christian life fail to grasp
that maturity involves developing the ability to under-
stand and appreciate the fullness of life. This failure
has had many damaging effects. Some have driven a
wedge between so-called ordinary and spiritual
activities, reducing spirituality to a set of religious duties
tucked away in some remote corner of life. A fresh
awareness of the wisdom themes of the Bible can
encourage us to form a healthier perspective on our
lives—our identities, relationships, employment, recrea-
tion, social involvement, stewardship and decision-
making.

Before leaving this unique part of Israel's heritage and its
profound fulfilment in Jesus, we should at least draw a few
implications about what should be going on in our own lives.

Christian thinking has often been shaped by false
distinctions, particularly the old distinction between the
sacred and the *secular*. For example, many books, conferences
and sermons paint a picture of the christian life in which
spirituality is limited to quiet times, evangelism and the like.
Which of the two models in diagram 5 represents your view
of spirituality?

Instead of exploring and proclaiming the Lordship of
Jesus in every walk of life (above right), we often follow the
false split (above left) and create a sub-culture characterised
by irrelevance, preoccupation with trivia and pious phrases.

So how do we start to think wisely—to think from the
gospel? Here are a few guidelines:

1   Jesus is the foundation of all our patterns of thinking.
    We seek to bring every thought captive to him
2   Our thinking and doing serves the Lord and should
    reflect our dependence on him. So we think prayerfully
    and self-critically

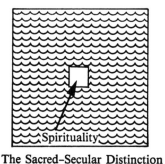

The Sacred–Secular Distinction   All of Life is Religious

Diagram 5: Two ways of defining what is "religious" or "spiritual"

3 Our relationship to the Lord doesn't depend on our ability to think. We should think and act as a response to his love, and as obedience to his word, not to be proud or to bolster our personal (in)security. We shouldn't compare our level of thinking to other people's

4 Thinking and doing are inseparable—neither is more important nor spiritual than the other

5 Every square inch of life is God's. He declared it is all good and he gave it to us to explore, rule and enjoy. It is a false question to ask whether preaching or ploughing is more pleasing to God

6 All of life is inter-related. God has established a remarkable unity and diversity in his creation. Consequently, we can and need to think in big pictures to see things properly. This same complex interrelatedness means that each part of life can serve as a window, a perspective on anything else. There is always more than one way to see anything

7 The world is no longer exactly how it was meant to be. In each situation, we must wrestle with the physical, social and personal effects of sin. We think through the broad pattern of creation, fall and re-creation

8 Every thought and act is religious because everything expresses a basic heart commitment. We are either God's servants, or his enemies. Yet even rebels remain in God's image. So all of us live in varying degrees of consistency with what we were meant to be

This list is anything but exhaustive. If a wise view of life (a worldview) is like a magnificent landscape, then all I've done is make a few broad sweeps of the brush in some rather bold colours.[5]

Our pictures of life are far too often like eating fast food, or like living under the shadow of a rule book, or like staring glassy-eyed out into the third heaven waiting for "a word from the Lord". Wisdom challenges all this. It says to us, warmly yet firmly, "Grow up!", "Mature!", "Move beyond childhood into adulthood!", "Use the mind God has given you!"

Wisdom is about learning to apply the gospel to every area of our thinking and doing. We will be tempted to justify our ignorance and mental laziness by saying that we're trusting the Lord. We may even appeal to Proverbs 3:5–6 to defend this attitude. But that's not what Proverbs 3:5–6 is about. Rather, it encourages diligent, careful, prayerful, intelligent and enthusiastic exploration of life in the light of the gospel.

DISCUSSION QUESTIONS

1 Many christians find making decisions hard and even frustrating. Others seem to take a magical, unreal or superstitious approach by looking for "a word from the Lord" in obscure Bible references, unusual experiences and inner peace. What do you make of these approaches? How do you make decisions? What light do the gospel and wisdom literature throw on this issue?

2 Christians often teach that making up lists of do's and don'ts is the best way to beat sexual temptation in a relationship. The writer of Proverbs 2 and 5 believed learning wisdom was the best way. Are these two ways the same? How could the gospel open up new ways of thinking about their relationship for a christian couple?

EXERCISES

1 This week listen to the wisdom and foolishness of the world. Identify a particular situation then think through what it means to be wise in the gospel in this situation.

2 Outline a Bible study on Proverbs 8:22–36. As usual make sure you work carefully through its connections to the gospel.

Notes

1 I consider the wisdom books to be Job, Proverbs, Ecclesiastes and Song of Songs. Many people do not see Song of Songs as a wisdom book. I see it that way because it deals with one of the mysteries of life and relates this mystery to the context of creation. The book is also traditionally associated with Solomon, the central wisdom figure in Israel's history.

2 Graeme Goldsworthy helpfully discusses how the perspectives of the wisdom books relate to the rest of the Old Testament in *Gospel and Wisdom: Israel's Wisdom Literature in the Christian Life*, Lancer/Paternoster, pages 129–146.

3 Many teachers of "the prosperity doctrine" today sound alarmingly similar to Job's misguided friends.

4 Goldsworthy details the development of wisdom in Israel's history in *Gospel and Wisdom*, pages 44–72.

5 A good introduction to thinking about christian worldview is B. Walsh and J. Middleton (1984), *The Transforming Vision: Shaping a Christian Worldview*, IVP.

10 THE PROPHETS BEFORE THE EXILE

Summary: The key to this study
The prophets were the guardians of the covenant relationship, first within the combined nation of Israel and then amongst the split kingdoms of Israel and Judah. They watched the domestic and international behaviour and policies of God's people—and especially the kings—and called the people to repent and reaffirm their allegiance to the Lord in the face of impending judgements against their sin. But the prophets shared a faith which transcended both their own times and the hardness of their countrymens' hearts, even in the face of an inevitable exile. They looked for a time of restoration in which God would fight to rescue and renew his people as he had done in their ancient past. The writers of the New Testament applied these hopes to the ministry of Jesus and in so doing reshaped the prophets' concept of history.

PROPHECY, COVENANT AND KINGSHIP

The role of God's word in Israel's life

God's word and his acts of salvation always went together in the Old Testament. The Lord used the great acts of salvation like the Exodus to draw his people to himself. The Lord based these events on the promises he had made to earlier generations. Furthermore, the Lord interpreted the meaning and significance of these acts for Israel's life.

Consequently, the Lord called his people to live by his word, and their condition as a nation always reflected how faithful or unfaithful they were to his word. And, since their hearts were frequently hard and stubborn, the Lord had to continually call them back to his word.

The role of the prophets

This is where the prophets fitted in. Although the Lord had bound the kings to rule by his word, they constantly resorted to their own wisdom, to the prestige of international alliances, or bowed to the pressure of the people. So, at the rise of kingship, God institutionalised the prophetic voice as a watchdog over the king's heart and, therefore, over Israel's fate.[1]

For the first hundred years or so after the north-south split in 922 BC, the prophets delivered their oracles in face-to-face encounters with the kings, their families and their court staff. The most notable of these prophets were Elijah and Elisha. These confrontations mainly concerned justice, idolatry, and whether or not the kings should go to war (e.g., 1 Kings 18:16–45; 20:13–28; 21:1–29). But, increasingly, as the kings resisted the prophets and excluded them from the royal courts, the prophets spoke to the people as a whole and began to write their prophecies. Why did the prophets change their strategy?

Perhaps the prophets turned to the people because it became obvious that the kings would never change their behaviour. Whatever the reason, they did shift their focus and, most importantly, they began to write. But why did they bother writing prophecies that few people ever read? Part of the answer lay in Israel's accountability to God's word. The point wasn't so much whether or not the Israelites would hear the word of the covenant, or even respond to it (Isaiah 6:9–12), but whether the Lord himself would keep his word and visit the covenant curses on his people. The prophets wrote to record that God had remembered his own oaths and that he would keep his word.

The prophets were covenant messengers to a nation of covenant breakers. They announced that God was still king of the covenant and that the covenant sanctions still stood. They insisted that the blessings and curses of Deuteronomy 28 still applied and that they would continue to shape Israel and Judah's history.

The prophets also realised that the Lord would remain faithful to his ancient promises. They knew that his love for his people was stronger than their sin. Thus they developed a tradition of preaching judgement and salvation, doom and promise, back-to-back. These two aspects were not only inseparable, one involved the other. The whole nation would experience judgement, yet the Lord would preserve a remnant. He would restructure their individual and national lives around a radical restoration of their ancient traditions. Thus the prophets began to speak of *new* patterns of kingship, and even a *new* covenant and creation, and a *new* people.

AN OVERVIEW OF THE PROPHETIC WRITINGS BEFORE THE EXILE

Joel

It is nearly impossible to date his ministry; it may have been as early as 835 BC, or as late as the exile. Joel witnessed an awesome locust plague and used it as a symbol of an army coming against Judah, and as an introduction to the natural disorders brought about by the day of the Lord (he may have been the first prophet to use that phrase). He saw that day as a future time when God would pour out his Spirit on the people after judging them (Acts 2:16–24).

Jonah

His ministry is also hard to date but may have been around 780 BC (or as late as the 400s BC). Unlike most of the prophets, he did not prophesy to Israel or Judah, but to a foreign nation (Assyria). Yet he probably also served as an example to his own people. Most of all, the book emphasises that God's word will be fulfilled (despite Jonah!), and that God's grace is as unpredictable as it is unfathomable.

Hosea

This prophet preached sometime around the year 750 BC. Israel, the northern kingdom, had abandoned the covenant in favour of a prosperous and idolatrous lifestyle. Israel was like a wife who had turned against her loyal, loving husband to become a prostitute. Hosea issued a radical call to the Israelites to stop worshipping the Baals, their lovers, and to recover their marriage vows to the Lord. Hosea promised a new exodus.

Amos

Amos was a contemporary of Hosea. After decrying the nations around Israel, including Judah, the prophet turned his attention to the injustice which lay behind Israel's wealth, and to their perverted worship at the shrines. Although the people expected a favourable day of the Lord, Amos believed that it would come only after the Israelites had experienced the Assyrians' swords.

Isaiah

Isaiah was also a contemporary of Amos and Hosea, but he preached to Judah, the southern kingdom. Despite the people's stubbornness and the inevitability of judgement, Isaiah reassured king Hezekiah that Jerusalem would not fall. Isaiah 40–66 presumes that the exile has happened (150 years after Isaiah) and records some of the Old Testament's most stunning pictures of restoration. These prophecies include a complete restoration of all of Israel's structures shaped around a new exodus and culminating in a new heaven and new earth.

Micah

A contemporary of Isaiah (around 720 BC), also in Judah, Micah preached about social inequalities which he probably witnessed in his own town. His most famous prophecy (6:1–8) is a covenant law-suit against Judah because of their injustice, idolatry and ritualism. Yet, Micah, like most other prophets, held that the Lord would keep his word to Abraham, and one day rule from Zion over a purified remnant.

Nahum

Like Jonah, Nahum prophesied against the Assyrian capital of Nineveh (probably around 640 BC). Yet Nahum was more than a narrow anti-Assyrian Israelite. His prophecy painted a landscape of the Lord's involvement in history as the ultimate judge and king of all men. Nahum left his readers at that point; their ultimate security lay in the Lord's control of history, not in any specific institution or event.

Habakkuk

Around 625 BC, Habakkuk saw the cruel Assyrians begin to weaken. But he was then horrified to witness the rise of the even more cruel Babylonians. He understood that Judah deserved judgement, but Babylon was worse! He began to resolve this tension in his classic statement on faith in 2:4 (the apostle Paul's "proof-text" for justification by faith). In the psalm found in chapter 3, Habakkuk recorded an awesome vision of the Lord's triumph as the warrior who fights for his people.

Zephaniah

Zephaniah was a contemporary of Habakkuk who called for reform while announcing judgement. He possibly influenced king Josiah's reform. But his prophecies went far beyond Judah to a vision of cosmic destruction and renewal in the day of the Lord. He saw this as a natural fulfilment of the promises to Abraham (Genesis 12:1-3).

Obadiah

Obadiah prophesied against Edom (the descendants of Esau), probably just after the fall of Jerusalem in 587 BC.[2] Like the prophets of the exile, Obadiah saw Edom as symbolic of Israel's enemies (compare Ezekiel 35). He too believed that the Lord would come to the aid of his people from Zion on the day of the Lord.

PROPHECY IN ISRAEL'S HISTORY: THE THEME OF THE DAY OF THE LORD

As the prophets wove together the themes of judgement and promise, they increasingly crystallised this two-sided picture into an expectation of a great future event. God would deliver the Israelites from all their enemies and a great new age would dawn. And, like the psalmists, who took up the word Zion as shorthand for the intersection of a wide range of themes, the prophets coined their own summarising term. That expression was *the day of the Lord.*

How did this term evolve?

Earlier, I stressed the connection between the rise of the offices of king and prophet. Yet there was actually another more ancient context for prophecy. Prophecy really started at the exodus when God raised up Moses and Aaron to confront Pharoah. Their message was simple and it became the model for every prophet that followed. Essentially the message was that the Lord was king over the whole earth, Israel was his special people, and the nations would be judged for oppressing his people and for their sins against the Lord (Deuteronomy 4:32-40; 9:4-5).

During the time of the conquest, the prophets and judges continued this basic message and model (e.g., Judges 4-5). The Lord held the Canaanites accountable and as Israel's warrior he secured his people and their inheritance by waging war against the nations. Yet Israel was far from innocent. The hard-heartedness and rebellion which began in the desert and developed at Mt Sinai led the Israelites into a cycle of sin-oppression-repentance-salvation during the period of the Judges. This cycle may well be the background for the way many of the prophets structured their prophecies:[3]

1   Judgement against the Israelites (e.g., Zephaniah 1:1–2:3; Ezekiel 1–24)
2   Judgement against the nations (Zephaniah 2:3–15; Ezekiel 25–32)
3   Salvation for the Israelites (Zephaniah 3:1–20; Ezekiel 33–48)

The Psalms further developed the themes associated with the exodus and holy war through their emphasis on Zion. The Lord was the universal king and warrior and Zion was his throne and he would continue to exercise his authority over the nations on behalf of his people. The psalmists also revived earlier sentiments by increasingly calling for judgement on the surrounding nations (e.g., Psalm 83).

The prophets Elijah and Elisha, and some of their less well-known contemporaries, developed the traditional involvement of the prophets in holy war. In 1 Kings 20:28, an unknown man of God prophesied against Ben-Hadad, the king of Aram (another name for Syria). The prophet announced victory for Israel and spelt out the particular sin of the Arameans; they had mocked Yahweh by saying his power was geographically restricted. The prophet probably saw this taunt as a denial of the Lord's universal rule over creation, which Israel traditionally understood as integral to his acts of holy war.

Isaiah developed this theme when he identified pride and rebellion against Yahweh as the root of the nations' sin. For example, Isaiah denounced the arrogance of the Assyrians who forgot they were simply an instrument in the Lord's hand (Isaiah 10:12–19). Against the Babylonians, he drew together the ancient holy war traditions and the theme of the nations' arrogance under the banner of the day of the Lord (13:1–13). And, in chapters 24–27, Isaiah extended his picture to cosmic proportions. In "that day" the Lord would come as the ancient warrior to destroy the earth and his enemies, and to restore his people (see also Joel 3:9–16; Ezekiel 30:1–4; Zechariah 9:14–17).

So *the day of the Lord* gradually became an expression for a time when the Lord would fight to restore the fortunes of Israel. The prophets believed that the people had a completely lopsided view of this day because they overlooked the consequences of their own sin. Thus the prophets insisted that the Lord would come in full fury against sin, whether it were sin of the nations or of the Israelites. The day would first of all be darkness, not light; judgement, not hope (e.g., Amos 5:18–20). The prophets believed that the Israelites would only experience salvation after they had experienced judgement.

THE PROPHETS AND THE GOSPEL

We will explore three connections between the gospel and the prophets:

1 Jesus as the greatest prophet
2 Jesus as the Word of the Lord
3 Jesus as fulfilling the prophets' messages

Matthew began his Gospel with Jesus re-enacting the exodus singlehandedly.[4] This introduction culminated in the Sermon on the Mount where Jesus became the new Moses giving the new law. In this respect, Jesus fulfilled the prophecy of Deuteronomy 18:15–16. This is also why he appeared alongside the two greatest prophets, Moses and Elijah, at his transfiguration (Luke 9:28–36). Like every other true prophet, Jesus lived by the word of God (Matthew 4:4; John 5:31–47; 8:12–59).

John went further than this. Jesus not only lived by the word, he *was* the Word of God, the greatest revelation of the Father (John 1:1–4). We have noted how all the events and structures of the Old Testment were temporary and incomplete. The covenants outlined how God would relate to his people, but they did not give the final picture of what that relationship would be. All these words from God anticipated and prepared the way for his final word in his Son (see John 14:6; Hebrews 1:1–4; 1 Peter 1:10–12).

Jesus believed that the Jews (and even the disciples) failed to understand him because they failed to understand the Old Testament (John 5:39-40; Luke 24:44-47). They failed to grasp that his coming fulfilled the Old Testament. But, after the resurrection and Pentecost, the pieces fell into place. Then the apostles realised that Jesus had brought the day of the Lord (Acts 2:16-36).

Yet the New Testament obviously reinterpreted the day of the Lord. Instead of the prophets' vision of a single event, the New Testament writers saw it as a two-stage event. The arrival of Jesus was the day of the Lord (Acts 2:20), yet they lived between two ages waiting for another day of the Lord (1 Thessalonians 5:2). Diagram 6 shows one way to picture it.[5]

Jesus revealed the mystery of God's plan for all history (Romans 16:25; Ephesians 3:2-6; Colossians 1:26-27). In fact, Jesus *was* that mystery (Colossians 2:3-4). Now we belong to the new age (Philippians 3:20-21) and experience its power and status (Colossians 3:1-4) while we wait to enter into its fullness (Ephesians 1:13-14; 1 Corinthians 15:42-54).

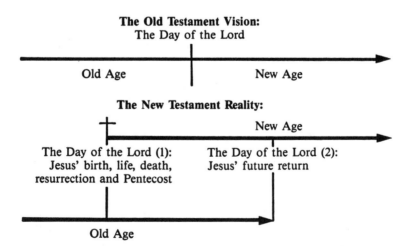

Diagram 6: The shift to the "Now and not yet" pattern of the New Testament

DISCUSSION QUESTIONS

1 The prophets faced a nation which rejected God's word and went its own way. Today many christians justify their beliefs and actions with the words "I feel right about it" or "The Lord has given me real peace about it". Do you see any similarities to Israel's attitudes? Where could attitudes like this lead us? How does the gospel clarify the issue of authority for us?

2 Read Amos 2:6-8; 5:4-16, Isaiah 61:1-3 and Micah 6:6-8. Do you think the prophets' social concern carries over to us through the gospel?

EXERCISES

1 The following passages all picture sin as a direct rebellion against God and as an arrogant assertion of human pride. Trace the connection between them and then draw your ideas together into a statement of how the main theme unfolds throughout the Bible:

Genesis 3:1-5; 11:1-9; Exodus 9:33-35; Isaiah 14:13-17; Ezekiel 28:1-19; John 19:4-16; Romans 1:18-25; Acts 12:19b-23; 2 Thessalonians 2:1-12; Philippians 2:6-11

2 Outline a bible study on Amos 4:1-13. Don't labour over every little detail, but concentrate on verses 4-5, 10-11 and 13. Try putting this prophecy into the broader picture of the Old Testament, and outline a few thoughts about how the gospel resolves the issues raised by Amos.

Notes
1 You might like to review at this point the few remarks made in chapter 7 about the interaction of the kings and prophets. The most notable of these prophets were Elijah and Elisha.
2 Verses 11-14 might refer to 2 Kings 8:20-22. If so the book dates around 845 BC.
3 This cycle is outlined in chapter 6.
4 These parallels are outlined at the end of chapter 3.
5 This model is adapted from G. Vos (1979), *The Pauline Eschatology*, Grand Rapids, page 38.

11 THE EXILE AND ITS PROPHETS

Summary: The key to this study
The prophets before the exile had warned repeatedly
that destruction would come to Israel and Judah. But
when the northern nation, Israel, collapsed in 721 BC,
the southerners in Judah failed to learn from the fate
of their cousins. Thus the prophets continued to warn
Judah until the inevitable happened in 588 BC when
the Babylonians destroyed the southern nation and took
many of them away into exile. This event shook the
people of God to the core; with no land, no Jersualem,
no temple, and no king, it appeared that the Lord had
deserted his people. The Lord raised Jeremiah, Ezekiel
and Daniel for these times. They explained why this
calamity had fallen on the people, they restored a right
perspective to the people's understanding of their
circumstances and pointed beyond the present suffering
to the time when the Lord would create a whole new
relationship with his people. That time and that
relationship came through Jesus.

THE EXILE, THE COVENANTS AND KINGSHIP

Israel's past would continue

In chapter 1, I introduced Graeme Goldsworthy's pattern
of *God's people in God's place under God's rule.* This pattern

helps us to understand the crisis which the exile brought to Israel.[1] Since the Israelites had lost their land (God's place) and the king and the temple (signs of God's rule), there seemed to be every reason for them to draw the conclusion that they were no longer God's people. It must have seemed to the Israelites as though God had cancelled the covenant, as though their traditional identity had come to an end.

In one sense, the conclusion was right. The prophets saw the exile as the final instalment of the covenant curses of Deuteronomy 28:15–68. God appeared to revoke the covenant which Israel and Judah had neglected continually throughout their histories.

Yet the exile did *not* mean a total end to God's people, nor to God's rule and God's place. The prophets of the exile remained convinced that the Lord loved his people and that he was committed to restoring them. The prophets believed that:

God was present with his people in Babylon
God was at work in their lives
The covenant still applied and would continue to do so
Israel would return to Palestine.

Yet the people themselves hardly inspired such confidence. Some maintained their faith in the Lord. They looked at him to act in their time as he had in the great moments of their past. But for many others, perhaps for the majority, the exile not only shattered what remained of their faith (if they had any), it increased their hard-heartedness. Those who remained in Judah and those who were in Babylon rejected each other, each group proclaiming itself to be the true remnant of the Lord. Alongside this elitism, many Israelites increasingly externalised the law so that the covenant bond became a legalistic formality, rather than the heart relationship God always intended it to be.

Israel's future would reshape their former hopes

Thus, the prophets of the exile were adamant that the future could not be just like the past. The Israelites needed a completely new beginning. In this emphasis, they continued the earlier prophetic tradition of building a vision of restoration which reshaped the concepts and structures of Israel's past. For example, there would always be a temple and a king, and Jerusalem would again become Zion, the glorious throne of God at the centre of the world. But there would be radical differences too. None of these structures would look the same in the future as they had in the past. Some of their future hopes might even look radically different to their ancient counterparts.

For example, Ezekiel's vision of a new temple in Ezekiel 40–48 defied any literal fulfilment. Its architecture is staggering: out of the centre of the temple flows a stream which widens and deepens into a mighty river eventually emptying into the Dead Sea. Ezekiel also avoided identifying the city with Jerusalem. The point of the flamboyant architecture was to symbolise a summary of different prophetic hopes. These included a purified new people, a return to the conditions of paradise, and God living face-to-face with his people in his rightful role as king of the whole earth. The point in not identifying the vision with Jerusalem was to ensure that the people placed their trust in the Lord and not in a return to the "good old days". They must look to the Lord, and not to any symbol of him.

THE PROPHETIC WRITINGS OF THE EXILE

Jeremiah

Although Jeremiah was technically not a prophet of the exile, he is included him in this chapter because he belongs to this period and its significance. Jeremiah witnessed the last days of Judah's internal decline and the rise of the Babylonian might. Furthermore, he belongs to the prophets of the exile because of his clarity of vision into the way the exile would unalterably transform the institutions and hopes of Israel's past.[2]

Jeremiah and the reforms of king Josiah We have frequently noted in these studies that the kings which followed Solomon led Judah and Israel into idolatry and unholy international alliances. This picture may give the impression that Judah and Israel experienced an unchecked decline from Solomon to the time of their respective exiles. But such was not the case. On at least two occasions, a king of Judah tried to introduce a widespread reform. King Josiah (640–609 BC) instigated the second of these reforms during the ministry of Jeremiah, perhaps even partly as a response to Jeremiah's preaching.[3]

Yet the general impression about Judah's decline still holds true. Josiah did try to reform the temple and city. His influence even extended to the outer areas of the kingdom. But the reform was ineffective. It did not bring lasting change because it did not change the people's hearts. Sadly, the people translated Josiah's call for repentance and faith into a revamped external religion.

This mistranslation of Josiah's reform probably lies behind Jeremiah's famous temple sermon (Jeremiah 7:1–29—the prophecy may extend to 10:25). The people saw the reform of the temple as an end in itself. They believed that the temple was tangible proof that the Lord would protect Judah indefinitely because the temple procedures now followed those prescribed in the law. Jeremiah mocked their false hopes with the very words they were using to reassure themselves: "the temple of the Lord, the temple of the Lord, the temple of the Lord" (7:4). This false trust in the temple "blocked...any return to the ancient paths" (see verses 21–26).[4]

Jeremiah and Israel's traditions   Jeremiah's ministry cut at the heart of Judah's simplistic and hypocritical trust in their institutions. Apart from the temple, the prophet also tackled the sacrificial system, the role of the ark of the covenant and the nature of kingship. We will look briefly at each of these.

Israel's oldest traditions showed that faith was first of all a heart response which looked to the Lord for forgiveness. Faith went beyond the sacrifices themselves, beyond the means of symbolising forgiveness to the God who forgave. If the people did not realise this and repent, then the Lord would destroy Jerusalem just as he had destroyed the abused shrine at Shiloh in the days of Samuel (Jeremiah 7:12-15, 21-23; see 1 Samuel 4).

Jeremiah preached that the ark, "the most solemn and most ancient symbol of all, the symbol which stood at the heart of covenant worship"[5] would become superfluous in the future kingdom (Jeremiah 3:17-18). But why would such a significant symbol lose its importance? The answer lay in Jeremiah's vision of an extended role for Zion. Like many earlier prophets, he looked to a day when Zion would be the focus of a *universal* pilgrimage, a day when all the nations would acknowledge the Lord's throne. Thus there would be no place for symbols which were strictly national. Israel would then be part of a "general worshipping community of nations".[6]

Jeremiah held that the Lord would continue the covenant he had made with David, yet perhaps not by way of lineal descent. After reviewing the performances of the descendants of Josiah who followed him as kings of Judah, Jeremiah announced that God would raise up another "branch from David" (i.e., a king) in the future to rule over a renewed Israel (Jeremiah 23:1-8; also 33:14-16; compare Isaiah 11:1). The king would stand in stark contrast to the present king. Jeremiah emphasised this by naming the future king "the Lord our righteousness", which was the meaning of the name of the king at the time of the prophecy, Zedekiah. In other words, the branch would be what Zedekiah was not.

Ezekiel

Ezekiel and Israel's understanding of the exile   Ezekiel lived and prophesied in exile in Babylon. His great contribution to the Old Testament came through his firsthand experience of the despair of the exiles and through his vision of the Lord's own explanation for Jerusalem's destruction. Ezekiel intimately understood the agony of exile and the idealised, nostalgic picture of Jerusalem which many of his comrades held. In that context, and for that hour, God raised up Ezekiel to set the record straight on two counts.

Firstly, Jerusalem and Judah deserved what they got. Israel and Judah had stubbornly and willfully abandoned their covenant with the Lord throughout their histories. In fact, the combined nation of Israelites had rebelled since their slavery in Egypt. Ezekiel dramatised this sin in his famous story of Israel the bride turned prostitute (Ezekiel 16; chapter 23 is similar). In the story, the Lord finds a newborn baby girl who was left to die in its own blood in the fields. The Lord bathed and protected the child and she grew into a beautiful young woman whom the Lord adorned and married. But the woman became a prostitute and participated in all manner of detestable practices, even sacrificing her own children. And, unlike other prostitutes, this woman chased and paid her lovers. This, Ezekiel says, is Israel's entire history.

When the Lord took Ezekiel to Jerusalem, the prophet saw that the woman had not changed. He saw first hand that the exiles' nostalgia for the city was totally misplaced. Everywhere he looked the city displayed idolatry and immorality of the worst kind. Finally, Ezekiel saw the glory of the Lord depart from the temple and leave the city (Ezekiel 10:1-5, 18-19; the whole incident is found in 8:1-11:25).

Secondly, the Lord was with his people in Babylon. Ezekiel's prophecy commences with his remarkable vision of the Lord symbolised by a storm, exotic living creatures and wheels full of eyes (Ezekiel 1:1-28). The details of the vision are notoriously difficult to understand. But its essential point is clear enough. The pattern of God's people in God's place under God's rule suggested that Israel was no longer his people if there was no land and if there were no tangible expressions of the Lord's rule. Israel could not see the land or the rule. But Ezekiel saw the Lord by the river Kebar in Babylon. In other words, the Lord was not bound to the land of Canaan. He was the King of the earth and he would still exercise this rule on behalf of his people.

Ezekiel and the new Exodus Ezekiel's vision of the Lord confirmed for him that the Lord remembered his covenant with the Israelites and that he would act on their behalf as he had in the past. In particular, the Lord would provide a second exodus for his people. The clearest way to see this is by noting how Ezekiel structured his prophecies.

The current order of Ezekiel's prophecies in the Bible is not the order in which they were given. Rather, they have been re-arranged to guide the reader through a deliberate sequence:[7]

Chapter 1—The Lord is king over the earth

Chapters 2-24—The Lord has judged his people for their sin

Chapters 25-32—The Lord will judge all the nations which stand against his people

Chapters 33-37—The Lord will lead his renewed people into a renewed land

Chapters 38-39—The Lord will personally destroy his arch enemy

Chapters 40-48—The Lord will live with his people forever in a city and land renewed like the garden of Eden.

The sequence guides us from the people of God in bondage through the Lord's judgement of their oppressors into a renewed promised land. This structure is obviously the same as the original exodus. If this were the only similarity, however, we could be making a lot out of nothing. But the parallels go much further. For example:

1 Ezekiel repeatedly used the phrase "that you may know that I am the Lord". This is the key phrase in Moses' encounter with Pharoah in Egypt. No other prophet used the phrase so deliberately

2 Ezekiel used the original exodus as a background for his prophecies of restoration (see e.g., 11:16-17; 20:32-38; compare 20:1-20)

3 Ezekiel identified the nations' sin as both oppression of the Israelites and personal defiance of the Lord, the two sins of Egypt in the original exodus

4 Ezekiel concluded his oracles against the nations with an extended and symbolic account of judgement against the Pharoah of Egypt

The reason for Ezekiel's use of the exodus tradition is obvious. The experience of the Iraelites in exile in Babylon mirrored that of their forefathers in Egypt. We have noted that their present dilemma questioned their identity and heritage. In this context, Ezekiel looked back to the greatest moment in their history to encourage his people in the knowledge the Lord was still the same and that he would redeem them once again.

Daniel

The book of Daniel makes two great contributions to the Old Testament. Firstly, it presents a portrait of the faithful Israelite in exile and how the Lord preserved him. Secondly, it clarifies how the Lord exercised his kingship over the earth. We will look briefly at both contributions.

Daniel the faithful exile   Ezekiel had set the record straight on three critical points: 1 Jerusalem was no longer the centre of God's activities; 2 the Lord did not favour his people in the homeland more than those in exile; and 3 the Lord was with his people in Babylon. But at least two questions remained: "How was an Israelite to express his or her covenant faith in Babylon?", and "What could he or she expect if they did remain faithful to the Lord?" The experiences of Daniel (and his friends) demonstrated the answers.

Daniel exemplified a faith which transcended nationalism. In the first few chapters of Daniel, our hero (like Joseph centuries beforehand) found himself alternately in high political positions and in prison. Both came from the hand of the Lord and both were the result of Daniel's faithfulness. Despite his topsy-turvy career, Daniel demonstrated a longevity which none of his masters could match. Surely this is the point of Daniel's life. The Lord caused the Babylonians and the Persians to rise and fall. Thus no individual or nation could create a lasting empire for itself (this is the point of Nebuchadnezzar's madness in Daniel 4:1–37). Yet the Lord's people endured beyond them all. Ultimately, it mattered little whether a person was from, or in, Jerusalem or Babylon. The Lord was king of the whole earth and he ruled to protect his people.

Daniel's vision of the Lord's rule over the earth   Daniel was written in two languages: 1:1-2:4a is in Hebrew; 2:4b-7:28 is in Aramaic;[8] and 8:1-12:13 is in Hebrew. This division has long puzzled interpreters. After all, what point could there be in using two languages? In diagram 7 I have tried to connect this phenomenon to another feature of Daniel's structure; namely, his movement between stories which probe the question of who has ultimate authority on the earth, and stories which describe God's delivering his people from human authorities.[9]

What was Daniel trying to say through this structure?

The book of Daniel largely conforms to a style of literature known as apocalyptic.[10] One of the chief features of apocalyptic writing is that God allows the author to see into

Hebrew Section: 1:1-2:4a—*The Lord prospers Daniel in a foreign king's court*

Aramaic Section: 2:4b-7:28: *The Lord is king over all the kings of the earth and he rules for the sake of his people*

> *2:4b-49—Authority:* The Lord reveals that he will establish an eternal kingdom which will overthrow all other kingdoms

>> *3:1-30—Deliverance:* The Lord rescues his people from the foolishness of the earthly king

>>> *4:1-5:31—Authority:* The Lord shows his absolute authority over earth's kings by humbling them when they exalt themselves

>> *6:1-28—Deliverance:* The Lord rescues his people from the foolishness of the earthly king

> *7:1-26—Authority:* The Lord reveals that he will establish an eternal kingdom through the one like a son of man which will overthrow all other kingdoms

Hebrew Section: 8:1-12:13—*The Lord will demonstrate his universal kingship in Israel's ongoing history*

Diagram 7: The structure of the book of Daniel in the light of its two languages

the mysteries of heaven and earth and the battles which take place between them, and how these mysteries shape the present and future experiences of God's people. There are several important ways in which Daniel may have conformed to this general pattern to convey his own message.

Daniel recognised that a heavenly dimension existed behind the scenes. In particular, the Lord ruled all the affairs of earth. Ultimately, national differences were irrelevant since all men were proud and defied the Lord—the rulers of earth were really all the same.[11] The use of the two languages highlighted both that the whole earth was to hear of the Lord's rule over it (the Aramaic section), and that the deeper significance of these visions remained a closed book to all those outside of the people of God (the Hebrew sections).

THE THEME OF THE NEW COVENANT

The need for a new covenant

The prophets of the exile never lost hope in the Lord's faithfulness. They fully expected that the covenants which the Lord had made with Abraham and David, and the essential framework of the covenant made at Mt Sinai, would continue to shape Israel's life. Jeremiah, for example, believed that these covenants would only cease if the Lord revoked his covenant with creation (Jeremiah 32:20–26). So long as day and night continued, Jeremiah said, the Lord would uphold his promises.

At the same time, we have frequently noted how each of the prophets re-expressed these covenants. No prophet expected the covenants to continue unmodified. Their conviction was grounded in their realism about the Israelites. They knew that the Lord was faithful and that there was nothing wrong with the way he had shaped each covenant. But no one was optimistic about the people. The prophets knew that if the future was to hold any real hope, then the Lord would have to deal with his people's hearts. The Lord would need to solve the problem of his people's hard-heartedness and rebellion. After all, it was their sin which had led to the exile.

The newness of the new covenant

Jeremiah's famous prophecy in Jeremiah 31:31–34 of a new covenant provided the definitive answer to Israel's problem in two ways. Firstly, the Lord placed his answer clearly within the context of their great past. Secondly, the Lord dealt with the core of the problem. So what made this prophecy so remarkable?

The new covenant is like the old   This new covenant would contrast with the covenant which God made with the Israelites at Mt Sinai. But if we only say this we may be misled. There are many ways in which the new covenant would be *like* the old covenant: The Lord initiated both— the Israelites did not create the covenants. Both covenants follow the Lord's acts of delivering his people—Mt Sinai followed the great exodus from Egypt (Jeremiah 31:32) and the covenant would be the natural endpoint of God redeeming and restoring his people (30:1–31:30). Both covenants involved law—both covenants demand perfect allegiance from each partner. And, finally, though Israel had broken the covenant bond, the Lord was her husband (31:32—Jeremiah alluded here to the fact that only the husband could divorce).

In other words, although the Israelites had behaved *as though* the covenant was dissolved, *in fact*, it wasn't. Thus the making of the new covenant presumed that the old still existed.

So much for how the two covenants are *not* dissimilar. But the text says that they *are* different. What is the distinctively new feature which made this covenant a *new* covenant? In answering this question we will explore the point that this new covenant proposed to deal with the core of the Israelites' problem.

The new covenant is quite unlike the old   We have noted already that the new covenant did not do away with the law.

Yet there was something new about the way the law would operate in this covenant. The Lord said that the law would be on the people's hearts (Jeremiah 31:33). In one sense, there is nothing new here since the Lord always intended his people to respond from the heart to the old covenant and its law (e.g., Deuteronomy 6:4–6; Psalm 51:10). Yet, unlike the old arrangement, the Lord would actually *put* the law on their hearts, rather than impress on them the *need* for it to be on their hearts.

The new covenant would do away with the need for instruction. Under the old covenant there was no guarantee that a person knew the Lord personally and intimately. If I knew the Lord intimately, but you did not, then I would exhort you to know the Lord for yourself. We were both in the covenant, but only one of us experienced this covenant as an intimate relationship. In the new covenant, however, every covenant person would have this immediate and intimate relationship (Jeremiah 31:34).[12]

God would forgive his people and no longer remember their sins (Jeremiah 31:34). The old covenant included an elaborate system of daily, weekly and annual sacrifices for the forgiveness of sins. Life in Israel was unimaginable without this ongoing ritual. Yet the Lord revealed that forgiveness would be final and complete as soon as the new covenant was made. Jeremiah obviously could not have understood how God would act in Christ to forgive his people. Yet he must have at least realised that God was going to do something which made sacrifice totally unnecessary. The problem of the old covenant, the problem of the sin of God's people, would be resolved in the new covenant.

So what is the newness of this new covenant? It is that the law will be on the *heart* of every covenant person. It is that every covenant person will *know the Lord intimately.* It is that every covenant person will be *forgiven for ever.* Most of all, it is that *every* covenant person will have all these blessings. The new covenant will mean that God's people will finally *experience* the full blessings of the Sinai covenant.[13]

THE NEW COVENANT AND THE GOSPEL

The genius of the New Testament's perspective on the new covenant is that God made this covenant with his Son, Jesus, and *not* with us. We need to explore here:
How Jesus attained this status
Why Jesus attained this status.

Jesus is the head of the new covenant

Under the old covenant, the Lord called the Israelites to live perfect covenant lives: they should love the Lord from their hearts; they should keep all the commandments without sin; and they should publicly demonstrate the character of their Lord. (The background I have in mind here includes Deuteronomy 6:4–6 and Exodus 19:5–6.) As we saw a moment ago, the new covenant did not make law obsolete. The new covenant still demanded absolute faithfulness.

In some previous studies,[14] we saw that Jesus fulfilled these obligations and promises concerning Israel's identity and calling. Jesus lived as the perfect son of the covenant, the perfect Israelite. This is why the New Testament transferred the Old Testament images and hopes for the Israelites to him. For example, instead of the Israelites being the vine(yard) (e.g., Psalm 80:14–16; Isaiah 5:1–7), Jesus now holds that title (John 15:1–5); instead of the nations gathering around the Israelites (e.g., Isaiah 60:3), they now gather around Jesus (e.g., John 12:32); and instead of the Israelites and their kings being the son(s) of God, now Jesus has that honour (e.g., Matthew 3:17).

Isaiah looked to the day when God would make his Servant a covenant for Israel and the nations (Isaiah 42:6). Jesus fulfilled this hope and became our covenant in the following all-important sense: the essential bond between God and his new people is *the bond between the Father and Jesus.* It is *not* first and foremost a bond between *us* and the Father. This is an important distinction and we need to develop the implications of it.

Jesus did everything in his life on our behalf. He

represented us in his perfect life, his complete sacrifice and his triumphant resurrection. The Father was totally pleased with his Son's life and he gave him a unique status in heaven because of his faithfulness (e.g., Philippians 2:9-11). The Father now views us in terms of his Son's actions and status. This is what Paul is driving at in his difficult argument in Romans 5:12-21: Jesus is now the representative of a new people, and God regards each of these people as having the same status as his Son. But why did the Father and Son make the covenant this way?

Why Jesus is the head of the new covenant

The answer returns us to what we saw about the problem of the old covenant. A covenant endures only if there is perfect faithfulness from *both* parties. In other words, it only takes *one* sin to break a covenant. This is why the new covenant will create a situation where no one sins (Jeremiah 31:34). Without this assurance, the new covenant would be no more effective than the old (Hebrews 8:7-13). Now imagine, therefore, what would have happened if the Lord had made the new covenant *directly* with us. If could not last because we still sin. But the Lord did not make it with us. He made it with his sinless Son.

Therefore, we enter into this new covenant with full assurance that neither party will ever break it. We have this confidence because we know that we enter through Christ. The covenant will endure not because we will always keep it, but because Jesus has kept and continues to keep it for us. The Father will not reject us for one all-important reason—he will not reject his Son.

DISCUSSION QUESTIONS

1 "We can talk about the idea of whether or not people can lose their salvation on the level of comparing one difficult Bible passage with another. But the gospel lies at the very root of the matter. If we say that we can lose the status Jesus gained for us on the cross, we deny that Jesus is really who

he says he is and that he really accomplished what he said he did." Discuss.

2 How does the death of Jesus allow us to accept the worst truths about ourselves and yet still have a healthy, positive view of our worth?

EXERCISES

1 Prepare a bible study on Hebrews 8:7–13 titled "Jesus our covenant".

2 Review the last series of devotional readings, bible studies or sermons which you read, wrote, attended or gave. Work through these three questions:

    a) Did they wrongly emphasise our faithfulness instead of Christ's? In other words, did they turn something which we should see as accomplished by Christ into something which we feel that christians still have to accomplish?

    b) What effects could this wrong emphasis have?

    c) How can we correct this mistake and re-emphasise Christ?

Notes

1 It may be helpful to repeat here the explanation given in chapter 7 about "Israel" existing as two related but distinct nations from about the end of Solomon's reign (922 BC) until the Babylonian invasion of Jerusalem in 587 BC. The northern nation was known as Israel. It ceased to exist in 721 BC. The southern nation was known as Judah (named after one of the tribes of the older *combined nation* of Israel). It went into exile in Babylon in 587 BC. Although both nations were exiled, we usually refer to the time after 587 BC as *the exile*. This is the period we are looking at in this chapter. From here on the word *Israel* will be used to describe the Old Testament people of God as a whole, even though after the exile these people were mostly from the old southern nation of Judah. When referring to the northern nation, Israel, as distinct from Judah, I will state that I mean the northern nation.

2 We will return to Jeremiah later to discuss his role in developing the idea of a new covenant.

3 You can read the account of Josiah's reform in 2 Kings 21:1–23:30 and 2 Chronicles 34:1–35:19. For the significance and impact of this reform see Ray Dillard (1987), *2 Chronicles*, Word Biblical Commentary, Word.

4 William Dumbrell (1984), *Covenant and Creation: An Old Testament Covenantal Theology*, Lancer/Paternoster, page 170. I have drawn a fair amount of the following discussion on Jeremiah from the outline on pages 170–172.

5 Dumbrell, *Covenant and Creation*, page 171.

6 Dumbrell, *Covenant and Creation*, page 171.

7 John used a similar structure in his Revelation. We will look at some similarities between Ezekiel and Revelation in chapter 22.

8 Aramaic is a language closely related to Hebrew. It was the common language of the Persian period. Jesus probably spoke in Aramaic more than in Hebrew or Greek.

9 I owe this insight into the movement between authority and deliverance to William Dumbrell. The way I have worked this out, including the chart, are my own impressions. The basic 1,2,3,2,1 of the middle section of the chart corresponds to an ancient literary device known as a chiasm. The significance of chiasms is discussed briefly at the end of chapter 22.

10 We will look at "apocalyptic" more carefully in the next chapter.

11 Two details in Daniel highlight this. Firstly, Daniel sets his accounts in the land of Shinar (Daniel 1:2). Genesis 11:4 identified Shinar with the great rebellion at Babel, and Zechariah 5:11 used it to locate the temple which housed the sins of the earth. Secondly, Daniel 2-7 alludes to different portions of Genesis 1-11, the story of mankind's earliest rebellions.

12 These differences between the old and new covenants are shown in a model in chapter 18.

13 If you would like to explore Jeremiah's prophecy further, see Dumbrell, *Covenant and Creation*, pages 172-185.

14 In this short section I am presuming the emphasis I have developed elsewhere about Jesus being the true covenant son, the true Israelite. We have explored this in the final sections of chapters 2, 4 and 8, and we will return to this emphasis in chapters 13, 14 and 18.

12 ISRAEL AFTER THE EXILE

Summary: The key point to this study
Jeremiah and Ezekiel laboured to make their people
see the inevitability and justice of the exile. But the time
came to move on from interpreting the past to rekind-
ling hope for the future. Ezekiel did this in his visions
of a renewed people, land, city and temple—visions
which reformulated the ancient themes of creation,
covenant and kingship (Ezekiel 34-48). As a result,
some of those who returned from Babylon to Jerusalem
had a new expectation and understanding of their
identity, calling and future as a people.

THE RETURN FROM EXILE, THE COVENANTS AND KINGSHIP

The bright prospects for those who returned

The exiles' hopes were realised in 538 BC. One year after
Cyrus, the Persian king, had overrun the Babylonians and
captured Babylon, he granted permission to the Jews to
return to their homeland and rebuild the city and temple
of Jerusalem (Ezra 1:1-4). Although many Jews remained
in Babylon, 42,360 of them journeyed home between 538
and 522 BC carrying with them the precious articles of the
temple and the hopes of reconstructing the ancient kingdom
of Israel-Judah (1:7-11; 2:64; 6:5; see 2 Kings 25:13-17).[1]
    The decree of Cyrus seemed to many of the Jews to be
the beginning of the fulfilment of the prophets' hopes:

Cyrus was one of the truly great men of ancient times, and one who stands in refreshing contrast indeed to the dreary succession of brutal conquerors who had preceded him across the pages of history. His policy was one of surprising moderation. Quite the opposite of what an Assyrian might have done, he made no effort to destroy national life in an orgy of pillage, deportation, and ruthless repression. On the contrary, he habitually respected the customs and honoured the gods of peoples subject to him. As far as he could do so, he trusted their native rulers. While the Persian government kept tight control of the whole structure and held it together by a complex administrative machinery, a very efficient army, and a well developed system of communications, it was apparently the official policy that conquered peoples be allowed as far as possible to live their own lives within the framework of the empire.[2]

Cyrus' enlightened and benevolent policies ensured that the Jews not only returned to Jerusalem, but that they did so under a leader from the house of David (Cyrus appointed Sheshbazzar then Zerubbabel as governors—both were heirs to the throne of David).[3] No wonder then that the Bible regarded Cyrus as the servant of Yahweh (see Isaiah 44:24-45:7).

The gloomy realities of a failed vision

Yet the visions of Ezekiel, the benevolence of Cyrus and a surge of enthusiasm failed to usher in the expected golden era. The building of the temple soon lapsed under the hardship brought by failed crops and the hostility of the surrounding peoples (Haggai 1:9-11; 2:15-19; Ezra 4:1-5, 6-24).

We must understand why the temple was so important in the struggles of the returnees. It was the key symbol of Israel's ancient traditions, the vision of Ezekiel and the (later) idealism of Chronicles. To cease rebuilding amounted to abandoning the restoration agenda and hope. This is the essential context for understanding the prophecies of Haggai and Zechariah, who both insisted that the temple restoration take precedence over residential development (Haggai 1:1-15; Zechariah 1:16; Ezra 6:14).

The temple was also the key symbol of the Israelites' distinctiveness from all other nations; it symbolised their history and faith. The temple distinguished the Jews from the surrounding peoples and even more importantly from those who had been relocated in the area by the Assyrians and Babylonians and who had intermarried with the remnants of Judah and Israel. The Jew's distinctiveness was threatened by the rulers of Samaria and other provinces who tried to stop the rebuilding of the temple by harassment and official appeals to the kings of Persia (Ezra 4; Nehemiah 4; 6:1-16). Moreover, if not stopped, intermarriage would in time have destroyed Jewish identity and culture (Ezra 9-10; Nehemiah 13:23-31).

Eventually, the people completed both the temple (Ezra 6:15—516 BC) and the city walls (Nehemiah 6:15-16—445 BC) and the city was repopulated (7:4-5; 11:1-2). Moreover, the two great reformers, Ezra (arrived from Babylon in 485 BC) and Nehemiah (arrived in 445 BC), reacquainted the people with the law of Moses, called them to repentance and reformed the priesthood (Nehemiah 8:1-10:39; 13:1-31). But the time and ministry of Malachi, the last of the Old Testament prophets, showed that the temple and reforms had never converted the hearts of the majority (Malachi 1:6-14; 2:11-16; 3:6-9). The true restoration of Israel waited a further four hundred years (3:1-4; 4:5-6; see Matthew 3:1-12; 11:10-14).

AN OVERVIEW OF THE WRITINGS AFTER THE EXILE

The Old Testament writers of this time viewed their people and circumstances from a variety of perspectives. Each book (except Esther) struggled to reconcile (1) the call to rebuild Jerusalem and its ancient traditions with (2) the reality of failure in this task and (3) a new prophetic vision of the future which both inherited themes from the former prophets and sought to re-express these in a manner appropriate to the life and times of the people.

Ezra and Nehemiah[4]

Derek Kidner provides the following helpful summary of the key events and personalities recorded in Ezra-Nehemiah:
  First there was the struggle to get the Temple rebuilt in the days of Zerubbabel (with Jeshua the high priest and eventually Haggai and Zechariah the prophets). This went on from 538 to 516, and it dominates Ezra 1-6, apart from a digression in chapter 4:6-23. Then we hear no more for nearly sixty years, when another expedition sets out from Babylonia. This time it is led by Ezra, whom the emperor has commissioned to enforce the law of Moses—a task whose immediate consequences bring the book to a painful and abrupt conclusion. The third great personality is Nehemiah, who largely tells his own invigorating story of rebuilding the city wall, of outfacing his enemies, repopulating Jerusalem and routing the traitors within his camp. By the end of these two books the former exiles have had their chief structures, visible and invisible, re-established, and their vocation confirmed, to be a people instructed in the law and separated from the nations.[5]
There is no doubt that many great things came out of those years. For example, the leaders revived the ancient traditions of Israel, including their tribal inheritance and their faith in Yahweh as the divine warrior (Ezra 2; Nehemiah 4:14-15); the law of Moses was restored to its rightful place in civil life; the cult was purified; and the remnant of the Israelites was preserved from being lost forever among the nations.
We cannot leave the two reformers without noting the down-side of their ministries. Ezra and Nehemiah had to call their people back to the law. But as the entire story of the Bible shows, law without an accompanying change of heart always leads to legalism and factionalism. Whether their ministries (unintentionally) initiated the drift, or whether they merely fuelled an older legalism and party spirit, the books finish on the "note of profound disappointment, with the community wracked by divisions between the priesthood and the laity".[6] And while those who adhered to the law perhaps opposed justifiably the powerful and political priestly faction, this emerging lay movement

contained within it the seeds of legalism which eventually flourished in Pharisaism between the Maccabaean revolt (167 BC) and the time of Jesus.

Haggai

The messages of Haggai and Zechariah epitomised the Jerusalem and temple centredness of the initial programme for Israel's revival. By the time of Haggai's ministry (520 BC), the returnees had been home for over fifteen years, the rebuilding had fallen into disarray and the people were experiencing drought and famine (Haggai 1:1–11).

Famine and no temple went hand-in-hand according to Haggai. Recalling the curse clauses of Israel's ancient covenant at Mt Sinai (see Deuteronomy 28:15–24, 38–42), the prophet drove home the critical issue of his day—the people did not recognise the rightful rule of their Lord, for if they did, they would finish rebuilding the supreme symbol of his kingship.

Unlike most of his forebears, this prophet's message achieved its desired effect; the people recommenced the building and Haggai responded with assurances that the Lord would restore the glory of Solomon's temple and that he would reestablish his rule over the world through the kingship he had promised to David's line (2:1–9, 20–23).

Zechariah

Zechariah lifted Haggai's prophecies to a new level both in terms of the richness of his drawing from the past and the fantastic proportions of his vision for the future. Like his contemporary, Zechariah centred his oracles on Jerusalem and the temple. But unlike Haggai's relatively straightforward preaching, Zechariah delivered most of his messages in powerful and enigmatic visions.

The book falls into two halves (Zechariah 1–8, 9–14), the second of which provides a commentary on the first (or perhaps a re-expression of it from another perspective). Both halves move from the rebuilding of Jerusalem and the Lord's return there (1:7-17; 9:9-17), to its role among the nations as the centre of the earth and the supreme symbol of the Lord's kingship (8:20-23; 14:1-9).

This Jerusalem centredness did not distract the prophet from the condition of the people to whom he ministered. In both halves, he addressed the problems of poor (and even corrupt) leadership and impurity (e.g., 3:1-10; 6:9-15; 7:4-12; 11:4-17; 13:1). But his oracles painted a vision of restoration which exceeded anything the returnees had known or would know—a vision which waited for the king who would enter Jerusalem on a donkey (9:9; see John 12:12-15).

Malachi

The book of Malachi may well be the last prophetic words which God spoke to his Old Testament people and passed on to us as his inspired scripture.[7] Following the finest traditions of prophecy, Malachi placed his message within the framework of the great events and truths of Israel's heritage.

The Lord still loved the Israelites and upheld the covenants he had made with Abraham and at Mt Sinai (Malachi 1:2, 6; 2:10; 4:4). This latter covenant called for an obedient response from the heart, but the people had broken faith prompting the prophet to utter a series of legal accusations against them: they had defiled the temple (1:6-14), perverted the priesthood (2:1-9), intermarried and broken their marriage vows (2:11-16), oppressed the vulnerable (3:5), and robbed and slandered God (3:8-15). The prophet called the people to return to the covenants or else face the fury of the Lord's coming (2:17-3:5).

But again like the prophets before him, Malachi held out a promise of protection and renewal alongside his threats. The day of the Lord would bring *both* judgement and purification—a remnant would pass through the fire. And the new Elijah would appear to turn the hearts of the people to a new experience of compassion (Malachi 3:1-4; 4:1-6).

Chronicles[8]

Chronicles was a tract for its times—a last call to revive a programme for rebuilding the old empire in the face of the collapse of the restoration under Ezra and Nehemiah. The Chronicler did this by presenting David and Solomon as the ideal kings and their reigns as the high point of Israel's history—patterns for the leaders of those who returned and for their hopes of a future king. The Chronicler used several parallels to show this.

He saw Solomon as a new David, then David and Solomon as a new Moses and Joshua. The Chronicler also drew numerous parallels between the building of the tabernacle and the temple. In particular, he presented Solomon and Huramabi (his chief builder) as the new Bezalel and Oholiab (the builders of the tabernacle). So what was the Chronicler trying to say through these parallels?

The Chronicler wanted the Jews to see Solomon's reign and the temple as the features of Israel's golden era. He wanted to show that this era had all the significance of Israel's experience at Mt Sinai, the events of the conquest of Canaan, and the promises made to David. Thus Solomon's era was the enduring model for Israel's kingdom, the pattern for those who had returned from Babylon to rebuild Jerusalem's glory.

Esther

We have already noted that many Jews remained in Babylonia after the decree of the Persian king, Cyrus. But what happened to them? Did they maintain their faith and identity? The story of Esther provides some answers.

The basic thrust of the story is that the Lord controls the nations and directs their histories for the good of his people—yet the book *never* mentions God! So how did the writer make his or her point?

The book is full of "coincidences": a Jewish girl just *happens* to be the most beautiful in the land; Mordecai, *happens* to overhear the plot against the king; Esther *happens* to survive her unlawful appearance before the king; Mordecai's rise to honour *happens* to occur between Esther's first and second banquet; the king *happens* to return and mistake Haman's plea as a sexual advance; Haman's gallows for Mordecai *happens* to be ready just in time to hang Haman.

The author seems to have structured the book as a chiasm, a literary device which arranges a story somewhat symmetrically and which puts emphasis on the "middle" section. That section is Esther 6:1-3—the story of the night on which sleep just *happens* to elude the king, and he *happens* to call for his scrolls, and the scribes *happen* to read about Mordecai's good deed, and the attendants *happen* to know that Mordecai was never rewarded, and Haman *happens* to be in the king's court!

The book plays on several "reversals", including these:

1 The Jews move from powerlessness to power and wealth
2 Those who support the Jews move from a low to a high status
3 Fasts and mourning lead to celebrations
4 Esther's entry warrants punishment, but the king rewards her (4:15–5:3)
5 Haman's glory passes to his arch-enemy, Mordecai—though Haman had come to the king to seek Mordecai's death
6 Haman dies on the gallows he ordered built for Mordecai

Esther's position, as a Jew who finds herself in the entourage of a foreign power, brings to mind such notables as Moses, Joseph and Daniel. And these stories convey the same theme of God preserving his people through his control over foreign powers.

Finally, the author identified Haman as an Agagite (Esther 3:1). This seemingly incidental detail links the story with an ancient chapter in Israel's past. At the time of the Exodus, God cursed the Amalekites (Exodus 17:14-15); yet the Amalekites continued to harass the Israelites; Saul was commanded to destroy them, but he spared *Agag* their king (1 Samuel 15); and by the time of Hezekiah the Amalekites were still around (1 Chronicles 4:43). Thus the death of

Haman is the last instalment of the curse and the episode serves our author's purpose of emphasising that God remembers and keeps his promises to Israel for all time.

THE CONTRIBUTION OF APOCALYPTIC LITERATURE

Reading Daniel and Revelation gives most of us the feeling that we are in strange and unfamiliar territory. We sense both that these books belong together and that they differ widely from most of the rest of the Bible. So what are these books: what is this style of literature which many call 'apocalyptic'; what distinguishes them from the rest; and, most importantly, what do they have to say to us?

Most discussions about so-called apocalyptic literature tend to bog down into debates about cataloguing its distinctive features; defining its relationship to prophecy; and, therefore, identifying which Old Testament portions are truly apocalyptic. It seems better to recognise that:

1 Certain distinctive traits, which do not appear in the bulk of the prophetic writings, do occur prominently in some parts of the books we call apocalyptic
2 Where these traits occur, the writers were using them to re-express "older" themes like creation, covenant and kingship from new and sometimes radical perspectives.

The following features occur quite frequently within Daniel and Revelation, and within many pieces of literature written in the two or three centuries before Christ and the century or so after him:

1 *Revelation*—a prophet or visionary comes to understand the heavenly councils and his times by being granted to see into the mysteries of heaven (e.g., in a dream, vision or personal appearance; sometimes an angel interprets the experience)[9]
2 *Dualism*—life is a conflict between two or more forces which control the physical and supernatural world (e.g., good/evil; light/darkness)
3 *Determinism*—history moves to the plan of God; the conclusion to the spiritual conflict is already known; the future is spelt out in definite periods of time and

sequences of events (e.g., "time, times and a half a time", "1000 years", "a little while", "and when. . . then will")

4 *Symbolism*—the key characters and events of the conflict and plan lie masked behind (usually) well-known and bizarre images (e.g., beasts, horns, numbers, ancient identities and traditions [like Adam and Enoch])[10]

The apocalyptic passages[11] and books used these features to re-express Israel's ancient and prophetic traditions and thus provide new perspectives on God's relationship to the world. The prophets were concerned chiefly with their own time; thus their message emphasised sin, judgement, repentance and renewal. But as the hope of a national renewal seemed more and more remote in light of the hardness of Israel and Judah's hearts, the prophets looked increasingly to the future for a time when God would reassert his authority and put all things right. Diagram 8 shows the relationship between the two. As John Bright puts it, apocalyptic meant "both the intensifying and the reshaping of Israel's historic faith in the triumph of God's rule".[12]

Thus apocalyptic had a deep interest in the approaching new era of God's dealings with the creation and the means by which that new era will dawn. Graeme Goldsworthy says it well: "It is generally accepted that the apocalyptic idiom gives much sharper definition to the transition from the old

	Prophecy	**Apocalyptic**
Writer's perception	"things are so bad that we must return to our origins"	"things are so bad that a whole new creation is needed"
Emphasis	Stresses *continuity* with the past while presupposing *discontinuity*	Stresses *discontinuity* with the past while presupposing *continuity*
Focus	Local (i.e., Judah, Jerusalem and Israel)	Cosmic
Call to the people	Repent!	Stand firm! Trust!

Diagram 8: The relationship between prophecy and apocalyptic

age to the new age of the kingdom of God".[13] Apocalyptic also often casts its message in universal and cosmic proportions—it concerns both the whole earth and the non-human beings involved in conflict behind the scenes of this world.

Although more Old Testament apocalyptic writing is associated with the exile (e.g., Ezekiel 38–48; Daniel) than with the return from Babylon (e.g., Zechariah), the return was a major stimulus to its development. In particular, apocalyptic writing flowered as those who began to lose faith in the reconstruction clung to the hope that God would not abandon his people. Perhaps God initiated this new expression at this time not only to reassure those who wondered what the future held, but to encourage their faith through a fresh realisation that God was still prepared to open the heavens and reveal himself to them anew.

In the centuries which led up to the time of Christ, apocalyptic visions and traditions increasingly leaned towards the bizarre and fantastic.

> This expected end event became in later writings virtually the exclusive centre of interest—indeed, well-nigh an obsession... This became, it need hardly be said, the pathology of Judaism. Forever scanning the times for signs of the coming end, drawing diagrams, as it were, of how that end should come, it moved in a dreamworld where the coming of the Kingdom was momentarily expected in clouds and glory.[14]

No wonder then that so few recognised the coming of the kingdom in the child born in Bethlehem, the humble worker of miracles and the suffering servant upon the cross.

The last word on our topic belongs to John Bright:

> ...strange though this 'apocalyptic mind' is to us, we must not forget that there lived in it a great faith that even those who sneer at it do well to copy. For all its fundamental pessimism about the world, it was in the profoundest sense optimistic. At a time when the current scene yielded only despair, when the power of evil was unbroken beyond human power to break it, there lived here the faith that the victory of God was nonetheless sure: God holds the issues of history; he is a God *whose Kingdom comes.*[15]

THE RETURN FROM EXILE AND THE GOSPEL

Throughout the first twelve studies, I have drawn connections repeatedly between the events, themes and hopes of the Old Testament and the person and work of Jesus Christ. Perhaps the time has come for me to stand back a little from this habit and to explain briefly *why* I make the sorts of connections which I have shared with you. But I would like to offer my reasons in a somewhat indirect way. Rather than focus on questions of methodology at this point, I would like to outline how one New Testament writer saw the wider significance of the coming of Jesus and leave you to judge whether or not my connections are faithful to his vision.[16]

Paul and the "mystery" of Christ

Paul the apostle used the expression "revelation of the mystery" or words to that effect several times in his epistles (e.g., Romans 16:25; Ephesians 1:9-10; 3:3-9; Colossians 1:26-27; 2:2). Taken together these passages associate the following ideas with the mystery of Christ:

the mystery concerns things long hidden but now revealed
it concerns the prophets
it centres in the gospel
it concerns all the nations
it concerns faith and obedience
it stands at the centre of God's eternal plans
it concerns God's plan to place Jesus at the centre of all creation
it was revealed by the spirit
it concerns the inclusion of the Gentiles within the one group of God's people
it concerns our sharing personally in what Christ has done, including the gift of his personal presence with us
the mystery is Christ himself.

We can formulate this complex web of connections into a simple set of propositions and a focusing question (see diag. 9).

Situation	God has always had a plan for all creation God has been revealing this plan
Complication	God chose initially to express this plan in a very limited way (i.e., through *one* nation) God has revealed his plan piece by piece and always in the limited terms of his dealings with this one nation
Focusing Question	When and how would God finally reveal and complete his plan for all creation?
Answer	In Christ! The mystery is now revealed and the plan has shown its final destiny

Diagram 9: The plan of God fulfilled and revealed in the mystery of Christ

The same insight enabled Peter to quote from the prophet Joel on the day of Pentecost (Acts 2:14-21; Joel 2:28-32). Much of the passage he quoted does not fit his own actual circumstances. Yet Peter believed passionately that the events concerning Jesus, which are described in the four Gospels, occupied the central place in God's plan of redemption and that they occurred as the natural consequence of all that God had done and promised through the history of the Israelites (1 Peter 1:10-12; Hebrews 1:1-4). This framework of understanding led Peter to make his connection with the prophet, and to create a precedent which he and other preachers were to follow (e.g., Acts 2:25-28, 34-35; 3:22-23; 4:11, 25-26; 8:32-33; 13:41,47; 15; 16-18).

Final reflections on Jesus and the Old Testament

I would like to finish this study, and indeed these first twelve studies, with two quotations from the reflections of others on the finality of the gospel and the way this fulfilled the longings of the Old Testament:

Speaking about apocalyptic, Graeme Goldsworthy has this to say:

Apocalyptic takes the concept of qualitative time to its high point by the symbolic use of numbers to express, not literal quantities of time in days, months, and years, but the quality of the time. The quality of the time is determined by the significance of God's action within it either to save or to judge. It was a failure to allow for this that gave strength to the scoffers who taunted the early Christians over their expectation of the imminent return of Christ (2 Peter 3:3-4). 'Where is the promise of his coming?' they asked. If God promised a 'day of God' on which all the prophetic words about the coming of the kingdom will come to pass, how is it that he still has not appeared in his reigning glory?. . . Peter shows us in that context that *the day* of the Lord is not confined to a quantity that we can discern as so many days or years or even millennia. But, it is still the day of God's action to bring in the kingdom. Of this new age which has intruded into the old through the coming of Christ, Paul says, 'This is the appointed time, this is the day of salvation' (2 Corinthians 6:2).

That the new age has invaded the realms of the old age is the cause of the apocalyptic conflict. But let us be clear about the perspective the gospel gives to this. As we have seen, the Old Testament views the two ages consecutively. . . The New Testament modifies this by showing that all the ingredients of the end are there in the gospel. Man's sin is judged in the person of Christ on the cross. The new humanity is resurrected in Christ and ascends to the right hand of God. Satan is confounded and cast out. His power is removed by the finger of God. The decisive conflict has taken place and the kingdom of Christ is victorious. The old age goes on but it can never be the same again. All history subsequent to the death and resurrection of Christ is history at the end.[17]

Starting his thoughts from the reconstruction of Jerusalem which followed the return from exile, John Job sees that the theme of restoration has received a deeper significance and wider application through the gospel of Jesus Christ:

The important truth which emerges is that while Christians regard the return from exile as ultimately a foreshadowing of heaven itself *(perhaps?)*, the kind of certainty of heaven that it is possible to have in this earthly life is one which comes from a relationship with

God that begins now. Christians see themselves as so little deserving or initiating the relationship, that they ascribe their privilege to God's choice before the beginning of the world. But the consciousness of it begins with the act of faith which both puts them in the right with God and sets them apart as members of Christ's church. This experience is enough, as we have seen, to translate those who were formerly subjects of the kingdom of darkness into freemen of the kingdom of God's Son (Col 1:13). It does not yet appear what we shall be. But in God's sight believers are already his sons. That is restoration indeed.[18]

DISCUSSION QUESTIONS

1 Ezra and Nehemiah tried to reform and revive their people (with mixed success). Many christian leaders take on similar challenges and often do so by introducing a new programme (e.g., small groups, evangelism strategies, discipleship courses, buildings, new leadership structures). Compare and contrast one such approach today with what Ezra and Nehemiah did. What emphasis and hope should we put on such "reformations"?

2 Preachers often use texts from the books of the return from exile. What do you think of the connections they make between text and punchline in the following three sermons:

a) 2 Chronicles 7:14—"God will heal and exalt our nation today if we repent"

b) Various texts from Ezra 6:13-22, Nehemiah 3-4, 6:1-7:3—"God called us to build this new church. Despite the opposition of Satan we have finished the task and now we dedicate it to God's glory"

c) Malachi 3:6-12—"You must not rob God; give him the full 10% of your income" or "Give God your tithes and he will bless you abundantly"

EXERCISES

1 The New Testament saw a connection between the following passages and Jesus:
Zechariah 9:9—John 12:15

Zechariah 11:12-13—Matthew 27:9-10
Zechariah 12:10—John 19:37; Revelation 1:7
Zechariah 13:7—Matthew 26:31
Study carefully the original context of each quote and the context of the New Testament use of it. What general principles of interpretation were the New Testament writers working from? How far can we follow their lead?

2 Create a bible study outline of Haggai 2:1-9. Remember to work with its context, the development of any themes throughout the Bible, and the way the gospel re-expresses the passage.

Notes

1 For an overview of the history of the return to Judaea, see J.J. Bimson and J.P. Kane (1985), *New Bible Atlas*, IVP-Lion/Tyndale, page 56 and John Bright (1953), *The Kingdom of God*, Abingdon, chapter 6. On the significance of the exile, see Bright (above), Peter Ackroyd (1968), *Exile and Restoration*, Westminster/SCM and Walter Brueggemann (1977), *The Land*, Fortress.

2 Bright, *Kingdom*, 156-157.

3 The exact nature of Sheshbazzar's role within the Persian administration remains debatable. The translation "governor" may be too strong. See Bimson and Kane, *Atlas*, 56.

4 The chronological relationship between the ministries of Ezra and Nehemiah has been debated for many years. You will find a helpful treatment of the issues in Derek Kidner (1979), *Ezra and Nehemiah*, Tyndale Old Testament Commentary, IVP, pages 146-74.

5 Kidner, *Ezra and Nehemiah*, 13.

6 William Dumbrell (1985), Unpublished notes on Ezra-Nehemiah.

7 Like many other Old Testament books, Malachi records very few historical hints for us. It is possible that he prophesied before the Ezra-Nehemiah reforms—though most conservative scholars opt for a time period between 450-400 BC. The lack of clues should remind us to be wary of dogmatic assertions about details like dating (and authorship).

8 This brief section summarises the section on Chronicles in chapter 7.

9 "Apocalyptic seems essentially to be about the revelation of the divine mysteries through visions or some other form of immediate disclosure of heavenly truths." Christopher Rowland (1982), *The Open Heaven*, Crossroads, page 70. Rowland's work provides a healthy correction to the usual emphasis on apocalyptic as being all about the future.

10 The role of images and symbols in the Bible are discussed more fully in chapter 22.

11 Apocalyptic features are in passages like Isaiah 24-27; Joel 2; Habakkuk 3; Ezekiel 38-39; Zechariah 9-14.

12 Bright, *Kingdom*, page 163.

13 Graeme Goldsworthy (1984), *The Gospel in Revelation*, Lancer/Paternoster, page 65.

14 Bright, *Kingdom*, pages 167-168.

15 Bright, *Kingdom*, page 169.

16 It is inappropriate at this point to enter into a full discussion of how the New Testament understood the Old Testament, or of how we are to read the Old Testament. Others have outlined the issues of this debate skilfully, e.g., John Goldingay (1981), *Approaches to Old Testament Interpretation*, IVP and Moises Silva (1983), "The New Testament Use of the Old Testament: Text-Form and Authority", in *Scripture and Truth*, edited by D. Carson and J. Woodbridge, Zondervan.

17 Goldsworthy, *Revelation*, pages 124–25.

18 John Job (1984), *The Teaching of the Old Testament*, SU/CLC, page 106.

13 THE COMING OF THE KINGDOM

Summary: The key to this study
When Jesus began to preach that the "kingdom of God was at hand" he was using an expression with which his audiences were familiar. Although it was not a common biblical expression, the Jewish writers after the Old Testament had used it frequently to describe the coming time of salvation associated with the appearance of the Messiah. But Jesus used the expression in an unprecedented way. While much of what he said was similar to other teachers of the kingdom, he did not offer his hearers any political or national liberation. Instead he pointed people to the humble way of discipleship and to his own suffering as the way of entry to this kingdom.

THE KINGDOM OF GOD

Jesus and the four Gospel writers used the expression *the kingdom of God* to say that God as King had broken into their world in a decisive way, pushing back the kingdom of darkness and releasing God's people from their bondage.

The term was *not* common in the Old Testament (Daniel 7:14, 27 is an exception), but the idea was.[1] In fact, the idea of the kingdom of God fits in so well with the Old Testament that it is like a bucket which captures and carries all the Old Testament hopes and expectations, including themes like exodus, law, prophets, temple, king, Zion, sabbath, ark, day of the Lord.

The Jewish hope for a messiah

We have seen in our studies in the Old Testament that the prophets envisioned a great future time of restoration. Different prophets saw this future through different and complementary perspectives. But all the prophets agreed that one ingredient was essential to each vision of the future. That ingredient was the Lord coming personally to his people.

During the period between the return from exile in Babylon and the time of Jesus, the Jews gradually refined this idea of God coming to his people into an expectation that God would come *in the person of his special representative* (we see glimpses of this in John 1:20, 41; 4:29; 7:31). In particular, the Jews looked to the arrival of a *messiah*, an "anointed one".[2]

Although the word messiah occurred only rarely in the Old Testament and the other Jewish writings, nevertheless the idea was well established in that the Old Testament had spoken about kings and prophets as the anointed representatives of God and his people (see 1 Samuel 2:10; 2 Samuel 7:12; Psalm 2:2). The prophets picked up this idea and used it to describe the king whom God would raise up in the last days (see Isaiah 11:1-3; Zechariah 9:9-10). Some of the later Jewish writings developed the expectation of a messiah, and especially a messiah-king like David of old. Consider the following examples:

"For my Son the Messiah will be revealed, together with those who are with him" (IV Ezra 7:28)

"And it will come to pass when all is accomplished that was to come to pass in those parts, that the Messiah will then begin to be revealed" (Apocalypse of Baruch 29:3)

"O Lord, you chose David...and swore to him that his kingdom would never fail before you.... Raise up to them their king, the son of David...that he may reign over Israel...and gather together a holy people" (Psalms of Solomon 17:4, 23, 28)

The hope for a kingdom of God

The phrase *kingdom of God* was common in the days before and during Jesus' life.[3] The Jews linked their hopes for the kingdom with their expectations of a messiah. Jesus linked these concepts and fulfilled the truth within them. Yet Jesus did not fulfil these hopes *exactly* the way the various visionaries and teachers had foreseen them. Jesus brought major changes to these expectations.

In Jesus the messiah was God himself (Matthew 1:18–23; Luke 1:68). Jesus brought the concept of the kingdom of God out of the distant future and into the immediate present in a way that the Jews could not appreciate. Howard Marshall, writing about the radicalness of Jesus' teaching concerning the kingdom, put it this way: "To say that the End was near was not unprecedented. To say that the future kingdom of God was *already* present was unparalleled".[4] At the same time, Jesus did not abandon the idea of the kingdom also having a *future* dimension. Jesus believed that there were two aspects to the timing of the coming of the kingdom:

1   The kingdom had decisively come both in himself (e.g., Luke 4:21; see Isaiah 61:1–2; Matthew 12:28; Luke 17:20), and in people's hearts (Mark 10:15)
2   The kingdom was still coming (Matthew 6:10; Luke 19:11; Matthew 25:31–46)

Jesus' concept of the kingdom ran against the popular ideas of what it would be like. In particular, he refused to identify his kingdom with a military overthrow of the Romans. Instead, he insisted that his presence had brought the sovereign rule of God to earth (Matthew 12:28), and that the kingdom commanded all people (including Jews) to follow Jesus in humble discipleship. He made his concept of the kingdom even more scandalous by tying it into servanthood and death (Mark 10:35–45).

So how did this kingdom come?

THE BIRTH OF JESUS

In the century or so before the birth of Jesus, God was setting the scene for his Son's ministry and creating favourable conditions for the spread of the kingdom through the first disciples. Three factors were particularly instrumental:

1 Alexander the Great's campaigns, three centuries or so earlier, led to the spread of Greek culture and the establishment of a common language (Greek) and many social similarities and advantages throughout the known world (e.g., easier communication, transportation, and trade)
2 The Romans, from about sixty years before Jesus, brought political order to the known world and the possibility of virtually unhindered travel within it
3 Jewish nationalism kept Israel's hopes alive despite the many failures and false hopes (e.g., the Maccabean revolts, Zealot movements, and religious and political splits between the Pharisees, Sadducees and Essenes)

Prophecy revived as Jesus' birth drew near (e.g., Luke 1:46-55; 57-66; 67-79; 2:28-32). These prophecies came to be seen as a link between the coming of Jesus and the Old Testament prophets' faith that the Lord would remember his covenants and be merciful to Israel (Luke 1:54-55; Psalms 105-106). These prophecies also recalled the wider prophetic picture of gathering in the nations (Luke 2:30-32; Isaiah 42:1-7) and they explain part of the significance behind the wise men visiting Jesus (Matthew 2:1).[5]

The place of Jesus' birth also provided clues about Jesus' identity and the significance of his appearing. Whatever note of humility the manger might strike (Luke 2:12), the location was highly significant. Bethlehem was the scene of another remarkable marriage among Jesus' ancestors (Ruth 4:11-12), the hometown of his most famous forefather, David (1 Samuel 16:18; Luke 2:4), and the prophesied origin of Israel's future king (Micah 5:2).

Likewise, Nazareth, the town of Jesus' youth, was significant for his identity and mission. Although it is difficult to relate this town to any specific prophecy (though see Matthew 2:23; John 1:46), Nazareth marked Jesus as a

Galilean. This both connected Jesus with Isaiah 9:1 and moved the centre of his ministry away from Jerusalem, the doomed city.[6]

The escape of Joseph, Mary and Jesus to Egypt created a parallel between Jesus' life and the experience of the exodus.[7] As Pharoah had tried to end the line of Abraham's seed (Exodus 1:15-22), so Herod had tried to cut off the line of promise (Matthew 2:16-18; Genesis 3:15). And like the ancient people of God and the prophet's vision (Hosea 11:1; Matthew 2:15), the Lord once again called his firstborn out of the land of slavery. When Jesus commenced his public ministry, he did so via three strong parallels to the original exodus and the events immediately after it:

His passage through the water

His trial in the wilderness

His giving the new "law" on the mountain.

Jesus' birth made it clear that the kingdom of God was coming with the full authority and power of the prophets, and that Jesus' ministry would be at least as significant as the greatest events of Israel's history.

THE MINISTRY OF JOHN THE BAPTIST

The Old Testament background to John's ministry

For centuries the prophetic voice lay all but silent, replaced by scribes, visionaries and withdrawn communities. The people of God lived under foreign domination, many of them yearning for the kingdom. Then, suddenly, they heard the last and greatest of the prophets crying out, "The kingdom of God is near" (Matthew 3:2; 11:7-15). Like all the prophets before him this prophet's message carried the twofold note of doom and promise.

The Old Testament background to John's ministry is rich. The Gospels used Isaiah 40:1-11 and Malachi 3:1-2 and 4:5-6 to associate him with some of the greatest of the prophets (Mark 2:2-3) and to place his ministry in the context of their prophecies of an era of salvation. As the new Elijah (Malachi

4:5; Matthew 11:14; 1 Kings 17–19), John called the people
to repent (Matthew 3:6, 12; Luke 3:3). In other words, he
called them to align themselves with and welcome the coming
kingdom. As the messenger of Isaiah 40:1–3, he prepared
the people's hearts for their coming king and redemption.
But, in the spirit of the covenant law, John also announced
that Israel was under judgement (Matthew 3:7–10,12; Micah
6:1–2).

Jesus would baptise with the Spirit and fire

John saw that the twofold message which shaped his ministry
would also characterise Jesus' ministry. Jesus would harvest
his people through a baptism of Spirit and fire (Matthew
3:16–17). Some details about John, his prophecy and its Old
Testament background help to clarify the meaning and
significance of the baptism which he believed Jesus would
administer:

1 John never gave any background to his practice of
baptism. There aren't any clear Old Testament
precedents, yet other groups of his time did similar
things. In any case, the crowd seemed to understand
its relevance

2 His baptism probably drew on a broad Old Testament
background, including ceremonial washings (e.g.,
Genesis 35:2; Exodus 19:10–19; Numbers 8:7,19:7–10),
prophecies of a future cleansing (Ezekiel 36:24–25, 33),
and perhaps an analogy with Israel's path through the
sea (Isaiah 43:2)

3 The threshing floor (Luke 3:17) was a common Old
Testament image for judgement (Isaiah 41:15–16;
Jeremiah 15:7)

4 Both Isaiah and Malachi prophesied that the Lord's
coming to save Israel meant that the people would
undergo a refining judgement (Isaiah 4:3–6; Malachi
3:1–4; 4:1–6).[8]

The context of Luke 3:16 leads us to see Jesus' baptism
of Spirit and fire as one baptism on one group of people;
namely, all the Jews. The above-mentioned Old Testament

prophets believed that the Lord would put all his people through the ordeal of judgement while preserving a remnant. John saw that Jesus would fulfil this by causing a radical separation in Israel (Luke 3:17).

In a sense, Jesus went through the same fiery baptism (Luke 12:49–50). Not that Jesus needed to be purified, but that he endured his people's judgement so that he could purify them. Jesus went through his own baptism of death, his own separation, so that he in turn could baptise with the Spirit and fire at Pentecost. This baptism at Pentecost was the final separating judgement on Israel. It ended any nationalistic hope for the Jews, any thought of a narrowly Jewish new covenant, and it marked the new people of God as those baptised into Jesus' death.

JESUS' BAPTISM AND TEMPTATION

Jesus was able to pour out the Spirit at Pentecost because of his unique identity as the Son of God. This title was first used to describe all Israel (Exodus 4:22). Later it passed on to David and his descendants in their role as Israel's representatives and as an expression of their special covenant relationship to the Lord (see Psalm 2:7; 2 Samuel 7:14; Luke 3:22). Therefore, when the Father spoke at his Son's baptism, he affirmed that Jesus was both the Messiah and the true Israelite, the true covenant Son.

The words "in whom I am well pleased" and the descent of the Spirit on Jesus strengthened his identity as the Messiah and the initiator of the day of salvation. They did this by connecting him with the great Messiah-Servant prophecies of Isaiah (Isaiah 11:2; 42:1–4; 61:1–4; Matthew 12:18–21; 3:16). The Spirit empowered Jesus for his ministry as the Messiah (Matthew 12:28; Luke 4:1,14), and confirmed him as the anointed one and the channel of the Holy Spirit (Luke 3:16; John 7:37–39; Acts 1:8).

Jesus' temptation (Matthew 4:1–11) acts out the struggle between the kingdom of God and the kingdom of darkness which characterised his life. The temptation replayed the essence of Israel's trial in the wilderness (see Exodus 15:22–17:7) and the original temptation in the garden (Genesis

3:1–5). On each occasion, God's people were tempted to find their identity and security in their own or the tempter's wisdom, rather than in God's words and the relationship they enjoyed with him.

In Jesus' case, Satan sought to undermine his messiahship and therefore the arrival of the kingdom of God (Matthew 3:17; 4:3,6). Jesus did not triumph over Satan through some mighty display of power, but through his obedience as the true Servant-Son and his confidence in his Father.

THE GEOGRAPHY OF JESUS' MINISTRY

After being baptised at Bethany (John 1:28), which is very close to Jerusalem, Jesus made the long journey to Galilee in the north to begin his public ministry. Matthew, Mark and Luke each make a point of this. Jesus only rarely ministered in Jerusalem. In fact, when the four Gospels focus on Jerusalem they do so as the scene of Jesus' rejection, the home of his accusers, and the place of his death. When Jesus confronted the disciples with the question of his identity (Mark 8:27), he did so at Caesarea Philippi—about as far from Jerusalem as Jesus ever got. He also met his disciples in Galilee after his resurrection (Mark 14:28).

But why emphasise Galilee and avoid Jerusalem? There are two sides to the answer: The kingdom of God was moving beyond Israel (Isaiah 9:1; 42:6; 49:6 and Matthew 4:15); and this meant that God would reject Jerusalem as the city of his special delight (Matthew 23:37). Once again, we see that the kingdom of God came in a way that was radically different to what people had expected.

DISCUSSION QUESTIONS

1 Some christians talk about "kingdom living" as some higher form of christian living. But if being a christian means sharing in the kingdom, how can there be any "higher levels" of christians? Does this teaching offer anything positive, or does it seriously distort the gospel?

2 "There is little evidence in the way christians live to support our claim that the kingdom of heaven is at hand. Rather, the evidence would suggest that, in most churches, the culture of economic, political and military systems of the United States (or Australia or Britain etc.) is at hand. The question must be asked why the churches do not live by their confession."[9] Discuss.

EXERCISES

1 Look up all the references to the kingdom of heaven/God in either Matthew, Mark or Luke. (You and your friends might like to look at different books and later on discuss what you find.) Catalogue them according to what they say about Jesus, the timing of the kingdom, its effects and what it means to belong to the kingdom. Draw your findings together into a one-page essay titled "What is the kingdom of God?" (Later you might like to use your essay as a discussion starter in a small group.)

2 Prepare a bible study on Matthew 4:1-11. Contrast the passage with Genesis 3:1-5 and Exodus 15:22-17:7. Make sure you think through some of the implications of Jesus' death and resurrection for how we face temptation today.

Notes

1 Our discussion in chapter 7, plus our repeated emphasis on the themes of creation, covenant and kingship, outline some of the Old Testament background to the phrase *the kingdom of God*.

2 The English word *Christ* comes from the Greek word *christos* which translated the Hebrew word *mashiah* which meant anointed. The word *messiah* is an English variation on *mashiah*.

3 The references include Enoch 1-36, Psalms of Solomon 17-18, Enoch 37-71, and the Assumption of Moses 10:1,3.

4 I.H. Marshall (1985), "The hope of a new age: the kingdom of God in the New Testament", *Themelios*, 11:1, page 7.

5 We will return to the theme of the gathering of the nations in chapters 19 and 21.

6 See the section on "The Geography of Jesus' Ministry" for a few thoughts on the significance of Galilee and Jerusalem in Jesus' life.

7 This connection is made at the end of chapter 3.

8 See also Isaiah 40:13, 44:1-5, Joel 2:28-32 and Zechariah 13:7-9.

9 Jim Wallis (January, 1980), "Rebuilding the Church", *Sojourners*, 9:1, page 10.

14 THE POWER AND MYSTERY OF THE KINGDOM

Summary: The key to this study
Jesus' teaching about the kingdom of God did not conform to the expectations of his audience. They thought it was far off—Jesus said it had come and yet was coming in greater power. They thought it belonged to them as a matter of course—Jesus spoke of no one being able to enter it unless his Father granted them this privilege. They thought it would be Jewish—Jesus spoke of the end of Jewish special privilege and status and the birth of a new people of God drawn from all nations. They thought of military power, political strength, wealth and status—Jesus spoke of suffering and humility. They thought the kingdom would arrive in splendour—Jesus knew it looked as insignificant as seeds and yeast. They expected great oratory that would rouse the masses to action—Jesus preferred to speak in parables.

THE KINGDOM OF GOD IN JESUS' TEACHING

Jesus taught with unprecedented authority (Matthew 7:28–29). He claimed an authority for his words which could only be justified if he was in fact the Son of God, the Messiah, the King of the kingdom of God (John 7:14–44). What did Jesus teach about this kingdom?

The kingdom of God and the Father

We need to start where Jesus' thinking about the kingdom started. The kingdom was the Father's gift to Jesus and the disciples (Luke 12:32; 22:29; Matthew 13:43; 25:34). Jesus made it clear that his special Father/Son relationship with God lay behind his and the kingdom's power and authority. In the Lord's prayer, Jesus linked the coming of the kingdom in power with a new-found intimacy for those who belonged to the kingdom; they could now call God, *Father*. So, first and foremost, the kingdom was relational; it was about God creating a new web of family relationships with his people through his own Son (Matthew 5:48; Luke 6:36; 8:21).

The kingdom of God and the Spirit

In our last study, we saw that Jesus carried out his ministry in the power of the Spirit and that this brought him into direct conflict with the kingdom of darkness (Luke 3:22; 4:1,14; Matthew 12:28). This is what made the Pharisees' attempt to attribute his ministry to Beelzebub so foolish and serious (Matthew 12:21,32): *foolish*, because it totally misunderstood the nature of Jesus' kingdom and totally disregarded the abundant evidence of Jesus' triumph over the demonic; and *serious*, because they were compounding their own guilt by blaspheming against the Holy Spirit.

Jesus extended this connection between the coming of the kingdom and the activity of the Spirit even to the question of how a person entered the kingdom (John 3:3, 5; later writers developed this—Romans 14:27; Galatians 5:21; 1 Corinthians 4:20). In this regard, he followed the Old Testament expectations that God would pour out his Spirit on his people as the distinctive gift of the new age and covenant (e.g., Joel 2:28; Isaiah 44:3; Ezekiel 37:14).

The kingdom of God and Jesus

It is clear that Jesus knew who he was (e.g., Matthew 3:15; 4:1-11; 16:13-20; Mark 10:45; John 8:12-30). It is equally clear that he did not want his identity, or at least a certain way of expressing that identity, revealed to all (Matthew 16:20; Mark 1:23-25, 34, 44-45; 3:11-12; 5:43; 9:9; but compare Mark 5:19, 20). How do these two ideas go together?

The connection is in the differences between how Jesus understood the title *messiah* and the sort of figure that the people expected. The Jews wanted someone to end the Roman occupation of Palestine, and they presumed violence was the only way to achieve this (John 6:14-15). Even the disciples misunderstood this for a while (Luke 9:33; John 2:20-25; 7:1-13).

This wasn't Jesus concept at all. So he did and said certain things in a deliberately ambiguous way to "clarify" his real identity. In particular, Jesus almost always called himself the *Son of Man* in a way which joined two seemingly contradictory titles or ideas: the Suffering Servant (Isaiah 52:13-53:12) and the glorious Son of Man (see Daniel 7:13-14).[1]

The kingdom of God and Israel

We have already seen how Jesus concentrated his ministry around Galilee and other places rather than on Jerusalem. This indicated that he was not bringing the gifts of the kingdom to the Israelites as a nation. The Jews believed that the kingdom would initiate a national restoration of Israel. They also believed that this kingdom was their unquestionable right because of their heritage (Luke 3:7-9). But Jesus rejected both their interpretation of the kingdom and their claim of ownership of it. Jesus only promised them judgement as a nation (Matthew 19:28; Luke 22:29).

Jesus was not saying that Jews couldn't enter the kingdom. But he said that a person's heart response to him was the essential decision which would either include or exclude them (Matthew 19:16-30). Jesus expressed this personal commitment to the kingdom in his words about discipleship. The kingdom was creating a new people whose lives followed the humble servanthood of their master (Mark 8:34-35; 9:33-37; 10:35-45; John 13:1-17).

The kingdom of God and the future

Jesus believed that the kingdom had already come in himself (Isaiah 61:1–3/Luke 4:21; Matthew 12:28) and that it was still coming (Matthew 6:10; Luke 19:11; Matthew 25:31–46). Howard Marshall summarises this two-sidedness in the following way:

> Perhaps the most fundamental fact . . . in Jesus' teaching about the kingdom of God was the way in which he looked forward to the future full manifestation of God's rule but at the same time proclaimed and brought into being that same rule during his ministry. For Jesus the future had already commenced in the present time. The Old Testament had prophesied the hope of God's future action as king, and it expressed its hope on the basis of the mighty acts of God which had already been experienced especially at the exodus. The early church was conscious of living in the era of fulfilment. Its hope for the future was based on what it already knew of the present working of God.
>
> Consequently, when we talk about the kingdom of God we are talking about something which is actually happening here and now, inaugurated by the ministry of Jesus, and now 'come in power' since his death and resurrection (Mark 9:1). . . Through his death and resurrection he has been shown to be both Lord and Messiah (Acts 2:38). The hope of a new age is thus a hope that has been coming true ever since Jesus first began to proclaim: "The time is fulfilled, and the kingdom of God is at hand" (Mark 1:15).[2]

JESUS' MIRACLES

Jesus' miracles were sermons in action. They were not raw demonstrations of power, but they said something about who Jesus was and what the kingdom was about.

Ever since mankind's first sin, the kingdoms of God and darkness have waged war with one another, and the kingdom of darkness has cruelly afflicted people. So, as the two kings of the warring kingdoms met head-on, the intensity of this age-old conflict grew. This is the drama behind Jesus' miracles over the demonic realms and death (Matthew 12:28; Mark 5:22-43; Isaiah 25:8). Jesus, the kingdom of God, was pushing back the kingdom of Satan, ending the curse of Genesis 3 and anticipating the blessings which would follow the resurrection of Jesus and his followers.

Alongside these more obvious and acute results of sin, there is a sense in which the whole created order is in conflict. Jesus, the Messiah-King, began to restore the earth in his miracles over nature, such as when he stilled the storm (Mark 4:35-41; Psalms 65:7; 89:9; 107:23-30) and walked on the water (Mark 6:45-52).[3]

THE PARABLES AND THE KINGDOM OF GOD

The parables relate to the kingdom in many ways. The parables are about the kingdom. The illustrations or starting points (soils, weeds, yeast, banquet, etc.) emphasise various aspects of the kingdom like its insignificant beginnings, irresistible growth, size, the way it separates people, the radicalness of discipleship (i.e., membership in the kingdom), the unexpectedness and swiftness of its final stages, and the movement away from Israel-centredness to a people drawn from every nation.

The parables made Jesus' audience come to grips with him, the King of the kingdom. They forced them to acknowledge that he was the one bringing the kingdom. To respond to Jesus was to respond to the kingdom (see Matthew 18:5-6). Yet the parables-kingdom connection is even bigger than just their content.

All communication is made up of three essential elements: *speaker, message,* and *audience.* Each of these, in the case of the parables, says something about the kingdom. In the case of the *message,* we need to go further and speak about both its *form* and *content.*

The parables were an unusually indirect type of communication. They did not appear to be indirect. In fact, they appeared to be simple, easy to understand stories. Yet the parables had *a mysterious way* of revealing and concealing at the same time; they seemed to hide as much as they gave. The parables were themselves *a mystery* in that they revealed the kingdom by producing *a mysterious reaction* in their hearers; hardening in some, illumination in others.

In the space of a few verses the various parables each highlights a different aspect of the kingdom. The effect on Jesus' listeners was to force them to make a decision one way or the other—either to "hear" or "not to hear" his message.

THE PARABLE OF THE SOWER: THE PARABLE ABOUT PARABLES

The parable of the sower, the parable about parables, highlights this bigger picture of power, fullness and mystery. (Matthew 13:1-23; also Mark 4:1-20 and Luke 8:4-15). When the disciples asked, "Why do you speak in parables?", Jesus gave one answer in two parts:

1 He used parables because they combined all the truths about who he was, what the kingdom was like, and how this affected people

2 The parable of the sower was about how people respond to the kingdom which was demonstrated by the disciples' and crowd's reactions to the parable at the time

In other words, the parable of the sower forced another question: why use parables at all? And that question in turn revealed a yet deeper question: what is this kingdom? The parable actually illustrated its answers to the two questions! Jesus used parables because they preserved the mysterious nature of the kingdom. In other words, people could not understand the kingdom by themselves. The parables, the kingdom, made hard hearts even harder unless the King of the kingdom granted eyes to see and ears to hear (Matthew 13:11).

Jesus also pointed to the Old Testament prophet Isaiah when he answered the disciples. We need to understand how Jesus used Isaiah 6:9-13 if we are going to grasp what he was saying and doing in the parable of the sower. It is important to see the passage in its context: Isaiah 1-12, a fairly self-contained section with a strong emphasis on kingship. I break down the section like this:

1:1	Set in the reigns of four kings of Judah
1:2–31	The kings and people were corrupt
2:1–5	Restoration would include Zion, God's throne
2:6–4:2	Judgement on Judah's leaders
4:2–6	Restoration would place the Branch in a new Zion/Sinai
5:1–30	Judgement on Judah
6:1–13	The Lord is the true king—the king would harden Judah's rebellious heart, yet spare a remnant
7:1–10:4	Judgement on Judah's kings—promise of a new king
10:5–34	Judgement on Assyria showed the Lord to be the true king
11:1–16	Judgement on Judah's kings—more promises of a new king
12:1–6	Summarising song of praise

Isaiah 6:1–13 was Isaiah's call to be a prophet and, in particular, to announce judgement on the Israelites. This judgement included the fact that the people would not be able to understand the prophet (losing the knowledge of God was itself a covenant curse). Yet the Lord would not totally destroy his people; he would spare a remnant (Isaiah 6:13).

Jesus was both the King and the Prophet (John 12:37–41; Matthew 13:53–58). Like Isaiah's original message of judgement and hope, Jesus' message hardened those who were already resisting him and his kingdom and it softened those he came to save (Matthew 13:53–58). So the coming of the kingdom meant the end of the Israelites' status as a privileged nation. They could now only enter the kingdom alongside the Gentiles and Samaritans through humble faith and the king's mercy.

Finally, the kingdom provided a boundary to the meaning of the parables. All the parables were about the kingdom. Yet that kingdom was as powerful and mysterious as Jesus' identity and all that he came to do and say. For these reasons we should perhaps see some wider relevance in Jesus' original parable, the parable about Jesus. Vern Poythress speaks

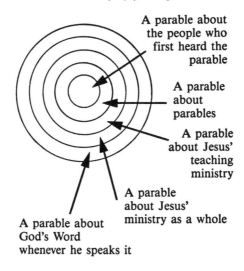

A parable about
the people who
first heard the
parable

A parable
about
parables

A parable
about Jesus'
teaching
ministry

A parable
about Jesus'
ministry as a whole

A parable about
God's Word
whenever he speaks it

Diagram 10: The different levels of relevance of Jesus' parable about the sower and the soils

about the parable of the sower as having ramified levels of meaning. He pictures it in this way.[4]

DISCUSSION QUESTIONS

1 You may have heard people say that Jesus spoke in parables to make it easier for his audience to understand him. How does that line up with Matthew 13:10–17? Why do you think the above explanation is so popular?

2 The motto of Jesus' ministry could well have been Luke 4:18–19. What do you think of the following quote?

... the New Testament letters are filled with discussions of the spiritual life that interweave the heralding of the good news with topics like racial intolerance, the eating of foods used in pagan ceremonies, the position of women, family relationships, prostitution, homosexuality, the relief of poverty. To equate the spiritual with the non-physical is completely unintelligible by New Testament standards. To isolate evangelism from the context of the world's concerns emasculates one and ignores the other.[5]

EXERCISES
1 Outline a bible study titled "The foolishness of being a christian". Base your thoughts around Matthew 13:31–33, 44–52 and 1 Corinthians 1:18–31.
2 In exercise 1 of chapter 13, you researched the references to the kingdom in one of the four Gospels. In the light of the present chapter review what you did then, and extend your essay to three pages. (Writing is one of the best ways to stimulate thinking.)

Notes
1 We looked at this title in chapter 7 and we will return to it in chapter 17.
2 I.H. Marshall (1985), "The hope of a new age: the kingdom of God in the New Testament", *Themelios*, 11:1, page 12.
3 For an even bigger picture of this restoration see Isaiah 35:5, 6, 42:7, 50:8, 61:1–3, Luke 4:18, 2 Corinthians 5:17, Colossians 1:20, and Revelation 22:1–5.
4 Vern Poythress, lectures on the Gospels, Westminster Theological Seminary, USA.
5 Harvie Conn (1982), *Evangelism: Doing Justice and Preaching Grace*, Zondervan, pages 68–69.

15 THE SCANDAL OF THE KINGDOM: JESUS' DEATH

Summary: The key to this study
Jesus' teaching about the kingdom of God pointed eventually to his own role in it. That role took him to his death. He was convinced that his death (and resurrection) was the key to fulfilling the Old Testament hopes of forgiveness. He believed also that his death (and resurrection) was the key to the kingdom coming in power and to his Father creating a new people of God. The writers of the letters in the New Testament confirmed this. They believed that Jesus' death (and resurrection) was the turning point of history and the ultimate basis of a new relationship with God. This event held such value for these writers that they searched for many different perspectives through which to explain its significance.

THE EVENTS SURROUNDING JESUS' DEATH

Jesus' understanding of his destiny

A deep sense of mission always characterised and energised Jesus. As early as his childhood, he knew that his unique relationship with his Father would shape his life (Luke 2:41–52). The four Gospels pictured his life as an unfolding drama, a series of events and experiences moving towards a specific goal—the time when his Father would glorify him (Luke 9:51; John 2:4; 7:1–9, 30; 12:20–28). Jesus knew that this time of glorification would be his death. Jesus knew that he had come to die (Mark 8:31; 9:12; 10:33, 45). This was part of the scandal of Jesus to the Jews. They knew the theology and necessity of sacrifice well enough, but they had not understood either that they needed forgiveness to enter the kingdom (Matthew 9:6), or that the suffering of the servant in Isaiah 53 was an essential part of the messiah's role. Thus the people rejected and persecuted Jesus as they had each of the prophets before him (Matthew 17:7–9).

Jesus was always aware that he was fulfilling the Old Testament and, as his death drew near, he wove a tapestry of Old Testament themes and hopes to help his disciples understand what he was doing. We will pause briefly to consider some of these.

The last supper

Jesus put his death and resurrection in the context of the passover (Luke 22:14–20). On the eve of Israel's exodus, their greatest experience of salvation, the Israelites slaughtered firstborn lambs as substitutes for their own children. They understood the act as a brutally graphic symbol of their need for forgiveness and redemption.

Although the original story emphasised Egypt's sin, Israel had its own sin also; each Israelite would have fallen under judgement without the substitute lamb. Thus the Lord warned them to stay inside their homes during the night in which he passed over the land in judgement. It is at this point that Jesus paralleled the original passover in a most remarkable way. After he ate the meal, he went outside the house while it was still night to put himself willingly into the hands of his betrayers. Jesus showed that the kingdom would only come if he bore the sins and guilt of his people.

When Jesus spoke of his blood as the blood of the (new) covenant he probably was referring to both Exodus 24:8 and Jeremiah 31:31–34 (Matthew 26:27–28). When God made the covenant with the Israelites at Mt Sinai, he had Moses throw the blood of the sacrifice over the Israelites to symbolise that God had confirmed the covenant. The passover lamb and the sacrifice at Mt Sinai both underlined the truth that the Israelites could only be in the covenant because of God's mercy shown in the sacrifice as a substitute for the people. Likewise, Jesus saw himself establishing the blessings of the new covenant (Jeremiah 31:34b) through his death for his people (1 Corinthians 5:7; 11:25; Ephesians 5:2).

The garden of Gethsemane

Jesus' actions in the garden reflected Old Testament themes. After Jesus and the disciples left the upper room, he quoted Zechariah 13:7 to predict Peter's denial (Mark 14:27). Although it is difficult to tell how far Jesus meant to apply this prophecy, he must have been aware of its broader context and of how relevantly that context suited his own situation. Zechariah believed the Lord would execute judgement on Israel and its leaders, and that he would purify a remnant through that judgement (Zechariah 12:10–13:1; 13:7–9). Jesus took that judgement and, at the same time, he became the remnant. He became the last true Israelite, and he gave that same status to his people as the new people of God because they had passed through the judgement *in him*.

In the garden, Jesus asked his Father to take away his cup (Luke 22:44). What was Jesus referring to? The answer lies in several Old Testament prophecies; Isaiah 51:17–22, Jeremiah 25:15–38 and Ezekiel 23:32–54. In each of these, the prophet pictured God's judgement as an overflowing cup given to his enemies to drink. Jesus understood the connection only too well. He was about to experience the full force of his Father's fury against our sin.

The trials

Why did Jesus die? Certainly not for his own sins or crimes. Jesus was tried by the Jewish legislative assembly (the

Sanhedrin, Mark 15:53-65), Pontius Pilate (the Roman governor, Luke 23:1-5), King Herod (verses 6-11), Pilate again (verses 12-25), and finally the crowd (verses 18-23). On each occasion, Jesus' innocence shone through his accusers' trumped up charges, false witness and self-righteousness.

So why did Jesus die? Was he unable to stop his death? On the last occasion that Pilate interrogated Jesus, the key issue was Jesus' identity (John 19:1-16). Pilate feared Jesus (and the crowd) because Jesus had been labelled the Son of God. This title must have suggested to Pilate that Jesus had an authority equal to or possibly even greater than his own. In any case, Pilate protested his authority over Jesus (verse 10). Jesus' reply takes us to the heart of why he died. Pilate had absolutely no authority over him (verse 11a). Nor did anyone else. Although the Jews were responsible for their actions (verse 11b; Acts 2:36; 4:27-28), Jesus died because he and his Father had decided that he would become a ransom for his people (Mark 10:45).

The crucifixion

Jesus knew the horror which waited for him on the cross, the horror which would lead him to cry out, "My God, my God, why have you forsaken me?" (Mark 15:34; Psalm 22:1). We might run into error if we say that there was a time when the Father completely severed his relationship with his Son. Yet, in some sense, this is what Jesus experienced on the cross. Along with the physical horror of crucifixion and the shame of carrying our guilt, Jesus endured the feeling of being utterly alone to bring us to his Father.

The various phenomena accompanying Jesus' death also revealed who he was and what he was doing. The eclipse and earthquake (Matthew 27:45, 51, 54) were in keeping with the awesome events the prophets had pictured concerning the day of the Lord (Isaiah 24:1-4, 18b-23; Joel 2:30-32). Jesus' death brought together both sides of the prophets' vision of that day, and in the order they had always anticipated: judgement first, and then blessing.

If these phenomena still left open the question of whether

or not Jesus was cancelling the Jews' status as God's people, then the tearing of the temple curtain removed all doubt of it (Matthew 27:51). After centuries of rejecting God and breaking his covenant, the Jews sealed their national fate by condemning the Lord of the covenant in order to preserve their own status (Matthew 27:18; 26:57-68; Luke 23:8-12). In the one great act, Jesus ended Israel's privileged status and began ours (Hebrews 7:19-20; 9:24-28).

THE SIGNIFICANCE OF JESUS' DEATH: GOSPEL WORDS

The New Testament drew from many different experiences and everyday pictures to explain the meaning of Jesus' death. Each picture provided a perspective or window through which to see what Jesus had accomplished. They are not different things or events or acts that happen to us, but partial pictures that together express something of the breadth of what he has done for us. We will look at five of the most important ones.

Propitiation: Jesus turned away God's anger

The picture here is the temple and particularly the sacrifices. Israel always lived under the shadow of God's holiness. Like the original passover, Israel's ongoing experience of the tabernacle, temple, priests and sacrifices reminded them that their Lord could not and would not tolerate sin, but through the sacrifices God turned his anger away from his people (Exodus 32:11-14; Psalm 78-38). The sacrifices were called atonements or propitiations because they turned away God's anger.

The New Testament saw the same concept behind Jesus' death. The Old Testament sacrifices were only ever incomplete and temporary (Hebrews 9:6-10; 10:1-4)—God patiently held back from demanding what sin really deserved (Romans 3:19-29, 25-26). Jesus' death was a perfect sacrifice perfectly satisfying the demands of God's perfect justice (Hebrews 9:11-15; 10:5-18). So Jesus' death turned away

God's wrath; it was a propitiation (Romans 3:25; 1 John 2:1-2; 4:10).

Redemption: Jesus paid for our freedom

The picture is a slave market—Jesus' death was a ransom. The Greeks and Jews believed that the ransom money for a slave or prisoner of war was an equivalent for a forfeited life. The Greeks used the idea in a religious sense too, but they paganised the idea by probing the question of *to whom* the ransom was paid.

The New Testament never went in that direction. Instead, it always emphasised *how much* redemption had cost God. All of us were slaves to sin (John 8:31-34; Romans 8:5-8) and its power was too strong for us to break. And the law only added to our debt and bondage (Romans 4:14-15; 7:7-13; Galatians 3:10-12). Christ broke the power of sin, cancelled the debt over us, and redeemed us from the curse (Romans 3:24; Galatians 3:13; 4:4-7; Ephesians 1:7). His death paid the price of freedom and life for us.

Like all the other pictures of salvation, redemption has a *now* and *not yet* flavour. We are *now* free from the world and its powers in that they are no longer our masters. *Yet* we still wait to experience that freedom in all its fulness (Luke 21:27-28; Romans 8:23; Ephesians 4:30).

Justification: Jesus made us right with God

The picture is a law court. God is just and his requirements must be kept. So to enjoy a right relationship with him we must keep his standards. But we can't and don't. We break the law and fall short of his standards (Romans 3:23). And our own efforts cannot make amends for what we've done (Galatians 3:1-11). So the verdict is guilty, and the sentence is death.

Unlike us, however, Jesus perfectly obeyed his Father and satisifed the requirements of his law. This is what the Bible means when it calls Jesus *righteous*. Jesus' righteousness meant that he could never be guilty of sin. It also meant that he could stand in our place and take our death sentence.

When Jesus did this he identified so fully with us, and the Father accepted his act so completely, that now we don't hear the verdict, "Guilty!" God now declares us innocent on the basis of what his Son did. Our legal system today leads us to associate innocence with someone who was let off through a loop-hole or technical hitch, and innocent people often live under a cloud of suspicion and accusation. But our justification isn't like that. God has credited the "rightness" of Jesus to us through faith (Romans 3:1–5:11). As far as the Father is concerned we are now as righteous as his Son.

Our justification means that we never have to fear judgement day. There will be no surprises for us on that day since God has already pronounced our verdict through his Son's death and resurrection (Romans 5:9–11).

Reconciliation: Jesus brought God and us together

The picture is warfare and family disputes. Sin is personal—it offends and alienates. We deserved God's hostility because we broke our relationship with him and we continued to fight against his authority and love.

But the Father wouldn't leave it there. Because he loved us, he initiated a plan to reconcile himself to us, to bring us back together. Jesus accomplished this by removing the barrier between us. His death and resurrection brought peace between God and us through turning away God's rightful anger and providing a way for us to be forgiven and welcomed home (Romans 5:10; 2 Corinthians 5:18–21; Colossians 1:20–22).

The New Testament took the picture of reconciliation beyond our individual and personal experience. In some sense, Jesus' death and resurrection reconciled the whole world order, or at least began a process of reconciliation and transformation that Jesus will finish when he returns (Romans 8:21; 2 Corinthians 5:17–6:2; Ephesians 1:10, 22; Philippians 2:9–11; Colossians 1:15–20). Peter O'Brien puts it this way: "the presupposition is that the unity and harmony of the cosmos have suffered a considerable dislocation, even a rupture, thus requiring reconciliation".[1] When Jesus comes again we will experience a new world in which everything has reached the potential which God intended it to have (Revelation 22:1-5).

Adoption: Jesus made us the children of God

The different pictures which we have outlined above add colour and depth to the overall story of what Jesus did for us through his death, and of the new status he won for us. We no longer fear judgement because the ultimate sacrifice has turned away the Father's anger and cleansed us; we are now free; we are perfectly righteous in God's eyes; and we are now his friends. But, as magnificent as these pictures are, the New Testament painted our new position even more intimately.

We are God's adopted children (e.g., John 1:12-13; Galatians 4:5-7; Ephesians 1:5; 1 John 3:1-10). As well as the common experience of being in a family, this picture also drew on an Old Testament image of the relationship between God and his people (Exodus 4:22; Hosea 11:1). We are now the children of Abraham, the children of God (Romans 9:7-8; Galatians 3:25-29; 4:6-7). Just as the Father announced that Jesus was his beloved Son, he has given us this same status (Romans 8:17; note also how 2 Corinthians 6:18 used 2 Samuel 7:14).

We now have the full privileges and inheritance that go with being in his family (Romans 8:17). However, the *not yet* of our experience of Jesus' death applies here as well in that we wait to fully enter our inheritance (Romans 8:19-21; Ephesians 1:14, 18; Colossians 1:12; 3:24). In the meantime, God gave us his Spirit to confirm our status as his children, to continually encourage us not to give up, and to lead us to call him boldly *"Abba!"*, our own dear Father (Romans 8:14-16; Galatians 4:6-7).

THE SIGNIFICANCE OF JESUS' DEATH: VICTORY OVER
DEATH AND SATAN

In our last two studies, we touched on the ancient warfare between the kingdoms of God and Satan and its climax in Jesus' ministry. John Stott has helpfully outlined this struggle and its resolution in Jesus like this:[2]

1 *Conquest predicted*—Genesis 3:15; 1 Chronicles 29:11
2 *Conquest begun*—Matthew 12:28; Luke 4:18-19; 10:18
3 *Conquest achieved*—Colossians 2:13-15; Hebrews 2:14-15
4 *Conquest confirmed and announced*—Acts 2:24; Ephesians 1:20-23; 1 Peter 3:22; Revelation 5:9-14
5 *Conquest extended*—Acts 26:18; Colossians 1:13; 1 Thessalonians 1:9
6 *Conquest consummated*—Romans 16:20; 1 Corinthians 15:24-28; Philippians 2:9-11; Revelation 7:15-17; 20:10

In his death and resurrection, Jesus conquered everything that stood against us. He overcame the power of the law (Galatians 5:18) and broke the tyranny of the world (Romans 6:6, 14; 12:1-2; Galatians 5:19-21; 1 John 2:15-16), of death (1 Corinthians 15:55-57; 2 Timothy 1:10), and of the powers of Satan (Ephesians 1:20-22; Colossians 2:13-15).

Once again, we see the *now* and *not yet* of the gospel. Jesus definitively defeated Satan and death through the cross. We now experience its liberating and cleansing power. We are now right in God's eyes and no one can accuse us. Yet Satan actively seeks to bring us down (Ephesians 6:10-18; 1 Peter 5:8-9) and we experience the pain of death (1 Thessalonians 4:13-14). So, we wait patiently for the Lord to return and to display publicly and fully the fruits of the triumph of the cross (Romans 16:20; Revelation 5:9-14; 7:15-17).

DISCUSSION QUESTIONS

1 A friend of yours says he wants to be a christian. He says that he has repented but he doesn't feel forgiven. Would you tell him to keep repenting till he does feel forgiven? Or perhaps that he should just get on with doing christian things

until he feels right? Does Jesus' death offer your friend any other ways forward?

2 Why does the New Testament label us as *saints* and not as *sinners*? After all, we do still sin!

EXERCISES

1 Read Hebrews 9-10. How many different shades to the significance of Jesus' death can you see there?

2 Prepare a bible study on Romans 5:1-5. Focus on how the gospel provides a solid base for our experiences and feelings.

Notes

1 Peter O'Brien (1982), *Colossians and Philemon*, Word Biblical Commentary, Word, page 53.

2 See John Stott (1986), *The Cross of Christ*, IVP, 231-239.

16 THE TRIUMPH OF THE KINGDOM

Summary: The key to this study
It is true and important to say that the resurrection of
Jesus proved both who he was and that the Father had
accepted what he did for us. But these truths do not
say enough. Jesus' resurrection was not only the proof
of what he did—it is itself something that he did for
us. Through his resurrection, Jesus became the new
Adam, the first person to experience all that God had
intended for humans since the creation. He became the
source of the resurrection life we enjoy now, and the
guarantee that at death we too will enter fully into the
same quality of existence.

THE OLD TESTAMENT BACKGROUND

The Old Testament hardly ever spoke explicitly about life
beyond the grave. Instead, it focused on life under the
covenant within the promised land. An Israelite could look
forward to the blessings of knowing the Lord intimately,
enjoying a secure prosperous life in Canaan and of passing
on his inheritance to his children. Alternatively, he faced the
curses of various physical and social calamities and of dying
with nothing to pass on. Thus the Old Testament focused
more on life now and the finality of death than on an
afterlife. Nevertheless, the Old Testament did look beyond
the grave in at least two important ways.

One of the ways was in relation to what an individual

could expect after death (e.g., Psalm 139:8; Job 19:25-27; Daniel 12:13). Although the Old Testament did not paint a full picture of life after death, it seems that at least some Israelites believed that God's covenant love and faithfulness would keep hold of them beyond the grave.

More important was the Old Testament emphasis that the Lord's plans were eternal. He had redeemed his people and would not allow death to have the last word. Despite the severity of his judgement on Israel's sins, the Lord would rescue them from death and grant them long lives in the new earth (e.g., Isaiah 25:8; 35:1-10; 43:1-13; 65:17-25; Hosea 13:14; 1 Corinthians 15:54-57).

This reassurance of God's overall plans undergirded the more specific promises regarding the messiah's eternal reign. There are two key people here. One is David. He became the model of what God had in mind for his messiah and his people. God had promised David an eternal kingdom (2 Samuel 7:1-16; Psalm 2:7-9; also Matthew 3:17; Acts 13:33; Hebrews 1:1-5; Revelation 12:5). The other figure is the son of man, in Daniel's vision, to whom the Ancient of Days handed an everlasting dominion and an indestructible kingdom (Daniel 7:13-14; Matthew 26:64).

However, Isaiah's last servant song (Isaiah 52:13-53:12) is perhaps the clearest and most dramatic picture of the Lord's determination to conquer death for his people. Although the Lord humbles the servant to the point of death and burial on behalf of his people (53:8-9), he then exalts him and hands him a people as his inheritance (verses 10-12). The servant's triumph over death provided a powerful focus for the broader pictures of restoration given in the other servant songs (42:1-9; 49:1-7; 50:1-11) and the rest of Isaiah 40-66.

THE NARRATIVES OF JESUS' RESURRECTION AND ASCENSION

The disciples' reactions

We have often noted that Jesus knew he had come to die and that his death would be the time of his glorification

(Mark 8:32; 9:12, 31; 10:33, 45; Luke 9:51; John 2:4; 7:1-9, 30; 12:20-28). At the same time, Jesus knew he was the Messiah. He knew that he would receive an eternal kingdom and, therefore, he knew that he would rise from the dead (Luke 9:51 [Daniel 7:13-14]; 24:26, 46; John 2:19-22; 10:17-18; 12:23-36).

For the disciples, however, it was a different story. Jesus' death shattered their hopes. They had failed to understand Jesus' predictions (Luke 24:6-8). In particular, they still expected Jesus to restore the Israelites physically and nationalistically (Matthew 18:1; 20:21; Luke 24:25-27, 44-49; Acts 1:6). That expectation ruled out the possibility of Jesus dying. Thus, in the hour of Jesus' greatest trial, all but one of his friends deserted him (Mark 14:50; Luke 23:49; John 19:26). Furthermore, when Jesus rose from the dead, he appeared to the women first (a scandal in a Jewish frame of reference) because his disciples were still hiding in fear (John 20:19).

Jesus' resurrection, however, turned their fear into excitement and boldness. A little over a month later the disciples were boldly proclaiming to their countrymen that Jesus' resurrection had fulfilled the Old Testament hopes and that now all people must submit to the resurrected Jesus as Lord (Acts 2:14-36; 3:14-15; 4:10-12). In fact, the resurrection became both the touchstone of their faith and the cause of their suffering (Acts 4:1-2; 5:29-33; 1 Corinthians 15:1-3).

Jesus' ascension

As Jesus left his disciples he lifted up his hands and blessed them (Luke 24:50-53). What was Jesus doing? There are several different sides to the idea of blessing in the Old Testament, and Jesus may well have had each of them in mind.

God's blessing of Adam and Eve (Genesis 1:28) followed and expanded his promise and commission to them (verses 26-27). Similarly, the blessing of Abraham through a priest Melchizedek (14:18-20) followed his promise to bless all nations through Abraham (12:1-3). It seems in these cases that the blessings sealed the promises. Yet, perhaps even more importantly, the blessings gave or promised the power to fulfil those promises. It was as though the blessings guaranteed the promises and then put them into action.

The high priest blessed the Israelites on the Day of Atonement and at other times (Leviticus 9:22-23). In that context, the blessing confirmed or guaranteed the covenant relationship and all its privileges (Numbers 6:22-27).[1]

Jesus' ascension was part of his exaltation. It confirmed him as the great king and priest at God's right hand (Psalm 110:1-4; Philippians 2:9-11; Hebrews 5:6). Therefore, Jesus had the authority, status and power to bless his disciples:

1 He confirmed the new covenant relationship with them, including his continued presence with them through the Spirit (Matthew 28:20; Ephesians 1:3; Philippians 1:19)

2 He guaranteed that he would fulfil all his promises, including the fulfilment of Adam's and Abraham's blessing (1 Corinthians 15:49; Colossians 3:10; Galatians 3:8-29)

3 He gave them the power of his own life to equip them to fulfil their commission (Galatians 2:20; Ephesians 1:18-21; Philippians 3:10-11)

THE SIGNIFICANCE OF THE RESURRECTION AND
ASCENSION FOR JESUS

Jesus the king

After Jesus rose from the dead and returned to his Father, the Father made his Son sit at his right hand in the heavenly realms (Acts 2:34; Romans 8:34; 1 Corinthians 15:25; Ephesians 1:20; Colossians 3:1). The idea of sitting at God's right hand recalled Psalm 110:1: "The Lord says to my Lord: 'Sit at my right hand until I make your enemies a footstool for your feet'." In the Old Testament, the Lord's right hand represented the position of supreme favour, victory and power (e.g., Exodus 15:6; Psalm 20:6; 80:18; 89:13; Isaiah 41:10; 48:13; Jeremiah 22:24). Therefore, the New Testament drew on Psalm 110 to emphasise Jesus' supreme favour and honour as the victorious and exalted king.

God has put all things under Jesus' feet and has made him the head over all things (Ephesians 1:22–23). These ideas go back to Psalm 8:6 which itself recalls Genesis 1:26–28. Paul took up the Genesis picture of dominion as part and parcel of being in God's image, and applied this to Christ as the last Adam. In other words, Jesus holds the full authority of God's image but on a far greater scale than Adam ever did (Ephesians 1:10). Jesus holds the highest position in heaven.

Jesus the priest

Hebrews provides the New Testament's most extensive discussion of Jesus' sacrifice and priesthood. But the book emphasises more than his death. The introduction (1:1–4) makes it clear that Jesus' exaltation is the foundation for the argument of the book as a whole. When God raised and exalted Jesus, he also appointed him an eternal priest who continually blesses and intercedes for his people (Psalm 110:4). Rather than standing at the ready, this priest sits because he has completed his sacrifice (Romans 8:34) and he now holds the power of an indestructible life (Hebrews 7:16).

Jesus the prophet

Jesus' exaltation ensures his role as the prophet par excellence, the last word to his people (John 1:1–4; Hebrews 1:1–4; Colossians 2:3–4). Although he was a prophet in the more normal sense throughout his life (Luke 24:19–20; Mark 6:4; Luke 13:33), he is now a prophet in this fuller sense. Jesus' exaltation marked him as God's greatest word.

Jesus the Last Adam

In 1 Corinthians 15, Paul offered some of the most profound and complex ideas in the New Testament. Starting from Jesus' resurrection as the heart of his faith and life (verses

1-19), Paul drew together a wide range of themes around a central question: "What is the significance of Jesus' resurrection?" The themes included creation, what it means to be human, history, death, the Spirit and heaven.

So how did Paul hold together these diverse ideas? At the heart of Paul's thoughts was a profound picture of who Jesus had become through his resurrection.

Ever since the creation, Paul said, God has planned a higher order of existence as his goal for humanity. When Paul focused his argument on our *future* existence, he described this goal as "heavenly" (1 Corinthians 15:44-49). Why? Paul was building his understanding of what it means to be human and of what our destiny is on his understanding of who Jesus was.

Paul believed that Jesus stood at the centre of all God's plans, including his goal for humanity (Ephesians 1:9-10, 18-23). Jesus, Paul concluded, was not only the greatest and most perfect human, he was the Last Adam, the leader or representative of a whole new order of human existence (1 Corinthians 15:45-49; Colossians 1:15-19). Thus, if the Corinthians wanted to know what God meant them to be, and what they would be, they only had to look at Christ. And, in particular, they would see God's goal for mankind in the heavenly existence into which Jesus entered after his resurrection.

Where does this leave us? In what way does Jesus' new status and resurrection affect us? Andrew Lincoln puts it this way:

Paul no longer has to look at what humanity once was to find God's design for it. Instead he looks to Christ, the true man. Because the resurrected Christ, whom he has encountered, was heavenly, he knows that it is also God's plan for a person's destiny that he or she is to be heavenly... The eschatological prospect held out to Adam (and to which he failed to attain) is realized and receives its character through the work of the last Adam who has become heavenly. In this way creation and the age to come...are correlated, the former pointing forward to the latter. From this passage in 1 Corinthians 15 it is not enough to say that the work of Christ restores a person to his or her original humanity, rather it brings that person to the goal for humanity that God intended but humanity before Christ had never reached.[2]

THE SIGNIFICANCE OF THE RESURRECTION AND
ASCENSION FOR US

Union with Christ

We have noted in earlier chapters that the New Testament has a *now and not yet* tone to it regarding the significance of Jesus for us. It always leaves us with a two-sided picture. For example, Jesus' death has changed our status with the Father and its power continues to work itself out in our lives. At the same time, its effects which we now experience are just a taste of what we will experience one day. This same two-sidedness occurs with the resurrection.

Jesus died for us to give us his death in exchange for ours. Likewise, he rose for us to give us his life (Romans 6:4; 10–11). Jesus now lives to God and since we are *in Christ* and identified with Christ in both his death and his life we are also to consider ourselves alive to God. Alongside of this *now* there is the *not yet*. Although God raised us with Christ, we will not experience the fullness of this resurrection life until Christ, who embodies that life, appears.

Jesus our firstfruits

In 1 Corinthians 15:20–23, Paul described Jesus' resurrection as the firstfruits of our own resurrection. The background to this picture is the firstfruits offerings of the Old Testament (e.g., Exodus 23:19; Leviticus 23:10; Numbers 15:20; 18:8; Deuteronomy 18:4; 26:2, 10). The Israelites brought a part of their harvests to the Lord as a representative portion for the whole. The idea wasn't that the offering was simply the first part, nor that this was the part which God owned.

Rather, the offering marked the beginning of the harvest and that the whole harvest was the Lord's.

The connection with Jesus' resurrection is profound. Paul saw that Adam and Jesus represented two orders of life and two groups of people. The experience of the first Adam characterised life until the coming of Jesus. When Jesus came, he inaugurated a whole new dimension of life and a whole new people. In fact, the contrast between the two figures was stronger than that between two orders of *life: death* came through Adam, but *life* came through Jesus, the Last Adam (1 Corinthians 15:20-22).

Now Jesus' life and experience characterises life for his new people. As we saw a moment ago, Jesus entered into a new dimension of life at his resurrection. His entry into this experience through his resurrection guarantees that we will also. Thus, Jesus' resurrection began the great harvest, the resurrection of all God's people. Jesus is the first fruits; his resurrection sealed our future. Now we wait for him to remove death's sting (1 Corinthians 15:25-28, 54-57).

Our future resurrection

Death could not hold Jesus. He overcame its power, and he did so on our behalf. Therefore, his resurrection assures us of victory. It assures us that he will transform us into a full experience of his resurrection life, his heavenly existence, when he returns (verses 45-54).

Since this resurrection life has both present and future aspects, heavenly existence too is also *now and not yet.* Heavenly existence began with the resurrection of Christ. We experience it now through the Spirit, but we are not yet fully heavenly. This will only occur when we express the image of the heavenly man (1 Corinthians 15:49); that is, when our bodies share in heavenly existence. Yet this doesn't mean our bodies are now irrelevant. Paul didn't teach some sort of unreal spirituality which saw the physical as evil. Rather Paul left us with a strong affirmation of the dignity and importance of our bodies both for now and for the life to come.

DISCUSSION QUESTIONS

1 "The resurrection opened up the way for Jesus to restore me in his image, and for me to express that in my own unique way—not as a clone or a stereotype." Discuss.

2 Your friend feels depressed. She has been sick and recently she experienced a major disappointment. Now she doesn't feel like praying, reading the Bible or being around other christians. A mutual friend suggests she should ask the Holy Spirit to "fill her with Jesus' life again". How do you react to this advice? Does Jesus' resurrection offer anything for your sad friend?

EXERCISES

1 In our last study we outlined some of the connections between the death of Jesus and words like propitiation, redemption, justification, reconciliation, and adoption. Using that section of the last study as a starting point, work through any connections between these words and the resurrection of Jesus.

2 Prepare a bible study on Colossians 3:1-4. In particular, how does this picture of the gospel:

Provide an antidote to the emphasis on misguided laws and experiences in 2:16-23?

Provide a solid basis for the behaviour changes Paul urged in 3:5-11?

Notes

1 This blessing is mentioned briefly in chapter 5.

2 Andrew Lincoln (1981), *Paradise Now and Not Yet*, Cambridge University, page 53.

17 JESUS THE KING OF THE KINGDOM

Summary: The key to this study
This book has explored the unity-in-diversity of the Bible. We have looked at various events in the Bible's story and the themes which emerged from those events as the writers of the Bible considered their significance. We have seen how these themes intersect and shed new light on each other. Most of all, we have seen how all the events and themes find their focus in Jesus Christ. In this chapter, we will consider this unity-in-diversity further, and then look at five impressive and interrelated pictures of Jesus found in the New Testament.

METAPHORS, PATTERNS AND PERSPECTIVES

The unity and diversity of the Bible

The Bible shows the most remarkable unity in diversity. Although it contains many people and events across different cultures over thousands of years, it all coheres as God's record of his plan to fulfil his original intentions for his people and their environment.

Ultimately every part of the Bible is related to every other part. The connections may be long and drawn out, and we may not have time to chase them all. But they are nevertheless there by virtue of the Bible's overarching plan.

This book has been divided into numerous topics, issues

and chapters because although the story is a whole, it can't be grasped all at once. The story has to be carved up into digestible pieces. But the separations may actually obscure the amazing interrelatedness and harmony that we are trying to explore because the whole Bible is *one* unified story. The purpose, plot, and climax all hinge on one central character, Jesus. That's why it is so hard to write a chapter on Jesus— the whole series is about him. Whatever could be said in this chapter could be and mostly has been said somewhere else.

So how can this complexity, this remarkable unity within diversity be understood?

The role of metaphors, pictures and perspectives in our understanding

All of us think and communicate in metaphors, pictures and perspectives all the time. No matter how aware or not we are of what we do, we constantly describe one thing by relating it to another. Designers, artists and writers (including the Bible's writers) do this consciously to capture our attention and tease our imaginations through unusual associations of ideas. But we all do the same thing, perhaps just not as self-consciously or as skilfully as they do.

Why do we think and communicate this way?

On the one hand, it's because *life is thoroughly interrelated.* God made everything according to one complex original design or plan.[1] This means that every detail has meaning in the whole and a place in the interlocking patterns. Therefore we cannot avoid seeing *connections* between things.

But, on the other hand, we *can't understand everything*, nor can we see all the ways in which any one thing is connected to any other. The patterns and plan are too complex for that. We can't see *all the connections* between what interests us and everything else. No matter how much we study a particular subject, there is not only more to learn about it, there are also many more ways of looking at it.

So what has this got to do with reading the Bible? In one sense, each of our studies so far has been about a small slice of the whole. And, in another sense, each has given a perspective on the whole. But there's another, perhaps even more important, point for us to remember.

The Bible operates within much the same human limitations as we do.[2] In other words, it must also communicate through metaphors, pictures and from limited perspectives. We mentioned this in the study on Jesus' death. There I made the point that justification, redemption, adoption and reconciliation are not different things or events, but different pictures of what Jesus has done for us. Similarly, the baptism, sealing, anointing and filling of the Spirit are not different things or events either. They are different metaphors for how the Spirit of Jesus works within us.[3]

So we need to multiply our own perspectives if we want to avoid being narrow, unbalanced or arrogant in our understanding. But where do all these ways of seeing come together?

The centrality of Jesus

Each one of our Old Testament studies included some thoughts on how it fitted within Israel's history as a whole, and each finished with an outline of how the gospel fulfilled that part or theme of the Old Testament. In other words, we've been working with the idea that everything in the Old Testament plays an important role in its unfolding story, and that the story climaxed in the coming, living, dying and rising of Jesus. Or, as a friend of mine puts it, we have been learning to tear out the blank page between the Old and New Testaments because the Bible is really one book, not two.

The New Testament writers expanded the idea of the centrality of Jesus in different ways, but they all confirmed that centrality.

Jesus has not only *completed* the Old Testament story (e.g., Luke 24:24-27, 44-47; Galatians 4:4-6; Colossians 1:25-27; 1 Peter 1:10-12), he also *continues to stand* at the centre of God's plan for history and the new creation (1 Corinthians 15:24-28, 50-58; Ephesians 1:20-23; Hebrews 2:5-9; Revelation 1:18; 5:1-6:17).

Jesus is the *key to understanding* everything in right perspective (Colossians 2:2–8). The New Testament writers always worked from the gospel as their starting point no matter what issue or problem they tackled.[4]

Now we must make "every thought captive to Christ" and pray to the Father to renew and enlarge our minds in the knowledge of who Jesus is and what he has done (2 Corinthians 10:5; Romans 12:1–2; Ephesians 1:18–23; Colossians 2:3). We must relate every experience and aspect of our lives, both individually and corporately in our church families, to the gospel of Jesus Christ.

FIVE PICTURES OF JESUS

In this section we will explore five different New Testament explanations of who Jesus was and is. We are doing this to illustrate what we have discussed above about metaphors, pictures and perspectives. These five are not the only explanations we could explore, nor necesarily the most important. As you study them, watch the way you use perspectives in your thinking. Consider the pictures in different ways:

1 Study their individual content
2 Consider the ways in which the different pictures overlap and explain each other
3 Treat each picture *as though* it was the most important and try to consider the others in the light of that one.

The glorious Son of Man: Mark 13:24–27

Jesus assured his disciples that the victorious and majestic coming of the Son of Man (Mark 13:26–27) would follow their time of suffering and distress (verses 9–25, 30–31). So who did he mean by this Son of Man?

In chapter 7, we noted that Jesus mostly drew his understanding of the title from Daniel 7:13–14. Now we need to look more carefully at Daniel's vision. The beasts who oppose God and his people unleash their terrifying strength and authority against the Lord's saints (Daniel 7:2–8, 19–25).

But God, the Ancient of Days, sits as the supreme ruler over the world, even over the power of the beasts (verses 9–12, 26–27). And the Son of Man represents the Ancient of Days in his victorious warfare against the beasts. Then he leads his people in triumphant procession back to the Ancient of Days (verses 13–14).

Jesus' prophecy in Mark 13 was strikingly similar to Daniel's in both its details and historical circumstances. As Daniel unfolded the realities of God's rule over history to bring hope to the exiles in Babylon on the eve of their new beginning,[5] Jesus identified the Son of Man as the one whom God had appointed as ruler and judge over all the affairs of men. The Son of Man would bring the present age to an end.

The judgement upon Jerusalem and the temple which Jesus had prophesied happened in AD 70. When the Romans destroyed the city, it marked the passing of one era and the establishment of another (Daniel 9:24–27; Mark 13:1–2, 14; John 2:19–22). The Israelites had centred their hopes on the temple of Jerusalem, the place where God's glory dwelt (e.g., 2 Chronicles 5:13–14; Isaiah 4:2–6). The prophets had looked to it as the gathering point of the scattered chosen people (Isaiah 2:2–5). But now the Son of Man had inherited the Lord's own role of gathering together God's scattered people—not around God's glory in the temple, but around himself (Deuteronomy 30:4; Psalm 50:3–5; Isaiah 43:6; 66:8; Jeremiah 32:37; Ezekiel 34:13; 36:24; Zechariah 2:6, 10).[6]

Mark's picture of Jesus' coming echoed both the great appearances of the Lord in the Old Testament (Joel 2:10; 3:15; Isaiah 13:10; 34:4; Ezekiel 32:7–8; Amos 8:9) and the triumphs celebrated by royal figures and heroes in the world of his own day.

So who is *this* Son of Man? He is Jesus, the triumphant ruler of heaven and earth and the redeemer of his people.[7]

The crowned Son of God: Romans 1:3–4

Paul's remarks about Jesus' life prior to his death and resurrection (Romans 1:3) highlighted two different but complementary things about Jesus.

He used the word *flesh* to emphasise that Jesus came in the weakness and temporariness of our existence; he spoke of Jesus being a truly normal human (1 Corinthians 15:47), the one "born of a woman" (Galatians 4:4). Thus Jesus lived and died in the same order of existence as Adam (2 Corinthians 5:16; Colossians 1:22).

But to Paul, Jesus was also the long awaited Messiah, the promised King from David's family; he was the Son of God (2 Samuel 7:13–14; Psalm 2:7; Isaiah 11:1–5; Amos 9:11).[8] Jesus brought the kingdom of God and the promised Spirit of God.

Jesus could not pour out this promise until he had endured death. To establish the new order for his people, he had to first live through the full experience of the old order, including its curse. He entered and inaugurated this new order of life, the order of the Spirit, through his resurrection (Romans 1:4).

The idea here is similar to what we discussed about Jesus when we looked at 1 Corinthians 15:45–49 in our last study. Jesus entered at his resurrection into such a thoroughly new *human* experience that Paul could speak of Jesus as having passed from one order of existence to another. So Romans 1:3–4 does not contrast Jesus' humanity and divinity, but two successive phases in Jesus' experience of humanity.

Paul staked his life and ministry on his conviction that Jesus' death and resurrection signalled the turning point of the ages. God had come to his people in his Son and had opened up a whole new possibility for them. The creating and recreating power of God, the Spirit of God, had equipped the Messiah to end the old age and to pour out his gifts without measure on the new people of God (Isaiah 32:15; 61:1; Joel 2:28–29; Zechariah 12:10).

The exalted Servant: Philippians 2:6–11

Paul probably had in mind four different background ideas when he painted this picture of Jesus in Philippians:
 1 God's Son always existed[9]
 2 Jesus, the last Adam, reversed the first Adam's actions
 3 Jesus was the Suffering Servant of Isaiah 53

4 When Jesus washed the disciples' feet he acted out in a small way the greater thing which he was about to do on the cross

Paul was saying that Jesus had always enjoyed equality with God but had refused to exploit this right for his personal gain (Philippians 2:6). Although this equality was his prerogative, he gave it up when he exchanged his heavenly existence for existence as a man upon earth. As the Last Adam, Jesus refused to follow the path of the first Adam. The first Adam tried to seize equality with God but found only disaster and misery. The Last Adam did not think of this equality as a prize to be seized, but chose to be given that equality at the end of his self-surrendered life.

In Isaiah's servant songs (Isaiah 42:1-4; 49:1-6; 50:4-9; 52:13-53:12), sometimes the servant seems to be an individual, and sometimes a renewed Israel. Ultimately, however, the two possibilities came together through Jesus acting on behalf of the people he was creating. Jesus was the Servant, the true Israelite—the only one who ever kept the covenant with perfect faithfulness (Matthew 3:17), the only son of Abraham who loved the Lord with all his heart, and all his strength (Deuteronomy 6:5).

One word sums up Jesus' earthly life and draws together the pictures of the Servant and the true Adam—obedience. Jesus obediently served his Father from the heart through his life (Galatians 4:4-5; Hebrews 5:7-10). Moreover, he carried this obedience to the farthest limit. He voluntarily put himself under the control of death, man's last enemy, even though it had no lawful claim over him.

In many respects, Philippians 2:6-11 parallels John 13:3-17. It is as though Paul saw in Jesus' demonstration of humility a bigger picture of who Jesus was and what he came to do. Here are the parallels:

1 Both writers begin by emphasising Jesus' authority and that he had come from God (John 13:1, 3; Philippians 2:6a).
2 Both emphasise his humility (John 13:4-5, 18-30; Philippians 2:6b-8)
3 Both point beyond his humility to his exaltation (John 13:31-14:4; Philippians 2:9-11)

4 Both writers present their portraits as models for behaviour (John 13:12-17; Philippians 2:1-5)

Jesus was simultaneously the true God, the true man, the ideal king, and the ideal representative Israelite who stood in the place of his guilty subjects. He established his rule over their hearts by conquering them through his humble love. Because of this his Father exalted him to the throne at his right hand and set a day when all the earth would acknowledge his kingship.

All the Old Testament descriptions of the Lord now belong to Jesus. God has proclaimed the humiliated and exalted Jesus as the Lord of all forces throughout the universe. All these powers fall down and submit to his God-endowed right. But we only see and experience his lordship in faith and hope. While we remain on the earth we experience conflict, persecution and tyranny.

Paul's hymn lifts our vision from earth to heaven, from the scene of conflict to the presence of the all conquering Lord.

The superior Son: Hebrews 1:1-3

The writer of Hebrews 1:1-3 depicted Jesus in terms of three key Old Testament roles: prophet, king and priest.

Jesus the prophet In the Sermon on the Mount, Jesus took the role of the new Moses giving the new law. Thus he fulfilled Deuteronomy 18:15-16. In his transfiguration, Jesus appeared alongside the two greatest Old Testament prophets (Luke 9:28-36). Thus Jesus was the prophet par excellence. But Hebrews went further than this.

We've often noted how all the events, structures and people of the Old Testament were temporary and incomplete. The covenants outlined how God would relate to his people, but they did not give the final picture of what that relationship would be. The heart of the argument of Hebrews is that Jesus is superior to everything in the old covenant.

All these Old Testament words from God anticipated and prepared the way for his final word in his Son (John 14:6;

1 Peter 1:10–12). In fact, Jesus not only lived by the word, he *was* the Word of God, the greatest revelation of the Father (also John 1:1–18).

Jesus the king "Since Christ is the Son, and more particularly the *only* Son, of God, he is also the Heir, the *sole* Heir, of all things. The concept of heirship is involved in that of sonship."[10] Both the ideas of sonship and heirship belong to the Old Testament pictures of covenant and kingship (Exodus 4:22; 2 Samuel 7:14; Psalm 2:7–9). Because Christ is God's true Son, the true covenant son, God has handed him the universe as his inheritance (Hebrews 1:2b), the universe which he created and which he upholds and renews (verse 3b; also Colossians 1:17). Because we are in Christ, we share in his inheritance (John 1:12–13; Romans 8:14–17; Galatians 4:4–7; 1 Peter 1:3–5). We share in the kingdom of the one who has sat down at the right hand of the Majesty in heaven (Hebrews 1:3c; Psalm 110:1).

So Jesus is the king. Yet, once again, our writer wasn't content to leave the picture there. Jesus' majesty is on a par with God's (Hebrews 1:3a). He possesses and radiates the Lord's glory, the glory which came down upon Mt Sinai as an awesome luminous cloud and which filled the tabernacle and temple (Exodus 19:16–18; 24:15–18; 33:9; 2 Chronicles 7:1–3; Isaiah 6:1–6; also John 12:41). This is why the writer could say that we have come to Zion by coming to Jesus (Hebrews 12:22–24).

Jesus the priest Finally, Jesus was also the priest (Hebrews 1:3c). "While the Son ceaselessly is 'the radiant light of God's glory' and 'the perfect copy of his nature' (JB) and continuously 'upholds the universe by his word of power', there is also something which he did once for all, namely, *he made purification for sins.*"[11] This is perhaps the greatest emphasis of the epistle. Unlike the temporary, partial and imperfect nature of the Old Testament sacrificial system, Jesus was the sacrifice and priest to end all others (e.g., 4:14–5:10; 7:21–28; 10:1–18). Now his people enjoy eternal forgiveness and unhindered direct access to the Father (10:14–22).

The Lion and the Lamb: Revelation 1:12-13

Like Jesus' own description of the Son of Man (see above on Mark 13:24-27), John's picture of Jesus in Revelation 1 came from Daniel 7. But John took the picture further by blending the description of the Ancient of Days (Daniel 7:9-10; 10:6) with that of the Son of Man (7:13-14).

John was saying that Jesus both possesses the glory of heaven and shares the likeness of God himself. The Son of Man is the First and the Last (Isaiah 44:6; Exodus 3:14), the initiator and the finisher of all things. The Son of Man is the man Jesus who is also true God. And because he died, he holds the power of death and hell, so that death no longer holds its terror for the people of God.

Here lies the heart of the paradox of the gospel: the eternally living one died! Speaking about John's vision in Revelation 5, Graeme Goldsworthy summarises the paradox this way:

When John turns to see the Lion he sees no such figure of glory and majestic power. Rather he sees a Lamb standing 'as though it had been slain'. Even that verbal conundrum, so typical of apocalyptic, only heightens the effect which is to shatter the visual image of the Lord of the beasts. A slain Lamb! That is the victory which overcomes and puts the truth of the kingdom of God within our reach. By a skilful use of apocalyptic images, John illuminates the central paradox of the gospel. The victory of God was the humiliation and death of his Son. The Lion assumes the meekness of the Lamb and dies in order to overcome. . . The vision of Revelation 1:12-20 is the vision of the now ruling Christ. . . And if Christ rules now, then he has overcome his enemies decisively in the past events of his life, death and resurrection. . . the finished work of Christ determines absolutely the nature of the present and future.[12]

The Bible ends in almost the same place as it started. In Revelation 21-22 (especially 22:1-5), we arrive at a new Eden, an Eden as much greater than the first Eden as Jesus is greater than the first Adam. The Son of Man has overthrown the confusion, frustration and chaos of life. Instead of war, there will be peace. Instead of death, there will be life.

Jesus is the slain Lamb who triumphed over death and the principalities and powers through his death and resurrection (1 Corinthians 15:54–57; Colossians 2:15). Jesus is the great warrior—the lamb who is also the lion (Revelation 1:12–18; 12:7–11; 19:11–21).

DISCUSSION QUESTIONS

1 Why is the Bible so important? Rather than going into some long-winded philosophical and theological argument about inspiration, revelation and truth, think through any connections between who Jesus is and what he's done and the authority and role of the Bible.

2 Do you think the gospel has lost its place as the centre of christians' thinking today? Look at denominations, colleges and churches. Are we basing our beliefs and actions solely on who Christ is and what he's done for us?

EXERCISES

1 Prepare a bible study on Ephesians 1:3–11 titled "The Supremacy of Jesus"

2 Get a group of friends together and tackle the second discussion question above. Run your thinking through four stages:

   1 What's happening "out there"?

   2 What difference should the gospel make?

   3 Where does the gospel really need to challenge and change what we think and do?

   4 How could we stimulate constructive criticism and change?

Notes

1 Already mentioned in chapter 9 in connection with the Old Testament Wisdom books.

2 The Bible is not incorrect or mistaken. It is God's true word for his people. But the authors expressed as much as they could see. The Bible does not and cannot include everything God says about everything.

3 One of the best discussion of the way christians think and formulate theology is Vern Poythress (1987), *Symphonic Theology: The Validity of Multiple Perspectives in Theology*, Zondervan.

4 This is less obvious in James than the others.

5 See chapter 11.

6 Chapter 21 returns to the theme of God's people gathering around him.

7 The issues and literature related to the title Son of Man are equally complex and voluminous. If you want to study this further, and if you have access to theological journals, then see David Jackson (1985), "The Priority of the Son of Man Sayings", *Westminster Theological Journal*, 47, pages 83–96.

8 The Old Testament background behind the title Son of God is outlined in chapters 7 and 13.

9 The title "Son" is a bit misleading in view of the status of Jesus apart from his conception in Mary's womb. The title properly describes how Jesus fulfilled the Old Testament ideas of kingship and the true covenant person. Thus the Father/Son language is only biblically appropriate when describing their relationship after Jesus came to earth. Before that time we can only appeal to the vague and sometimes unhelpful language of his place in the Trinity.

10 Philip Hughes (1977), *A Commentary on the Epistle to the Hebrews*, Eerdmans, page 38.

11 Hughes, *Hebrews*, page 46.

12 Goldsworthy, *Revelation*, page 104.

18 THE PROMISE AND POWER OF THE KINGDOM: THE HOLY SPIRIT

Summary: *The key to this study*
The permanent, personal presence of the Holy Spirit with us is the unique blessing of the new covenant. The Israelites had seen the Spirit work amongst them from time to time, but even the most famous Israelites had not experienced the Spirit's presence the same way as we do. Like everything else we must start from the gospel in order to understand the gift of the Spirit. Jesus has given the Spirit equally and fully to all his children. Much teaching today about the so-called baptism of the Holy Spirit ignores this gospel foundation, distorts the evidence in the book of Acts and leads christians to think of each other as "haves" and "have-nots".

THE OLD TESTAMENT PROMISE OF THE SPIRIT

The Old Testament linked the Spirit's presence with creation (Genesis 1:2; Psalm 104:30), the exodus (Nehemiah 9:19,20; Isaiah 63:11–14; Haggai 2:5), and the activities of the judges (Judges 11:29; 13:25), kings (1 Samuel 10:10; Psalm 51:11) and prophets (Numbers 11:29; 2 Kings 2:15–16; also 1 Peter 1:11). The presence and power of the Holy Spirit wasn't just a New Testament phenomenon. The Old Testament had already lain the groundwork for understanding the Spirit's work of creating, empowering and renewing, and therefore for his place as the special promise of the new covenant.

Although the people of the old covenant did experience God's Spirit in their life as a nation, their personal understanding and experience fell short of ours. They did not experience the Spirit as a permanent blessing. Even the kings and prophets only experienced God's Spirit as a temporary visitation to empower them for their ministries. And only *some* of the people under the old covenant received the Spirit. But in the new covenant *everyone* has God's Spirit. We could represent this difference as in diagram 12.

The Old Testament writers were aware of these inadequacies and they longed for a more permanent and total experience of God's Spirit:

1 Moses desired that all his people would prophecy by the Spirit (Numbers 11:26-29; compare Joel 2:28-32)
2 The prophets longed for a new heart for each Israelite (e.g., Jeremiah 31:31-34; Ezekiel 36:25-27; 37:13-14; Isaiah 44:3; 59:21)
3 The prophets believed God would empower the future king with his Spirit (e.g., Isaiah 11:1-3; 42:1)

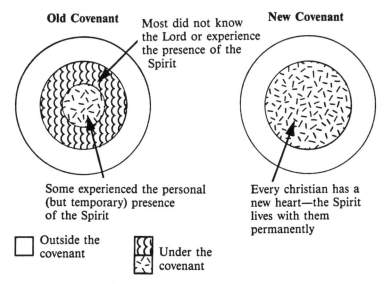

Old Covenant   Most did not know the Lord or experience the presence of the Spirit   **New Covenant**

Some experienced the personal (but temporary) presence of the Spirit

Every christian has a new heart—the Spirit lives with them permanently

☐ Outside the covenant   ▨ Under the covenant

Diagram 11: The difference in personal experience between the old and new covenants

4 The prophets associated the coming of the Spirit with
their broader hopes (e.g., Joel 2:28–32; Isaiah 34:16; 4:4;
Ezekiel 39:29)

So the Old Testament looked to a time when God's Spirit
would enlarge his creating, restoring and empowering
ministry within the hearts of his people.[1]

THE SIGNIFICANCE OF PENTECOST

On the day of Pentecost, Peter quoted Joel 2:28–32 and
included the initial words "in the last days". For Peter, then,
the pouring out of the Spirit signalled the beginning of the
new age of God's grace, the fulfilment of the Old Testament
hopes, and the creation of the new people of God. We need
to explore the connections between Pentecost and the Old
Testament a little further, in order to discover the significance
of the day of Pentecost.

We have often noted that in many ways the exodus was
the cornerstone of the Old Testament. It was the Lord's
greatest saving act for the Israelites. It gave them a model
of what salvation meant. It led to God's confirmation of
the covenant at Mt Sinai when he came to live with his
people, and commissioned them as a kingdom of priests and
a royal nation (Exodus 19:5–6). God's presence in the cloud
was their deliverance and commissioning for subsequent
ministry (Exodus 13:21–22; 14:19–20; 19:16–18; compare
Isaiah 63:11–14).

Pentecost had a similar background. Jesus had completed
the great event of his death and resurrection and he had
appeared on the mountain as the exalted Lord to commission
his new people (Matthew 28:19–20; Luke 24:50–52; 1 Peter
2:4–10). At Pentecost, he poured out the Spirit in fulfilment
of the prophets (e.g., Isaiah 42:1; 44:1–5; Joel 2:28–32), John
the Baptist's predictions (Luke 3:15–17; John 1:29–34), and
his own promises (John 7:39; 14–17; 20:22).

Pentecost marked the creation of the new people of God.
It confirmed the new covenant. From this perspective we gain
fresh insight into the ministry of the Spirit. He directs the
people's attention to their covenant Lord (John 14:27; Exodus

14:19-20). He makes the people into the new tabernacle/ temple, God's new dwelling place (1 Corinthians 3:16; 12:13; Ephesians 2:22; 1 Peter 2:4-10). Through him the people are drawn together in unity (Ephesians 4:4; 1 Corinthians 12:13) and they receive gifts necessary for their life together and their role in the world (Ephesians 4:8; Romans 12:3-8; Ephesians 4:9-13; 1 Corinthians 12-14).

In summary, Pentecost marked:

1 The fulfilment of Jesus' promise to remain with his people
2 The creation of the new people of God
3 The end of Israel's monopoly on the covenant
4 The inauguration of the new age

JESUS, THE SPIRIT AND OUR EXPERIENCE

Jesus' experience of the Spirit

The bond between Jesus and the Spirit went much further than the Spirit empowering Jesus for his ministry, or than Jesus initiating the Spirit's new ministry. The Spirit was with Jesus in a more radical sense than any Old Testament prophet or king had ever known.

Paul explained the Spirit's presence with Jesus in terms of creation and new creation (1 Corinthians 15:35-49). As we mentioned in our study on the resurrection of Jesus, Paul's contrast in 1 Corinthians 15 between the physical/earthly and the spiritual/heavenly was not a contrast between what is evil and what is good. (That last contrast comes from Greek philosophy, not Paul.) Rather Paul contrasted two *ages* which were represented or characterised by two figures: the first Adam, and the Last Adam. His argument seems to be that, at his resurrection, Jesus began a new way of existing that went far beyond what Adam knew. At the same time, this new existence was what God had intended for us ever since the beginning of creation (verses 44-48).

So what is this new order of existence? Firstly, it is not

vague or unphysical. Paul carefully silenced any idle speculation about what it will be like for us to experience this new order (1 Corinthians 15:35-41). Our only model is Jesus: we will be like him (verse 49). Secondly, Paul explained this new order in terms of the Spirit's presence. The Spirit totally characterised Jesus', the Last Adam's, life (verse 45). As a result of the resurrection, Jesus entered a new dimension of human existence.

This new dimension of life was so closely associated with the presence of the Spirit that Paul identified Jesus with the Spirit (1 Corinthians 15:45; also 2:10; 2 Corinthians 3:3, 18; Philippians 1:19; Galatians 4:6). Not that Paul confused Jesus and the Spirit. He certainly recognised them as unique persons. Rather, the point seems to be that Jesus' will and personality now characterise the Spirit.

Jesus remains in heaven at the Father's right hand (*not* "in our hearts"). Yet because the Spirit is *his* Spirit (Philippians 1:19; 1 Peter 1:11), Pentecost signalled the coming of Jesus to his people just as he had promised (Matthew 28:20b).

Our experience of Jesus' life through the Spirit

Paul particularly linked the Spirit with Moses' experience of the Lord's glory and Israel's failure to enter into that experience (2 Corinthians 3:6-18). The point seems to be that all we who believe in Jesus enter an experience like Moses' because we have the Spirit.[2]

This brings us back to what we said a moment ago about Jesus' new order of existence and the Spirit being the Spirit of Jesus. Paul identified this new experience of the Spirit, this experience which is like Moses' experience yet better, as the experience of being transformed into Jesus' image. Like the argument of 1 Corinthians 15, Paul here affirms that Jesus was the Last Adam and that Jesus' special glory was due to his own experience of the Spirit.

There's so much here that we need to explore in order to get a clear idea of what it means for the Holy Spirit to be with us now. I think Paul leads us away from any unreal or airy-fairy pictures of what it means to have the Spirit. I think he forces us to realise that we must think of the Spirit in terms of Jesus. Jesus has come to us through the Spirit to hold us within the power of his death and resurrection and to enable us to experience an ongoing transformation into his likeness.

Because Jesus is the new man, the Last Adam, then he is the model of what it means to be human. Therefore, spirituality is a gradual rediscovery of the richness and fullness of life as God intended us to experience it. Spirituality is not a matter of weird experiences, individual ecstasy and other-worldly practises. It is the joy of rediscovering authentic humanness through a growing application of what Jesus has done for us (Colossians 3:10, 17).[3]

The Spirit keeps us and guarantees our future

The Old Testament person was always in danger of falling away, and did not experience the Spirit's presence in any permanent way. The two are connected. It is the presence of the Spirit under the new covenant that keeps the new people of God loyal (Jeremiah 31:31-34; also 32:38-40). He does this by giving them a new heart (Ezekiel 37:13-14; John 3:1-16).

The Spirit keeps us in such a way that we are sealed (2 Corinthians 1:20-22; Ephesians 1:11-14). His presence guarantees that:

1 Jesus has finished his work for us
2 We experience the Father's intimate love for us
3 We will experience the same order of existence and intimacy of relationship which Jesus now experiences

In other words, we are already experiencing the blessings and power of the future because we have the Spirit. He fills us through and through so that he characterises our lives as "life in the Spirit" (Romans 8:1-17; Ephesians 5:15-21). In this daily experience, we hunger for the final instalment of what we now know in part as a downpayment or pledge (Romans 8:22-25; 2 Corinthians 1:22; 5:5; Ephesians 1:14).

In and through all our present experiences, the Spirit's

presence and ministry assures us of our union with Jesus, of his Father's acceptance of us, and of the reality of the kingdom to which we now belong as he changes us into the image of Jesus (Romans 8:12–27; Galatians 5:22).

A THORNY ISSUE: THE BAPTISM OF THE HOLY SPIRIT

The New Testament used several word pictures to describe our present, permanent and common experience of the Holy Spirit. Three of these images come through the words baptised, filled, and sealed. Sadly, some christians believe that these pictures only apply to some christians, and that the rest miss out on what Jesus accomplished for them.

Looking for a pattern in Acts

Several key passages in the book of Acts (namely 2:1–13; 8:14–17; 10:34–48; perhaps also 11:15–18 and 19:1–7) are taken by some christians as teaching that after conversion every christian can and should receive the baptism of the Holy Spirit as an *extra* or *second* baptism. Many also say that this

	Acts 2	Acts 8	Acts 10	Acts 19
Receiving the Spirit at faith	(v38?)	–	(v44)	(see vv2–4?)
Receiving the Spirit after faith	(1:4–5; 2:1–2?)	(vv14–16)	–	(vv5–6?)
Water baptism	(v41?)	(v16 pre HS)	(v48 after HS)	(v5 pre HS)
Laying on of hands	–	(vv17–19)	–	(v6)
Tongues	(v11)	–	(v46)	(v6)
Apostles present	(v14)	(v18)	(v44)	(v6)

Diagram 12: The book of Acts presents no standard order for conversion and receiving the Holy Spirit

extra experience should (usually) happen through the laying on of hands and with the gift of tongues as evidence.[4] But do the passages reveal this simple pattern?

The way the passages break down according to the key details as shown in diagram 12.

If we want a standard order for conversion, baptism and baptism in the Spirit, and a standard pattern which includes tongues, apostles or laying on of hands then we must either make one of the examples in Acts *the* standard or make up our own order and pattern. In other words, the simple pattern of so many teachers of "the baptism of the Holy Spirit" simply doesn't exist in the Bible. However, a different type of pattern emerges if we view these passages as a whole.

Acts and the unique role of the apostles

The only constant feature in these passages is that the apostles were present in every instance. In their foundational role within the new covenant community (Acts 1:8 and Ephesians 2:20), the apostles were on hand to witness and validate the coming of the Spirit to the Gentiles.

Jesus had outlined to his apostles how the kingdom would spread geographically (Acts 1:8—Jerusalem, Judea, Samaria, the ends of the earth). The key passages noted follow this basic order of moving from the Jew to the Gentile: Jews and God-fearers in Jerusalem (Acts 2); Samaritans in Samaria (Acts 8); a Roman God-fearer in Caesarea Philippi (Acts 10); and converts of John the Baptist in Ephesus (Acts 19).

But why is this important? Why did the apostles need to witness the coming of the Spirit as the gospel spread beyond Jerusalem?

For nearly two thousand years the Israelites had been God's special people. It was hard for many Jewish christians to accept that the gospel had cancelled all their national privileges and put them and the Gentiles on an equal footing. Many of the Jews insisted that Gentile christians were inferior to them, and that they should compel the Gentiles to keep the Jewish laws.[5]

But the apostles silenced these criticisms on two grounds. They argued that Jesus' death-and-resurrection, not the law was the only basis for membership in the new covenant. And they witnessed to God's pouring out of the unique new covenant gift of his Spirit on both Jews and Gentiles without favouritism (Acts 10:34–36, 45–47; 11:1–18; 15:5–21).

By the time the earliest churches had been established in Gentile countries, the apostles no longer needed to defend the Spirit's presence with the Gentiles. It was then an accomplished and recognised fact. But in the earliest days it was critical that the apostles be on hand to watch God pour out the distinct gift of the new covenant to these non-Jews. This is the logic behind the "pattern" of Acts; it is not a reconstructed scenario that offers "three easy steps" to the baptism of the Spirit, but the record of the unique and unrepeatable beginnings of the new people of God.

The gospel and baptism in the Spirit

By the time Paul wrote 1 Corinthians (one of his earliest books), he was equating baptism in the Spirit with membership in Jesus' body. According to Paul, if you hadn't been baptised in the Spirit, then you were not in Jesus—you weren't a christian (1 Corinthians 12:13). Paul was not saying that every Corinthian christian should have the *second* experience which many people teach today. Rather, he said that the word-picture of baptism was an appropriate description of how *every* christian experiences the Holy Spirit.

If they trusted Christ, then the Spirit of God *had* baptised and filled their lives.

Paul built his idea of God's people functioning as the Lord's body on this concept. If it was accepted that only some people had the baptism of the Spirit, then it would follow that only they were in the body, only they had gifts, and only they were christians—which was just the sort of superiority he had slammed at the start of the letter (1 Corinthians 1:10–17). (Sadly, today's version of this error encourages the same elitism.) But Paul denied any hint of hierarchy or difference in status in the body. He emphasised that all christians knew the same Lord, were equally saved and equal sharers in his Spirit.

If you are trusting Jesus to save you, then he has baptised you with the Holy Spirit.

DISCUSSION QUESTIONS

1 There are groups today who teach the "baptism of the Spirit" as a *second* experience beyond conversion, and therefore as something which only some people experience. Why do you think this teaching has become so popular? What effects have you seen it have on people?

2 "Christians use expressions like 'spirital' and 'unspirital', 'the Lord's work' and 'worldliness' to justify the things they will and won't do. Phrases like these sound spiritual, but often they hide an avoidance of the real challenges of following Christ in the normal day-to-day experiences of life. Such people refuse to climb outside of their ghetto to live authentic and involved lives in a dying, hurting world." Discuss.

EXERCISES

1 Outline a bible study on what Romans 8 teaches about the way the Holy Spirit works in our lives. In particular, how does his presence with us and work with us relate to our relationship to Jesus. You might find it helpful to summarise your ideas under three time headings: our past, our present experience, and our future.

2 A research project. Christians often speak about Jesus living inside them. Is this either helpful or accurate?

Notes

1 See chapter 11.

2 See chapter 4 where we discussed Moses' experience at Mt Sinai after the golden calf incident and Paul's use of Moses' experience to explain our present experience of God's Spirit. You might like to review that section at this point.

3 There is a stimulating discussion of the relationship between Jesus, the Spirit and us in James Dunn (1975), *Jesus and the Spirit*, SCM/Westminster, pages 301–342.

4 I am, of course, referring to the idea of the baptism of the Spirit as many Pentecostal and Charismatic christians teach it. However, the idea of seeing this as a second experience after conversion is much older than the so-called Charismatic movement. There are numerous other groups and individuals who teach this idea and even some who are opposed to the Charismatic movement.

5 The central controversy of the first christians concerned the opinion of certain Jewish christians about the status of their Gentile brothers and sisters. (See Acts 15 and Galatians 1-3.) Although it is hard for us to relate to this issue directly, we must not dismiss its role in shaping the New Testament history.

19 THE ADVANCE OF THE KINGDOM

Summary: The key to this study
The kingdom of God is not to be associated with any political realm or earthly ruler. There can be no such thing as a christian nation, state or political party. But this is not to say that the kingdom is weak or that it is unconcerned about social change. Rather, the kingdom's power is the Spirit of God working through the frailty of God's people to bring others to repentance and new life. When this happens the social structures feel the presence of a people who will not compromise the message of the gospel, nor accept the claim of the state over their hearts.

THE KINGDOM OF GOD AND MISSION

Old Testament background

Responsibility for upholding God's name goes as far back as Genesis 1:26–28. When God made mankind in his image, he specifically designated our role on the earth as maintaining order and increasing the fruitfulness of the creation. This commission presumed a perfect world. There was no hint that mankind would face opposition in carrying out the task. But sin complicated all this. After the first sin, God's people had to struggle to fulfil their role (3:15).

But God intended to totally undo all the effects of sin by bringing about a total restoration (e.g., Isaiah 35:5; Ezekiel

36:35; Revelation 2:7; 22:1-5). Despite the opposition, God established the Israelites as his people on the basis of his covenant promises (e.g., Genesis 12:1-3; Exodus 6:1-8). Yet creating a new people was not an end in itself. The Lord's plans still included the *whole* earth. Thus, when the Lord drew his people into covenant with himself, he made it clear that he had a task for them. They were the agents through whom he would extend his rule over the whole earth.

Therefore, the nations played an important role in God's great plan. For example, God's promise to Abraham (Genesis 12:3b) was in direct contrast to the curse of Babel (11:1-9). God would eventually regather the scattered peoples of the earth under his lordship. Furthermore, when the Lord called Israel to himself at Mt Sinai, he commissioned the Israelites to represent him before all the nations in the knowledge that he was in fact the Lord of the whole earth (Exodus 19:5-6).[1] So although the biblical story focused on the Israelites, their existence and identity as God's people was never meant as an end in itself. The Lord intended something much bigger.

The prophets held on to this bigger picture in their vision of the age to come. Alongside the various blessings which God would give to the Israelites, the prophets believed that God would gather in the nations on the last day (e.g., 1 Kings 8:60; Isaiah 52:10,15; Psalm 87:4). Thus all the earth would join in the march to Zion, the palace and temple of God, to acknowledge his kingship over the whole earth (e.g., Psalm 48:2; Isaiah 22:2-4; 49:6).[2]

The triumph of the gospel

Jesus fulfilled the prophets' vision by personally taking the role of the Israelites and then passing this role on to God's new people (Exodus 19:5-6; Isaiah 5:1-7; Matthew 28:19-20; John 15:1-8; 1 Peter 2:4-10). Jesus took the images which had defined Israel's role and hopes and fulfilled them in himself.

The harvest of Pentecost   The Old Testament had often used the image of a harvest to describe the great day of universal judgement and salvation (e.g., Isaiah 27:12; Joel 3:13-18; Amos 9:13). Not surprisingly, the four Gospel writers adopted it and John the Baptist understood Jesus this way (Luke 3:9, 17). Jesus also frequently used this picture (John 4:36). It was a particular favourite in his parables: as the Son of Man he came to sow the seeds of the kingdom (Matthew 13:37,19); this kingdom would grow and spread (Matthew 13:31-33) until the great harvest (Matthew 13:40-41).

Pentecost began the harvest. At the start of Jesus' ministry, John the Baptist had anticipated what Jesus would do at Pentecost in terms of the images of baptism and harvest (Luke 3:15-17).[3] The symbolism of the feast of Pentecost was ideal (Exodus 23:16; Leviticus 23:16). This Jewish festival celebrated the possession of Canaan and God's ownership of the harvest. The New Testament took up this image and saw the pouring out of the Spirit at Pentecost as the event which marked the believers in Christ as God's special possession and the firstfruits of his harvest (Romans 8:23).

The powerful advance of the kingdom In Acts, Luke emphasised the spectacular growth of the kingdom among the nations in the power of the Holy Spirit (e.g., Acts 2:41, 5:14, 6:7, 8:6, 9:35, 11:21, 24; 13:44, 49; 17:4, 6). Now that God had lifted up Jesus he was drawing all men to himself with such power that not even the opposition of Satan could stop it.

We read an example of this power in Acts 12. Herod Agrippa[4] had opposed the first disciples and killed some of them (verses 1-5). The believers responded in the power of the Spirit. They knew Herod's might, but they looked to a greater king in prayer. Subsequently, the Lord miraculously delivered Peter from prison (verses 5-17). Herod was furious (verses 18-19). Moreover, he continued to defy God even to the point of accepting the worship of the crowd (verses 20-22). The Lord's answer was swift. Herod died suddenly (verse 23), his plans were thwarted (verse 24), and the word of the Lord continued to spread and bear fruit.[5]

The end of nationalism Jesus broke down all nationalistic boundaries and opened up the way for universal peace through his death and resurrection (Ephesians 2:11–22; Colossians 3:11). The first christians, however, took a long time to accept this.[6] For a long time, many Jewish christians insisted that Gentile converts must become "Jewish". This hindered the spread of the gospel by perverting its clear message that God accepted people through Christ rather than through their observance of the law. It also placed believers under an unnecessary and futile bondage to the law. This is why Paul wrote such stern warnings about perverting the gospel (e.g., Galatians 1:6–9; 3:1–5; 4:8–20; 5:7–12).

Nevertheless, despite the many sectarian and petty attitudes of some early believers, the kingdom advanced throughout the Mediterranean region.

The new people of God and mission

Jesus passed on and amplified the role of the Israelites (Exodus 19:5–6) to, and in, the new covenant community (1 Peter 2:4–10). Jesus created a new community of disciples loyal to their master's calling (Matthew 10:34–38; 26:31; 12:50). He demonstrated the power and claims of the kingdom to them (Luke 4:18–19), and he commissioned them to carry on this same ministry through the power of the Spirit (Luke 10:1–24; Matthew 28:19–20; Acts 1:6–8). In that power, his people went about the task of seeing all things bend the knee to Jesus (Ephesians 1:10; Philippians 2:10–11; 1 Corinthians 15:28).

This reworking of Israel's role in the ministry of the disciples takes us back beyond the covenants with Abraham and the Israelites to the commission of Genesis 1:26–28. Jesus now fulfils this commission; *he* is the new Adam who perfectly establishes dominion and fruitfulness on the earth (Hebrews 2:5–9). And he calls us to increase his dominion by calling all mankind to acknowledge that he is Lord (Matthew 28:19–20).

THE EMPHASES OF THE KINGDOM'S MISSION

Speaking about Jesus and his kingdom

The four Gospels had emphasised the kingdom of God. The book of Acts and the epistles shifted this emphasis somewhat to proclaiming Jesus as the crucified and risen Lord. In other words, as the kingdom grew and advanced, the believers focused on Jesus rather than on the more general kingdom statements found in the four Gospels. They were convinced that Jesus stood at the centre of God's kingdom strategy and they increasingly realised that all of life hinged on who he was and what he had done.

The sermons in Acts provide a clear picture of this emerging focus on Jesus the Lord. The speakers emphasised several key ideas:

1   Jesus had fulfilled the Old Testament; he was the long awaited Messiah
2   God had vindicated Jesus by the mighty acts of the Spirit
3   Jesus was crucified
4   God raised Jesus from the dead
5   God enthroned Jesus as his right hand, and the Spirit bears witness to him
6   God's mercy is for all mankind
7   Everyone must respond to Jesus by repenting and believing[7]

The epistles endorsed this newer emphasis by insisting that the gospel was all about Jesus. Paul went so far as to insist that his only message was Jesus (1 Corinthians 1:18–2:5) and that his ministry was wholly that of reconciling God and people through the message of Jesus (2 Corinthians 5:11–6:2).

Practical demonstrations of the kingdom

We have noted before that the kingdom brought liberty and relief for people in all kinds of distress (e.g., Luke 4:18–19). Jesus came to bring justice and righteousness for "the poor of the earth" (Isaiah 11:1-5; 61:1-2; Luke 4:17-21), and he called his people to give their lives passionately for the same cause (Matthew 5:6).

James expressed a similar thought by saying that our faith has to work; words, he said, are useless without deeds (James 2:14-17, 24). Paul believed that good works on behalf of both christians and non-christians should characterise a christian's life (e.g., Ephesians 2:10; 1 Timothy 5:10, 25; 6:18; Titus 3:1, 8, 14; 1 Peter 2:12; Galatians 6:9-10). These good works are not separate to the business of the kingdom of God. Rather, they are the practical fruits of the kingdom and the things which demonstrate the reality of what is proclaimed.

THE STRATEGY OF THE KINGDOM'S MISSION

The message met the context

In his earthly ministry, Jesus demonstrated that the kingdom was able to meet people where they were. For example, Jesus crossed national and cultural barriers to speak with the woman at the well (John 4:1-42). According to the Jewish traditions and social expectations, Jesus should have avoided the person at the time because she was not only a Samaritan, but possibly a prostitute. Yet Jesus always insisted that he had come to call the sinners, not the righteous.

In Acts, the apostles and others went to normal meeting places to speak about Jesus; places like synagogues (Acts 17:2; 18:4,19), market places (17:17), the Areopagus (17:19,22) and homes (18:24-26). Similarly, they varied their message from audience to audience; they always centred on Christ but they saw that they could do this in many ways. For example, when they spoke to Jews, they emphasised the Old Testament context behind what Jesus had done (e.g., Acts 2:14-36). When they spoke to Gentiles, they sometimes found a natural starting point in their audience's culture (e.g., Acts 17:22-31). In each case, they sought wisely to make the most of every opportunity (Colossians 4:2-6).

What liberated the apostles and first christians to move

and speak freely among diverse types of people? Speaking about Paul, Harvie Conn explains that these believers had

...a sense of solidarity with a wide ethnic spectrum of hearers (1 Corinthians 9:19-20). When Paul says, 'I have become all things to all men, so that by all possible means I might save some,' he is not engaged in gospel modification, homiletical cutting and paring. He is 'under orders' to the changeless gospel (9:16). But it is precisely this changelessness that liberates him to change in terms of the life-situation of his hearers. He is not talking about the mere act of adjustment, proposing one more curriculum for one more Successful Church Seminar. In the light of the coming of the kingdom, he is exhorting us to circumcise our half-Jewish Timothys (Acts 16:3), to take our temple vows (Acts 18:8), to participate in our purification rites for suburban Nazarites (Acts 21:17-26). His focus, and ours, is not on the technique of adjustment but on the demands created by the 'now' of the kingdom.[8]

It was the gospel of Jesus that drove the first christians on. The same gospel liberated them to share their lives openly and naturally with the people around them. No law, tradition, person or government could threaten them in any ultimate sense. Nor did they worry about preserving their religious or social status. They understood that their identity and worth was secure in their relationship to Christ.

Planting local churches

Paul the sometime tentmaker (Acts 18:1-4; 20:32-35), sometime fully supported missionary (Philippians 4:18), established local churches wherever he went (Acts 14:21-27). Yet it is perhaps misleading to think of his church planting as a *strategy*. Paul didn't establish these communities merely as a means to an end, as though evangelism was more important than community, or as though he measured the *success* of the kingdom in terms of numbers rather than the quality of life which people experienced in these churches. Instead, these communities were the natural outcome of preaching Christ. They are also God's appointed way of experiencing and demonstrating the Gospel's power to transform people's lives.

Robert Banks explains it this way:

> In the wake of Paul's travels throughout the Mediterranean, Christian communities sprang up, consolidated and began to multiply. This was the outcome of a deliberate policy on his part. He not only proclaimed the message about Christ and brought people into an intimate relationship with God, but drew the consequences of that message for the life of his converts and led them into a personal relationship with one another. . . for Paul the gospel bound men and women to one another as well as to God. Acceptance by Christ necessitated acceptance of those whom he had already welcomed (Romans 15:7); reconciliation with God entailed reconciliation with others that exhibited the character of the gospel preaching (Philippians 4:2-3); union in the Spirit involved union with one another, for the Spirit was primarily a shared, not individual experience (2 Corinthians 13:14; Philippians 2:1; Ephesians 4:3). The gospel is not a purely personal matter. It has a social dimension. It is a communal affair.[9]

Prayer and a vital lifestyle

The Old Testament prophets included prayer in their panoramas of the blessings, privileges and activities which would characterise the messianic age. These prophets believed that the new covenant would cause God's new people to experience a new intimacy which they would express in the boldness, immediacy and effectiveness of their prayers (e.g., Isaiah 56:6-7; 58:9; 65:24; Malachi 1:11).

Not surprisingly, then, prayer played a central part in Jesus' life on earth and in the arrival of the kingdom through him (e.g., Luke 1:10, 46-55, 67-88; 2:29-32, 38). Jesus demonstrated this new intimacy and power of the kingdom throughout his ministry (Hebrews 5:7). As the new Adam, the true covenant Son, he staked his life on his Father's love, and showed this most clearly in the way and circumstances in which he prayed (Luke 3:21; 4:1, 14; 6:12; 9:18, 29-31; 22:39-46; 23:34, 46).

"Jesus entered the new age of the Spirit. Now his people enter that same age after him."[10] When Jesus returned to his new people at Pentecost through the Spirit, he drew them into the same experience of prayer which he had known. As the Spirit filled them with life and power, they took hold of their new status with the Father and boldly called on him to show the kingdom's power through their words and deeds (Acts 2:17; 6:6; 9:40; 12:12; 13:2-3; 14:23; 16:25; 28:8). Thus the kingdom came in the power of the Spirit and the King, not in the strength of its people.

Paul's prayers enlarged on these themes (Ephesians 1:15-23; 3:14-19; Philippians 1:3-11; 4:4-9; Colossians 1:9; 4:2-6; 1 Thessalonians 1:2-3; 2 Thessalonians 1:3-4; 2 Timothy 1:3). Like the rest of his thinking, Paul built his ideas and practice of praying on the gospel. He thanked God that the gospel had taken hold of his friends' lives and he longed for them to understand and appreciate their Lord better and better.

Along with this new vitality and frankness in prayer, there seems to have been a vibrancy about the early christians which radiated life, joy and enthusiasm (e.g., Acts 2:42-47; 4:32-35; 1 Thessalonians 1:4-10). The kingdom grew because the exalted Lord Jesus was in control and because his people consciously staked their lives on his love and power.

DISCUSSION QUESTIONS
1 Do you think planting new churches is a helpful and necessary strategy for today? If so, how do you think it should be done in order to take account of (a) the biblical teachings and (b) your context? Could you see yourself becoming involved in such a venture?
2 "We'd get a lot further with evangelism if we stopped treating it as something separate or extra in a christian's life, and got back to helping each other live full and natural lives." Discuss.

EXERCISES
1 Harvie Conn suggests an exercise for local churches. He suggests we survey our neighbourhoods by asking
"What do you believe the church should be doing in this

community to help people?" Ask shopkeepers, teachers, unskilled labourers. Ask them if the church has helped in the past... Take their suggestions to the elders and deacons, share them with your congregation. Settle on several priorities... Go back to the people who made these suggestions and share your conclusions. Invite them to join you in this expression of ministry.[11]

2 Make a list of the analogies which the New Testament used in explaining the gospel (e.g., law courts, slavery, marriage, adoption). Now think about your context: what analogies do the people around you understand? Try expressing the gospel in *new* pictures which *they* will understand.

Notes

1 See chapter 4.

2 See chapters 8 and 21.

3 For the significance of the saying "he will baptise you with Spirit and fire", see chapter 13.

4 Agrippa the Elder, who was known as Herod, should not be confused with the two earlier Herods: Herod the Great (Agrippa's grandfather) who tried to kill Jesus as an infant; and, Herod Antipas (Agrippa's brother-in-law) who was involved in Jesus' trial and execution.

5 This story is explained in greater detail, including its relation to Ezekiel 28:11-19, in my, "An Old Testament Background to Acts 12:20-23", *New Testament Studies*, 32 (1985), pages 289-292.

6 Peter's struggles to accept this truth probably reflect what many other Jewish christians first experienced (see Acts 10:1-11:18). We looked briefly at this tension in chapter 18.

7 Acts 2:14-39; 3:11-26; 4:8-12; 5:29-32; 7:2-53; 10:34-43; 13:16-41; 17:22-31; 20:18-35; 22:3-21; 24:10-21; 26:1-23; 28:17-20, 25-29.

8 Harvie Conn (1982), *Evangelism: Doing Justice and Preaching Grace*, Zondervan, page 13.

9 Robert Banks (1980), *Paul's Idea of Community: The Early House Churches in their Historical Settings*, Eerdmans, page 33.

10 Conn, *Evangelism*, page 78.

11 Conn, *Evangelism*, page 56.

20 THE LIFESTYLE OF THE KINGDOM

Summary: The key to this study
A great deal of teaching on christian experience is misleading. It regards the gospel as only the starting point of our experience and it urges us to go on to "deeper" things. It frequently speaks of what Jesus has done for us (e.g., "union with Christ", "righteousness", "peace" and "life in the Spirit") as things which we must obtain and/or secure for ourselves. Rather than understand "growing in the knowledge of Christ" as a life-long journey of appreciating more carefully the work of Christ on our behalf, it points us to rules, "spiritual exercises" and experiences as the key to maturity. We may need to recover the simple and profound vision of the New Testament writers that the gospel of Jesus Christ secures and shapes our acceptance by God, our ongoing experience of life and our final destiny.

THREE MAJOR PERSPECTIVES ON CHRISTIAN EXPERIENCE

Discipleship

To which part of the New Testament do you turn for a description of what it means to be a christian? Personally, I tend to favour Paul's letters because they give such clear directions on how I need to relate my status and responsibility to the death and resurrection of Jesus. Yet, increasingly, I've come to realise how much I lose if I ignore the words of Jesus on being a disciple. Perhaps I favour Paul, John and Peter because I find Jesus' words a bit too demanding—perhaps even radical.

In writing to the Christians of Galatia, Paul was able to affirm, "There is neither Jew nor Greek, slave nor free, male nor female, for you are one in Christ Jesus" (Gal 3:28 NIV). In doing so, Paul was only affirming in writing what Jesus had already demonstrated in deed. In associating with Gentiles, Samaritans, "sinners", lepers and others, Jesus broke through the barriers which had been built up over years and years of Jewish life. In upholding a Gentile soldier as a model for faith (Lk 7:1-10), in counting women among his followers (Lk 8:1-3), and in calling a tax collector to discipleship (Mk 2:13-14), Jesus demonstrated that the good news of God's salvation knew no boundaries. Activity of this nature could only be regarded as scandalous in its day, but through such deeds Jesus embodied his gospel, proving its message was not empty.[1]

Whatever else we say about the picture of discipleship in the four Gospels, we must say that it is radical. Radical, because it equally cut Jew and Gentile to the heart, calling both to put aside all hopes of entering the kingdom through national and social status, and to abandon themselves to following a social misfit and peaceful extremist. In this calling, Jesus promised homelessness, persecution, misunderstanding, accusation, even death—and the kingdom of God (e.g., Luke 9:23, 59-62; 12:8-9; 14:26; Matthew 10:38; 19:21; 5:3-12).

Jesus overthrew the then current expectations and securities and called people to make a radical decision; either they could choose the kingdom of this world and death, or else follow the one who would love his enemies and voluntarily choose death to bring life to his people. The call has not ended.

No-one who takes the Bible seriously and Jesus Christ seriously should be content with a comfortable undemanding form of Christianity (though many of us and many evangelical churches easily slip into that)...we do need to hear the challenge to follow Jesus radically—in every aspect of our lives, and not only to hear but also to begin to work it out in practice. This might seem a hopeless task; but it is not: Jesus inaugurated the revolution of the kingdom of God; he gives us his Spirit so that we may live the revolution here and now, and he will one day bring what he has begun to completion.[2]

In Christ, with Christ

Paul took the general statements of Jesus acting "for us" or "on our behalf" and coined a new expression, *in Christ.* Rather than simply speaking of what Jesus had done for us, Paul spoke of how we were and are represented by Christ, and of how Jesus included us in all that he did. Paul was not suggesting that we would be made into gods, nor become part of some sort of mystical union. Rather he always focused on the historical life, death and resurrection of Jesus.

One key to Paul's idea lies in the parallel between Christ and Adam (Romans 5:12-21 and 1 Corinthians 15:20-28, 42-49).[3] The two Adams represented two worlds, two ages, two groups of humanity. What each one did, he did for all the people he represented. Thus we were included in everything that Jesus did.

The practical effect of this was that Paul based his pleas to his friends to die to the old world on the historical reality that *they had already died with Christ* (Romans 6). In other words, their inclusion in Christ's death and resurrection had transferred their status from one world to the other. Thus Paul steered away from any language about christian growth that might give the impression that our status in Christ depended on the stability of our day to day experiences.

Romans 6 was Paul's classic expression of all this. In diagram 13, I have tried to outline his argument.

In many ways, verses 11-14 are the most pointed and perhaps difficult part of Paul's argument in Romans 6. Diagram 14 might help.

Paul knew the temptation of going back to the law as the

	Past	Present
Introductory Remarks	Before the coming of Jesus: law always leads to sin; grace to righteousness.	"If we keep on sinning we will get more grace? No! Remember what your baptism stood for."
Jesus	Jesus died and rose again.	He lives with his Father. Nothing can shake that relationship. He overcomes sin and death.
Us	We died and rose again with Jesus.	We live with Jesus and the Father. Nothing can shake this relationship. We overcome sin and death through Jesus, even though it often seems as if we don't.

Diagram 13: The relationship between our history and Jesus' history according to Romans 6

	Romans 6:11 and 14	Romans 6:12–13
Yes! The Positive Implications:	If we think of ourselves in the way verses 11 and 14 describe us, then...	We will experience the positive side of verses 12–13, because we will structure our lives around our identification with Jesus
No! The Negative Implications:	If we do not think of ourselves in the way verses 11 and 14 describe us, then...	We will experience the negative side of verses 12–13, because we will structure our lives around rules and emotions

Diagram 14: The positive and negative of Romans 6:11-14

guide to christian living. After all, his friends wanted to serve the Lord faithfully and they desired clear directions for how to do that. Thus many of them tended to think in terms of laws, rules and codes of conduct for deciding which behaviours were or were not appropriate. Some found this in the Old Testament laws (as the Galatians tried to—Galatians 3:1-14), while others mixed parts of Old Testament law with their own rules (as the Colossian troublemakers did—Colossians 2:16-23).

Paul rejected both approaches. Instead, he dogmatically pointed his friends back to the gospel and to the presence and role of the Holy Spirit. So how did he understand our experience of the Spirit?

Living in the Spirit

The peculiar gift of the new covenant was that everyone in it received the Holy Spirit. Under the old covenant, believers did not experience the Spirit in a permanent and personal way and thus they were always in danger of falling away from the Lord. But in the new covenant, the presence of the Spirit ensures that God's people have a new heart and remain loyal to him (Jeremiah 31:31-34; also 32:38-40; Ezekiel 37:13-14; John 3:1-16).

One way the New Testament described the Spirit's role was to say that he sealed us (2 Corinthians 1:20-22; Ephesians 1:11-14). The idea here is that the Spirit's presence assures us of our union with Christ, of the Father's acceptance of us, and of the reality of the kingdom to which we now belong (Romans 8:12-27). One day we will experience the same order of existence and intimacy of relationship with the Father which Jesus now experiences. Thus the Spirit leads us to hunger for the final instalment of what we now only know in part (Romans 8:22-25; 2 Corinthians 1:22; 5:5; Ephesians 1:14).

In the meantime, we experience life as a struggle between the flesh and the spirit (Romans 7:7-8:17; Galatians 5:13-25). But what does this language mean? Many teachers speak of flesh and spirit as though they were lower and higher parts of our nature. They then point us to various experiences, acts of obedience, or rules as the way to tame and destroy our "fleshly" side while liberating our "spiritual" side? But is this what the New Testament meant?

Paul's use of flesh and spirit is not a description of our *inner* condition. We are not split personalities comprising flesh and spirit. Rather, the terms follow on from what we have seen in earlier chapters about Paul's picture of Christ and Adam. To be in Christ means to have passed from one order of existence to another. The first Adam no longer defines us; the second Adam does.

Paul is saying that Jesus came to the people of the old age, the age of the flesh or weakness (2 Corinthians 5:18). But he brought in the new age, the age of the Spirit, by his resurrection. Consequently, our lives are characterised by the presence of the Spirit (Romans 8). Since we have Christ and his Spirit, we are members of the new creation (2 Corinthians 5:17). Therefore we no longer model our lifestyle on the law and this world (Colossians 2:16-23), but on the gospel (Galatians 3:15-5:1). At the same time, we must take up our cross and identify with the sufferings of the crucified Christ (2 Corinthians 11:23-12:10; Philippians 3:10; Colossians 1:24).

Paul does not lead us to think of ourselves as having two natures. Nor does he encourage us to think of the Spirit as a vast reservoir of power waiting for us to tap into it. Rather he points us to the cross and resurrection and urges us to live consistently with the facts of Jesus' death and resurrection and the Spirit's presence with us. Thus, as I have said before:

Paul leads us away from any unreal or airy-fairy pictures of what it means to have the Spirit. I think he forces us to realise that we must think of the Spirit in terms of Jesus. Jesus has come to us through his Spirit to hold us within the power and the radical demands of his death and resurrection and to continually transform us into his likeness. Because Jesus is the Last Adam, the model of what it means to be human, then spirituality is a gradual rediscovery of the richness and fullness of life as God intended us to experience it. It is not a matter of weird experiences, individual ecstasy and other-worldly practices, but of rediscovering authentic humanness, even authentic suffering, through a growing appreciation of what Jesus has done for us (Colossians 3:10, 17).[4]

For this reason, Paul never defined our progress as

christians in terms of getting-better-at-obeying, but as a renewal or a constant transformation (e.g., Colossians 3:1-4, 9-11; Ephesians 4:24; Romans 12:1-2; 2 Corinthians 3:17-18; 4:1-5:10). Paul was even bold enough to link the certainty of our progress into the gospel and the faithfulness of Jesus (Galatians 2:20; Philippians 1:6). In other words, his death, resurrection and present reign guarantees our ongoing growth.[5]

A MODEL OF CHRISTIAN EXPERIENCE: COLOSSIANS 1:9-14

We need to spell all this out more concretely. At the start of his letter to the Colossians, Paul gave his friends a helpful overview of what christian growth is all about (1:9-14). I like to think of this as a spiral (see diagram 15).

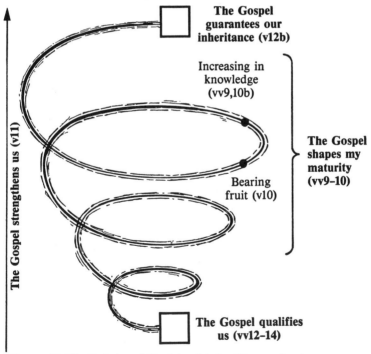

Diagram 15: The "spiral model" of the christian life according to Colossians 1:9-14

What are the main features of the model? Firstly, the work of Jesus, the gospel, secured both our starting point and final destiny. Secondly, it is his strength and presence (through his Spirit) which provides the energy to keep going. Thirdly, we should encourage an ongoing interaction between practical experiences and deepening our appreciation of the gospel (Colossians 1:28-2:5). In other words, Paul's "cycle" of knowledge and deeds (1:9-11) was not about the experiences, rules and secret knowledge of the troublemakers (2:16-23). It concerned knowing more of the gospel (1:15-20; 2:2-5) and expressing this in everyday circumstances (3:18-4:6).

Perhaps the clearest way to see the practical value of Paul's model is by restating it *without* the gospel. In the next diagram 16, I have taken the last model (diag. 15) and labelled it with the feelings of those who try to base their lives on laws and experiences rather than on Christ.

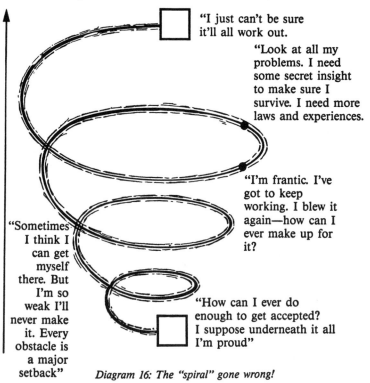

"I just can't be sure it'll all work out.

"Look at all my problems. I need some secret insight to make sure I survive. I need more laws and experiences.

"I'm frantic. I've got to keep working. I blew it again—how can I ever make up for it?

"Sometimes I think I can get myself there. But I'm so weak I'll never make it. Every obstacle is a major setback"

"How can I ever do enough to get accepted? I suppose underneath it all I'm proud"

Diagram 16: The "spiral" gone wrong!

APPLYING THE BIBLE TO OUR LIVES: SOME IMPORTANT ISSUES

Finding appropriate pictures and patterns

Presuming that we read the Bible in order to apply it meaningfully to our personal and social lives, I believe that to do this intelligently and powerfully, we must keep in mind the bigger picture of the Bible as a whole. In particular, we must not skip over the significance which the gospel (Christ's life, death and resurrection) brings to each time period within the Bible, each major idea, and each passage. So, presuming that we don't ignore the gospel, how do we now bring the Bible into our lives?

I am convinced that many people find it hard to relate to the New Testament's images for personal experience and development—fruit, armour, race, fight, building, boat— and Old Testament features such as the temple. Perhaps it is because they are images from another world; perhaps it is because many Bible teachers make them sound so other-worldly and artificial; or, as I suspect, perhaps it is because we don't relate them to equally basic images and concepts more familiar to our own experience.

When I seek to apply the Bible to life, I often focus on three key issues:

1 *Knowledge.* What new dimensions and perspectives have I gained on the Bible's story and the gospel? What implications do they have for my everyday life—work, leisure, purchasing, debts, family, friendships and pace of life? What should I believe now?

2 *Attitudes.* What should I feel now about Christ, myself, my family, friends, enemies and the wider world? Where do my commitments, opportunities and responsibilities lie?

3 *Behaviour.* What should I do now? What sort of strategies and plans should I create to bring these concepts into my life in a meaningful way? How can I implement these plans (etc) realistically, taking account of any limiting factors such as availability of time and other resources? What radical demands am I in danger of playing down?

At the same time as we discover overarching patterns like these, perhaps we need to recover and explore other biblical and non-biblical images like creation/new creation, community, and authenticity.

The cult of the individual

Most christians seem to accept that individual rights and needs are central to our culture and to the business of being a christian. Thus many studies on the christian lifetyle emphasise such things as personal quiet times. Such studies may encourage fellowship, yet they give the impression that an individual's personal relationship with the Lord is the most important part of christian experience.

One way this preoccupation with the individual has surfaced in recent years is through the issue of self-image or self-worth. We need to explore this issue and to develop a strong gospel perspective on it. In our day, more than ever it seems, our minds are bullied by salesmen and media who feed our immaturity with hopes of instant popularity and quick solutions to life's problems. Ronald Conway, an Australian psychologist and sociologist, notes:

Our how-to-do-it culture, with its glossy magazine and media images of superficially glamorous people, only consolidates the growing problem of narcissism in male–female relationships. By propagating such images the world itself appears to be endorsing the message, originally imparted by shallow, materialistic parents, that style is more important than substance and that the ultimate crimes are to be uncomplicated and boring... Psychiatrists' consulting rooms are becoming cluttered with such personalities who bemoan the lack-lustre quality of their lives and the meaninglessness of their existences.[6]

The gospel offers a powerful and uniquely balanced vision of the individual's worth. The Bible pulls no punches about our depravity and rebellion outside of Christ. We deserve judgement. Yet, Christ loved us to the point of dying for us while we were still his enemies. Jesus' death and resurrection mean that we never need to see ourselves as worthless again.

But we need a third dimension to the concept of self-worth. We need to see ourselves more as people in community than as individuals. The fact is, the more we chase after a positive self-image, the more elusive it seems. Yet, when we cease focusing on feeling good about ourselves, and move towards recapturing the dignity of being a servant to others, then we actually discover a far deeper sense of personal worth and satisfaction.

Once we begin to read the Bible with an eye and ear for what it says about God's people as a community, a whole new dimension of freedom and responsibility opens up:

(Paul) does not view salvation as simply a transaction between the individual and God. A person prior to his encounter with Christ belongs to a community, however much his actions incline him to pursue his own (or his immediate circle's) self-interest. And it is into a *new* community that his reconciliation with God in Christ brings him, however much he experiences that event as an individual affair.

So this freedom granted by God not only transfers men and women out of a broken relationship with God, and a defective solidarity with men, into a new community with both, but also inclines them to live the kind of life that will extend and deepen that new community itself.

The gospel is not a purely personal matter. It has a social dimension. It is a communal affair.[7]

We need to develop a sense of community where together we can wrestle honestly with the Bible and life.

Relating faith to everyday life

If we begin to develop such a sense of community, then hopefully our agenda will concentrate on the details of everyday life. All too often yawning gaps lie between the curriculums that filter down from theological and denominational centres and the real questions we face each day. Without minimisng the value of systematic Bible reading and teaching, we must reckon with the fact that many christians feel alienated and second-class because they cannot relate their faith to their everyday experiences of decision making, work, child care, shopping, budgeting and recreation. In place of a holistic and dignified view of their own roles in life, they believe that only ministers and other professionals paid by christian organisations are "living by faith" and are really employed in "spiritual" work.[8]

We must not ignore the need for developing a sense of intimacy with our Father through prayer, reading and meditation. And, at the same time, we must, as Robert Banks encourages, relate our faith to our work (or unemployment), to our spare time activities, to our routine or monotonous activities, and to the values that shape our society.

DISCUSSION QUESTIONS

1 How many ways have you heard the reason for our obedience being described? Why should we be *better* christians according to many books, conferences, etc? How do these compare with Paul's view?

2 Do you accept and support the idea that some people's work is more spiritual than others? What does this leave you feeling about yourself and them? Is there another way to assess the value of work?

EXERCISES

1 Try to develop an outline of 2 Corinthians 3:7–6:2. What are the major points? How are they connected? Write a brief summary of the passage.

2 The pictures of discipleship which Jesus gave in the four Gospels often seem different to the lifestyle teaching of people like Paul, Peter and John. Try to construct an overall picture for yourself:

Develop summaries of:
a) Matthew 8:14–17; 9:9–17
b) Galatians 5:8–21
c) 1 Peter 1:13–2:1

Place these summaries side by side and try to create an overall statement about the christian lifestyle. As you do this:

a) Be careful to consider the wider context of each passage
b) Try to keep the impact of each passage

Notes

1 Joel Green (1987), *How to Read the Gospels and Acts,* IVP, page 137.
2 David Wenham (1982), Editorial in *Themelios,* 7:3, page 3.
3 See also chapters 16 and 18.
4 Chapter 18.
5 The relationship between Christ and the Spirit, the idea of flesh and spirit, and our present experience of the Spirit are each complex and crucial topics to understand. If you want to explore these issues further and in depth, see James Dunn (1975), *Jesus and the Spirit,* SCM/Westminster, pages 301–342.
6 Ronald Conway (1984), *The End of Stupor? Australia towards the Third Millenium,* Sun.
7 Robert Banks (1980), *Paul's Idea of Community,* Lancer/Paternoster/Eerdmans, pages 25, 27 and 33, emphasis his. On this theme, see Harvie Conn (1982), *Evangelism: Doing Justice and Preaching Grace,* Zondervan.
8 See Robert Banks (1987), *All the Business of Life: Bringing Theology down to Earth,* Albatross/Lion.

21 THE COMMUNITIES OF THE KINGDOM

Summary: The key to this study
When God gathered the Israelites to himself at Mt Sinai, he established a precedent for his people of all ages. In every case, their common bond was what God had done for them and they gathered to remind themselves of these great truths and to spur each other on to know the Lord better. Such assemblies were the meeting place of heaven and earth. When the New Testament writers wanted to explain the significance of their home gatherings, they found a word—ekklesia—tailor-made for what they wanted to say. The churches, the ekklesia, inherited the meaning of Israel's great assemblies without any of the "religious" connotations of worship, priests or rituals. The churches were simply God's people meeting together in homes to encourage each other in the gospel.

GOD'S COMMUNITY PLANS

When Jesus and the first christians used the word which we normally translate "church" (the Greek word is *ekklesia*) to describe the people of God, they had at least two reasons for doing so.

Firstly, the word simply meant a gathering of people (see Acts 19:39 where the word for "legal assembly" is simply *ekklesia*). The word didn't imply worship or ritual or temple. Thus the word was tailor-made for conveying the simplicity and people-centredness which the New Testament wanted to emphasise.

Secondly, the idea of a gathering or assembly enabled them to tie their ideas about being God's people back into some key Old Testament ideas about the same reality. In fact, the Greek translation of the Old Testament (known as the Septuagint) frequently used *ekklesia* to translate the Hebrew word for assembly, *qahal.*

All this is far more than academic or linguistic trivia. As we discuss some major Old Testament features, Jesus' words about his new people and the first christians' experiences, we will see that the idea of God's people as "assembled" tied Jesus' kingdom to the history of Israel and gave the new christians a powerful perspective on the significance and dignity of their life together. Through their simple home meetings, they expressed a rich theological and historical heritage, and an unpretentious down-to-earthness which was remarkably appropriate to the world around them.

Sinai, Zion and the assembled people of God

After the Lord rescued Israel from Egypt, he led them to Mt Sinai where he assembled his people around himself (Exodus 19:9–19). This assembly set a pattern for what it meant to be the people of God. Israel was the people gathered around the Lord, hearing of his mighty deeds on their behalf and acknowledging his kingship over them in worship. At Mt Sinai heaven came down to earth, to show its glory on earth and to give its blessing on the new people of God (Psalm 68:1–18; also Deuteronomy 33:2–3 where Moses seemed to see a connection between the hosts of heaven and Israel).

This pattern continued in Israel's history. Israel looked to the Sinai assembly as *the* assembly which stamped their character (Deuteronomy 4:10; 9:10; 10:4; 18:16). At key points in their later history, Israel assembled before the Lord to renew the covenant with him and/or to announce some new development in God's relationship with them (e.g., Deuteronomy 31:11–12; 32–33; Joshua 8:30–35; 1 Chronicles 28:2; 29:10; 2 Chronicles 5:2; 6:12; 20:5; 23:5; 30:1–31:1).

The significance of the Mt Sinai assembly eventually passed on to Zion (Psalm 68:17-18).[1] After all, Zion was the site of the temple, the throne room of the Lord, and therefore the place to which all Israel came for the appointed feasts. Thus the idea of heaven meeting with earth became associated with Zion, so that Israel increasingly saw it as an earthly representation of God's heavenly palace (2 Chronicles 6:18-21; Psalm 134; 135:1-2, 6-7, 21; compare 144:5-7 with 132:1-8; 150:1).

Israel's gatherings at Zion assumed enormous significance. They were the focal events in their ongoing history, the living symbol of their identity as the people who worshipped and lived in the presence of the Maker of heaven and earth. At least that was the *intended* significance. Sadly, however, the Israelites' practice rarely matched their theology. Increasingly, the people neglected the appointed assemblies and thus lost sight of their identity and calling.

Remnant and the hope of a new community

In the context of decline and indifference, the prophets revived the image of glorified Zion as the heavenly dwelling of God on earth and as the rallying point for his renewed people (Isaiah 2:2-4; 51:1-11). Not that the prophets' grandiose visions blinded them to Israel's condition, however. Instead, their hopes for the people developed in new directions.

The true Israel would be a remnant the Lord preserved for himself through the fires of judgement (e.g., 1 Kings 19:17-18; Amos 5:15; Isaiah 6:13; 10:21-23; Jeremiah 30:11; Ezekiel 11:13, 17; Zechariah 13:7-9). Unlike the Israel of old, this remnant would never turn away from the Lord for he would give them his Spirit and write his covenant bond on their hearts (Isaiah 59:21; Jeremiah 31:31-34; Ezekiel 37:11-14); and the Lord would gather people from *all* the nations around himself at Zion (Isaiah 2:2-4; 56:6-8; Psalm 87).

Thus the assembly of God's people at Zion was at the heart of the prophetic vision of the end of the age (Isaiah

56:3-8). God would fulfil his promise to Abraham to bless all nations (Genesis 12:2-3) through an assembly of the people of God, an assembly even greater than the original gatherings at Mt Sinai and Zion.

Jesus' pictures of the community

As we have seen in our earlier studies on the kingdom,[2] Jesus cancelled any special status for physical Jerusalem/Zion and transferred to himself the hopes which were traditionally associated with the city. Yet Jesus did not contradict the prophetic visions; he fulfilled them. A purified remnant *would* gather together with the Gentiles around God's presence and throne just as the prophets had foretold. But the gathering point was no longer a city, or even a temple. It was Jesus himself.

The temple, priesthood, sacrifices and kingship could no longer serve as Israel's focal point. At best, they had been symbols of great truths about the Lord and his ways; at worst, they had distracted the people's attention from the One who stood behind the symbols. But now, in Jesus, the perfection, reality and person behind the symbols had appeared (Matthew 1:21-23; John 2:19-22; 8:48-58). Therefore, Jesus began to draw together the new people of God around himself (Matthew 4:18-22; 8:5-12; John 10:14-18). We need to look at other passages in the four Gospels which expand on this theme—Matthew 8:32, John 12:23-34 and Matthew 16:13-20.

Micah had prophesied that before the day of the Lord would bring blessing to Israel, it would first bring calamity and cause a deep rift among them (Micah 7:1-20). Jesus picked this up in Matthew 8:34-36 (he quotes Micah 7:6). As he sent out his disciples, he made it clear to them that the decisive question was, "Will you acknowledge me (Jesus) before others?" (Matthew 8:32) A person could only enter and remain in the kingdom by choosing to identify with Jesus. Moreover, this identification might divide their homes and society (verses 34-39).

Jesus saw himself as the Son of Man who would draw

all people to himself (John 12:23, 32-34). The context and details of Jesus' remark makes his point all the more vivid. The Jews had only just (hypocritically) welcomed him as their new king and messiah in the words of Zechariah 9:9. Yet Jesus reversed Zechariah's expectation. Instead of the Lord judging the nations (Zechariah 9:1-8, 13) and restoring the awaiting Jerusalem, Jerusalem rejected Jesus while the nations rallied around him (John 10:37-40, 20-22). This switch was so significant to Jesus that he recognised the coming of the Gentiles to him as the signal for his final hour (12:23). Israel had assembled at Zion to hear God's word for the last time (verses 27-37).

Jesus' commendation of Peter (and the disciples) in Matthew 16:13-20 drew together many of the features we have noted above. Peter recognised that Jesus was the new focus of assembly. Moreover, Jesus stated that Peter could only see this because God had spoken it from heaven above. Jesus pulled together these ideas (and others) through a play upon Peter's name (Greek *petra* = rock or stone). This wordplay alluded to the Old Testament use of the rock symbol which had grown from their assembly around both the rock in the desert and rocky Mt Sinai (Exodus 17:6; Deuteronomy 32:4; Psalm 18:2; 78:35).

Jesus would build his new people around their confession of him as the Messiah and Son of God. And the power of heaven would come down and remain with these people, guaranteeing both their survival and that their actions would mirror those of the heavenly assembly (Matthew 16:19).

Pentecost and the earliest communities

The early christians saw their own gatherings in the light of this rich Old Testament background. At Pentecost, the Lord created his new people in "one great assembly of fulfilment at Jerusalem".[3] They knew that each of their meetings, their churches, was "not merely a human association, a gathering of like-minded individuals for a religious purpose, but a divinely-created affair".[4] And they readily used the symbols and words of Israel's great assemblies to explain their own identity, dignity and calling (see how Peter used Exodus 19:5–6 and Isaiah 43:20–21 in 1 Peter 2:4–10).

We turn now to look at some New Testament images for God's people.

MORE ON METAPHORS, PICTURES AND PERSPECTIVES

In chapters 15 and 16, we noticed how the New Testament used different images to explain Jesus' death and resurrection. If we don't recognise these images for what they are—namely diverse, complementary and rich perspectives on a particular reality—we may end up making some serious mistakes.[5]

We may consider each perspective as separate or in isolation. This is what often happens with the image of being "born again", and the images associated with the Holy Spirit such as "baptised", "filled" and "sealed"; when we separate these perspectives, we run the risk of making one more important or central than the others. Some have done this with the images of "justification by faith" and being "baptised in the Spirit". It is helpful to use different perspectives from time to time *in isolation or as if they were unique*, but we mustn't use any one of them exclusively.

Emphasising one perspective, while forgetting that it is a *perspective*, also often leads to creating an artificial technical language. For example, it is popular to say that "sanctification" is the process through which God makes us more like Christ. But, for many people who use this definition, "sanctification" is no longer one of many pictures of what it means to be a christian, but *the* literal process happening in a christian's life. So the word acquires the precise meaning of "the ongoing work of the Holy Spirit in a believer's life", and people often stress that it is totally unlike justification by faith.

Yet the New Testament wasn't so careful! Passages like Hebrews 10:10 use basically the same words to describe our status in Christ. In these passages our "sanctification" is as past, complete and finished as Jesus' death and resurrection.

In fact, the passages describe something which sounds far more like the scholars' definitions of justification than sanctification. To handle such passages the scholars coined another technical term—"definitive sanctification". I suspect that we will get further by simply realizing that language is flexible and that meaning comes through context and sentences, not through individual words.[6]

What has all this got to do with the communities of the kingdom?

As in explanations of Jesus' death and resurrection and the Holy Spirit, the New Testament writers used images to describe what it means to be God's people. Words like "church", "body" and "community" offer different snapshots of a common reality; they are not different realities nor are some more central than others. But, like the examples above, we often forget this. We forget that we are dealing with images, and thus we create inaccurate, misleading and unhelpful ideas about what it means to be God's people.

Think for a moment about some of our traditional ideas about church. Why do so many people believe that only Sunday meetings and denominations are "church"? Similarly, why do we keep the word "body" exclusively for the "whole group" or even all the christians in the world, and not for a smaller mid-week or spontaneous gathering? Why do we talk about "visible and invisible" churches? Does the New Testament really talk about a "universal church"? Why do we believe that we gather primarily for "worship"?

These questions give some idea of the way in which we can limit our understanding through relying on one perspective more than others. It's time now to look at four New Testament images for God's people.[7]

DIFFERENT NEW TESTAMENT PICTURES OF
KINGDOM COMMUNITIES

Household gathering

Earlier, we saw that the Old Testament used the word we normally translate as "church" (Greek *ekklesia*), to describe

Israel's special assemblies. But it also used the word for ordinary meetings (1 Samuel 17:47; Psalm 25:5). Most importantly the word was commonly used in the Greek world and simply meant "a regular 'assembly' of citizens in a city to decide matters affecting their welfare".[8] Thus when Paul began to use the word he had in mind either an actual gathering of christians or a group of christians who regularly gathered together (e.g., 1 Thessalonians 1:1; Galatians 1:22; 1 Corinthians 11:18; 16:19).

These gatherings met in people's homes (Acts 2:46; 1 Corinthians 16:19; Colossians 4:15; Philemon 2). Robert Banks suggests that many house churches and occupation-related churches existed in the larger cities like Corinth, and indeed in any locality, as more and more people were converted. Most likely, these groups gathered together in larger meetings from time to time (1 Corinthians 14:23; Romans 16:23). But the smaller home churches probably remained the most frequent and influential meetings.

Heavenly reality

Small did not mean insignificant for Paul. He knew the Greek Old Testament and was aware of how it had used the word *ekklesia* for Israel's assemblies. He also understood how the psalms and prophets linked the earthly assembly to a heavenly assembly and how the prophets looked forward to a great gathering of all God's people at the end of the age. So how did Paul tie these ideas together?

He looked forward to a great assembly at the Lord's return (1 Thessalonians 4:15-17). Yet, and perhaps more importantly for his idea of "church", Paul believed that christians were already a part of the heavenly assembly. Jesus had ascended to heaven and sat down at his Father's right hand on high. And because believers are "in Christ" then they have taken their place in heaven as well (Ephesians 2:5-6; 1:3; Colossians 1:13; 3:1-4). They now belong to the "Jerusalem above" (Galatians 4:25-27; also Hebrews 12:18-24) and are citizens of heaven (Philippians 3:19-20).

Paul was not talking about some kind of universal or

invisible church as many talk of it today. Nor were the local gatherings a *"part* of the heavenly one any more than they are a part of any alleged universal church. . . . (Rather) each of the various local churches are tangible expressions of the heavenly church, manifestations in time and space of that which is essentially eternal and infinite in character".[9]

Furthermore, Paul did not move by analogy from the idea of common membership in the heavenly assembly to suggest that local assemblies should be bound together by an organizational framework. Certainly their common experience of being "in Christ" welded their hearts together and led them to pray for each other, exchange letters and gifts, send people to help out and pass on greetings (2 Corinthians 8:11–14; 4:16; 13:13; Romans 16:1). But these intimate bonds were never formalised into a constitutional framework. Our present day denominations not only lack New Testament support, they often hinder fellowship by seeking to institutionalise it.

Paul's idea of churches as simple meetings which represented a heavenly reality was tailor-made for its context.

Comparison of Paul's understanding of *ekklesia* with the intellectual and social climate of his day emphasizes both the comprehensiveness of his idea and its appropriateness for his times. Attention has already been drawn to three aspects in the contemporary scene that were particularly significant: those aspirations for a universal fraternity which captivated the minds of educated Greeks and Romans and devout Jewish leaders; the significance of the household as a place in which personal identity and intimacy could be found; the quest for community and immortality pursued through membership in various voluntary and religious associations. In a quite remarkable way, Paul's idea of *ekklesia* managed to encompass all three:

1 It is a voluntary association, with regular gatherings of a relatively small group of like-minded people.

2 It has its roots in, and takes some of the character of, the household unit.

3 These small local churches were invested with a supra-national and supra-temporal significance. They were

taught to regard themselves as the visible manifestation of a universal and eternal commonwealth in which men could be citizens.

Only Paul's understanding of *ekklesia* embraces all three ideas of community to which people gave their commitment in the ancient world at the time. This means that, psychologically speaking, Paul's approach had a decided advantage over its first century competitors, since it offered so much more than any of them and offered things which elsewhere could only be found by adhering to more than one religious group. Sociologically, the distinctive element in Paul's conception was its combination of all three models of community. I am not suggesting that Paul systematically related each of these models, or even consciously viewed his idea as the fulfilment of contemporary strivings, merely that his view was conceptually richer and more socially relevant than others advanced in his day. In all this, by his use of the quite ordinary term for assembling in the ancient world *(ekklesia)* and by his setting such gatherings in ordinary homes rather than cultic places, Paul shows that he does not wish to mark off his gatherings from the ordinary meetings in which others, including church members, were engaged... Paul did not see such gatherings as more religious in character than any other activity in which Christians were involved.[10]

Family

Part of the normalness and significance of churches for the New Testament writers came from the association of these groups with homes. Houses were not only the context for these gatherings, they provided an essential perspective on what living as christians meant. Christians were family and, once again, this experience mirrored the heavenly reality.

The New Testament almost always used the Father/Son image to explain the relationship of Jesus and God. It was, therefore, natural to describe christians as adopted into this family (e.g., 1 Thessalonians 1:10; Galatians 4:4-6). Thus christian growth was a matter of maturing from infancy to adulthood (Ephesians 4:11–16; Hebrews 12:4–9) and of learning to relate to each other intimately and responsibly as in an ideal family (e.g., 1 Corinthians 8:11–13; Galatians 6:10; Colossians 3:12–14; 1 John 2:28–3:3).

We need to reflect on the implications of this image for *our* experiences of church. We frequently talk of churches and act as though they were branches of an organisation, rather than as extended families. We often reduce the lists of qualities in passages like Galatians 5:22 and Colossians 3:12–14 to a purely individual affair. We lift ourselves out of our family context and speak about confidence and generosity etc. in some vague and abstract sense, rather than as a call to love deeply from the heart those people with whom we church. Without concrete long-term evidence of such love for each other our "christian" communities are a farce (John 13:34–35).

Body

"While the term 'body' did not originate with him, Paul was apparently the first to apply it to a community *within* the later community of the state, and to the *personal* responsibilities of people for one another rather than for more external responsibilities."[11] Paul used the image in two different ways.

Firstly, Paul called Jesus the head of the body (Ephesians 1:22–23; Colossians 1:18; 2:19–20). Various religious groups of Paul's day believed that cosmic powers existed as intermediaries between their god (or gods) and mankind and that these powers could assist followers to contact their god. Apparently, some christians were tempted to regard these same powers as similarly influential in their own faith. Against this, Paul declared both the supremacy of Jesus over every other power and the perfect and unhindered access to the Father which christians enjoyed because of Christ (e.g., Colossians 1:15–20; Ephesians 1:21). Paul's friends must disregard the claims of these powers and their followers, for Christ is their head.

Secondly, the image described each group of christians

who gathered together. While using the label church *(ekklesia)*, emphasised the act of gathering, the body image focused on the unity and diversity within the group. There are several things we should note here:

1 *Each* group is *the* body of Christ, not *a* body of Christ amongst others. We find *the* body wherever Jesus is through his Spirit (1 Corinthians 12:13)

2 The community contains a wide diversity of gifts and ministries, each unique and irreplaceable (1 Corinthians 12:14-21)

3 The body must honour those who exericse the less spectacular ministries (1 Corinthians 12:22-25; Romans 12:3-6)

4 The bond between the members of the body is so close that they *do* share each others' experiences (1 Corinthians 12:26; Romans 12:15)

A common pattern runs throughout the images of house and heavenly gatherings, family and body. Christians receive their identity, dignity and calling through what Jesus has done on their behalf. They express this new status and responsibility through the simplicity of their times together. At these times, and whenever else their lives intersect, they express the gospel through the quality of their relationships. In other words, they are free to honour and serve each other as Christ has honoured and served them (Colossians 3:12-14; Philippians 2:1-11).

LIFE WITHIN THE COMMUNITIES

Once we understand the above framework, the details of life in those early communities become both clearer and richer. The framework should also help us to critically evaluate our own experiences and traditions. I would like to sketch some of the issues as I see them.

Unity in diversity

The gospel provoked the early christians to expose and tear down many of the social distinctions of their world. Their appreciation of the radical equality which came through being in Christ ended all grounds for racial, class and sexual bigotry (Galatians 3:28; Colossians 3:11). As they churched together they rejected all distinctions between priests and laity, holy men and common people. All found their identity in Christ and all shared equally in his Spirit. A stinging rebuke answered any attempt to place people under religious and social rules and expectations (e.g., Galatians 1:6-3:14; Colossians 2:16-23; James 2:1-13; 4:1-12; 5:1-6).

Yet there were real and necessary differences between christians. In fact, the diversity among these people was a gift which promoted their unity (Ephesians 4:1-16). The Lord gave each group a wide cross-section of gifts which the members would use to serve each other (Romans 12:3-16; Phlippians 2:1-4). In particular, when they assembled, the members had the opportunity, privilege and responsibility to use their respective gifts for the benefit of the others present (1 Corinthians 12:4-31; 14:26).

The common meal clearly expressed both the centrality of relationships in the believers' meetings and the corresponding rejection of religious and social prestige. The meal was not a "service" or special ritual, but simply an ordinary meal in someone's house. It seems that the christians adopted the standard Jewish practice of commencing their meal with the breaking and sharing of bread and ending by drinking wine. They would also pray at both the beginning and the end of the meal. In this regard, no outsider familiar with Jewish custom would have noticed anything unusual.

Yet some things were different—radically different. Greek and Jew, Roman citizens and non-citizens, slaves and free men sat together without regard for positions of honour. In fact, an owner might even serve his slave. There was no priest present even though the prayers, singing and conversations had an unmistakably "religions" tone about them. Thirdly, and most importantly, the hosts and other regulars saw a far greater significance in the bread and cup. They spoke openly of the death and resurrection of Christ, of how he had given his life for theirs and of how they would eat with him one day. And the meal expressed the solidarity and intimacy of the group. It did so, not so much because of the idea of "unity" in the symbolism, but because a common meal is perhaps the most tangible expression of love, care and service.[12]

We seem to have lost more than we have gained over the years. For example, why have we sophisticated this "primitive" practice with our clergy, altars, rails, delicate linen, silver chalices, minute pieces of bread, sips of wine and silence? Some fundamental issues lurk beneath such questions.

Service and responsibility

For example, *why* do we church together? The most common answer is "to worship". Yet the New Testament *never* gave that answer. There was certainly Old Testament precedent for this answer, and descriptions of the activities of the heavenly assembly point in that direction (e.g., Hebrews 12:22; Revelation 4-5). But it is not the answer to be drawn from New Testament practice. Some propose that we meet for evangelism. But again the New Testament disappoints us.

The consistent answer is that we meet to build each other up in our faith through pointing each other to Christ in prayer, scripture, song, teaching and prophecy etc. (e.g., 1 Corinthians 12:4-6; 14:26; Ephesians 4:11-16; Colossians 3:15-16; Hebrews 11:24-25). To say that we meet *explicitly* for worship would be like saying that we meet to be christian. They are one and the same since our whole lives are worship (Romans 12:1-2; Colossians 3:17).

Once again, we see the New Testament emphasis on relationships. We do not live individual "christian lives". We *are* christians. Thus everything we do will express our allegiance to Christ and, like Christ, we must use our lives to serve each other. My welfare, discipline and growth always remain my brothers' and sisters' responsibility—and theirs remain mine (Galatians 5:13-6:10).

Freedom and authority

Robert Banks has captured the radicalness of the early christians' belief in the gospel and fellowship as the basis, context and expression of their understanding and practice of freedom and authority:

According to Paul's understanding, participation in the community centred primarily around *fellowship*, expressed in word and deed, of the members with God and one another. It demonstrates concretely the already-experienced reconciliation between the individual and God and the individual and his fellow-men; the gifts and fruit of the Spirit being the instruments through which this is expressed and deepened.

This means that the focal point of reference was neither a book nor a rite but *a set of relationships*, and that God communicated himself to them not primarily through the written word and tradition, or mystical experience and cultic activity, but *through one another*.[13]

But surely, we ask, we can't adequately guard against error and promote purity without some form of constitution and/or formalised membership. Surely, we ultimately need some form of regulation to preserve both freedom and authority. There may be dangers in ordination (as we usually know it) and denominational hierarchies, we argue, but then we must be realistic about the possibilities of schism. Such is often our reasoning.

I believe that Paul's theology and life rebukes us here. He knew only too well the realities of schism and error. (Think about the immorality and chaos at Corinth; the legalism at Galatia; the weird rules and experiences at Colossae.) Yet he never countered error with law. He did not offer a constitutional safeguard. Rather he pointed people back to their freedom in Christ. He knew the farce of regulations. He knew that they appeared wise and spiritual, but that they lacked any value in controlling sin (Colossians 2:22-23). Today, we often think that it is naive to expect that people can church together without some form of membership and constitution. But who is the more naive?

Paul was not naive. He knew how easily a church could lose sight of Christ and, therefore, of its true identity and calling. He knew that some people would use his proclamation of freedom in Christ to justify their sin (Romans 6:1-2). Yet he hung on to his agenda of building up his friends in the knowledge of the gospel, firmly believing that Jesus would guide and keep them through his Spirit and the intimacy of their friendship. He knew that if they did not love Christ and serve each other, neither constitution nor clergy would make them live as a body.

Do we know better?

DISCUSSION QUESTIONS

1 "The debate about women's ordination totally misses the point. It is not a matter of denying *women* their privilege in Christ, but of denying the dignity and ministry *of the whole body*. If we put down women, it is because the model of ordained ministry as we know it prohibits *all* people from ministering as they can and should. The model makes them second-class christians." Discuss.

2 Where does your church put its money: administration; denominational organisation; buildings; evangelism; aid for your own people; relief for the poor? How do you feel about this? What should you do?

EXERCISES

1 Read the following passages and put together a list of the required characteristics of a leader within the body. Write him or her a job description. The passages are: John 13:1–17; Romans 12:3–6; 1 Corinthians 2:1–5; 2 Corinthians 12:7–10; Ephesians 5:21; 1 Timothy 3:1–7; 1 Peter 5:1–5.

2 A group of you might like to explore the issue of leadership training. Create a big picture around the following questions:

a) Who decides who trains for leadership?
b) What qualifications does the person need? Why?
c) Do your answers to a) and b) sound like what happened in the New Testament?
d) What knowledge, attitudes and skills does a leader need?
e) What knowledge, attitudes and skills do theological colleges impart, either intentionally or unintentionally?

f) Do your answers to a) and b) sound like what the New Testament emphasised?

g) If you could design a leadership training programme, what would you do?

Notes

1 See chapters 7 and 8.

2 Chapters 13 and 14.

3 Edmund Clowney (1979), *The Biblical Doctrine of the Church*, Westminster Theological Seminary, page 25.

4 Robert Banks (1980), *Paul's Idea of Community: The Early House Churches in their Historical Setting*, Lancer/Paternoster/Eerdmans, page 37.

5 I believe the question of how perspectives work in our thinking is critical to applying the Bible meaningfully to life. If you want to explore this further, once again I refer you to Vern Poythress (1987), *Symphonic Theology: The Validity of Multiple Perspectives in Theology*, Zondervan, especially chapters 3, 6 and 7.

6 For an overview of some of the linguistic knots we tie ourselves in see Poythress, *Symphonic Theology*, chapter 6. If you want to dig deeper, you won't do better than Moises Silva (1983), *Biblical Words and Their Meaning: An Introduction to Lexical Semantics*, Zondervan.

7 Throughout the next section I have largely followed the basic outline of Robert Banks, *Paul's Idea*, chapters 3-6. I have also adopted many of his ideas.

8 Banks, *Paul's Idea*, page 34.

9 Banks, *Paul's Idea*, page 47.

10 Banks, *Paul's Idea*, page 49.

11 Banks, *Paul's Idea*, page 70.

12 Robert Banks has reconstructed what he thinks these early home meetings would have been like. See Robert Banks (1985), *Going to Church in the First Century: An Eyewitness Account*, Hexagon.

13 Banks, *Paul's Idea*, page 111.

22 THE FULNESS OF THE KINGDOM

Summary: *The key to this study*
The New Testament writers focused on the importance of Jesus' return for the lives of their audiences rather than on the details of how it would happen. They inherited the Old Testament writers' love of imagery and drama and described our present experience and future hope in terms of a battle. But once again, they grounded this hope in the gospel. We do not wait nervously for Jesus to return, feverishly scanning the newspapers for "the signs of the times" and living in fear of mistakenly receiving the mark of the beast. Christ secured his victory and our inheritance on the cross and in the empty tomb and he has marked us as his people for all time to come.

THE END OF THE BEGINNING

Back in chapter 17, I mentioned that I found it hard to write a chapter on Jesus in a book which was all about Jesus. I now face a similar dilemma. Traditionally, this present chapter should be about *eschatology*, which is the study of the last things, or how God will draw the present age to an end and begin a new one. But throughout our studies we have seen that God has progressively unfolded his plan (to create a new heaven and new earth for his people) ever since the first drama in Eden. Furthermore, the last days and new creation began at the resurrection of Jesus. In this sense, I have written twenty-two chapters on eschatology.

Nevertheless, the New Testament did look forward to Jesus' return knowing that it would bring new realities and experiences for believers and the creation. The New Testament also related our *present* experience to the Lord's return. Yet, once again, these writers saw that the events of the end were shaped by the history which led up to them, and especially by the Lord's death and resurrection. Therefore, as William Dumbrell expresses it, the New Testament anticipated the very last moments of history more as the "end of the beginning" than as the "beginning of the end".[1]

WHAT THE NEW TESTAMENT EMPHASISED

The topic of the Lord's return often has generated considerably more heat than light, not to mention a bewildering array of interpretations and theologies. At one extreme, some people rarely discuss the topic and then only as a dry, cold article of doctrine rather than a rich source of encouragement and hope. At the other extreme, many books, videos and conferences delight in futuristic speculation about current events, nations and dates. In both cases, the discussions and debates seem to focus on a handful of obscure passages and details like the mark of the beast and the so-called millenium in Revelation 13:16–18 and 20:1–3 respectively.[3]

The New Testament writers were far more down-to-earth. Instead of indulging in dry theology or wild speculation, they focused on how the certainty of Jesus' return could help christians to follow him more faithfully.

Jesus: the exalted Lord returns

The events from Jesus' birth to the pouring out of his Spirit on the day of Pentecost caused a fundamental shift in the way God's people thought about the end of the age. Until the time of Jesus, the prophets and visionaries expected a singular day of the Lord which would thoroughly end the old or present age and begin the age to come. But the incarnation of Jesus recast this expectation. Diagram 17 expresses this contrast.[3]

The gospel provides this new shape. Christ became the heavenly man through his resurrection and he took his rightful place at the Father's right hand (1 Corinthians 15:45–48; Ephesians 1:20). Jesus has removed the sting of death for us (the power of the old age) and our identity is secure in heaven (Philippians 3:19–20; Colossians 3:1, 3). Thus we can say that the new age has begun for us (1 Corinthians 10:11; 2 Corinthians 5:17).

Yet we still experience sin and the powers of this age continue to wage war against us and our Lord (Ephesians 6:10–18). In this sense, we continue to live in the old or present age and experience a tension between it and the age to come (Romans 8:38; 1 Corinthians 3:22; Galatians 1:4; Ephesians 1:21; Hebrews 8:13; 1 John 2:15–17).

This tension will continue until Jesus returns to transform heaven and earth. The same power which raised Jesus from the dead will transform his people into his heavenly likeness and bring all things in heaven and earth under his authority

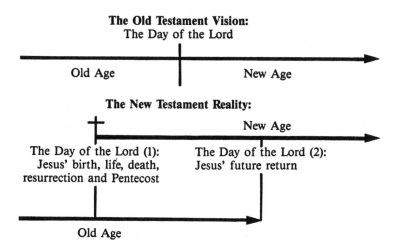

Diagram 17: The shift to the "Now and not yet" pattern of the New Testament

(e.g., Romans 8:20-21; 1 Corinthians 15:22-26; Philippians 3:20-21; 2 Peter 3:10). Thus Jesus will return to complete what he began by unleashing the full power of his death and resurrection:

> In this magnificent finale attention will be riveted on the figure through whom all this has been brought about. Jesus Christ is the one who unites heaven and earth. In Ephesians 1:9, 10 the apostle indicates that God's plan is that the goal of history should be embodied in Christ as he sums up and restores to harmony everything in heaven and on earth and this redounds to the glory of the one who created it all. In this way the drama ends on a (note of praise), for as Christ's cosmic lordship is openly confessed God the Father is glorified (Philippians 2:9-11; 1 Corinthians 15:28; cf. also Romans 11:36).[4]

Jesus' people: heaven's citizens wait to go home

So we experience life essentially as a tension between our struggles with this age, our present experiences of heaven and our hope for a final redemption. We need to explore this further.

Jesus' death and resurrection not only gives us our identity and security, it also shapes our present experience. We are used to thinking about Jesus' death and resurrection predominately in positive terms. In other words, they gained our forgiveness and new access to the Father. But they were also judgement against sin and the enemies of God. Thus, when Jesus and Paul spoke about identifying with the cross, they understood this as an invitation to suffer since the hosts which Jesus defeated would turn their fury against his people (Matthew 16:24-25; John 15:18-20; Philippians 3:10; Colossians 1:24). Like Jesus' own life, we express our heavenly identity and power precisely in the midst of humiliation and weakness.

We know that our destiny is to be with the Lord. If we die before he returns, then we will join him in his heavenly existence (2 Corinthians 5:6-8; Philippians 1:23). Yet that is not our *final* glory. When the Lord returns, he will gather up his people in one great triumphant procession and transform them into his likeness (1 Thessalonians 4:15-17). On this last point, we should note that the New Testament does not teach that we have a soul which lives forever (an immortal soul). Rather, Jesus will (re)create us through the power of his resurrection (1 Corinthians 15:42-57).

Jesus' return should influence the way we live. Paul expected his friends to practise "heavenly-mindedness" because Jesus was in heaven and our lives were now hidden there and would be revealed from there (Colossians 3:1-4). Yet Paul was not saying that our *real* lives were heavenly. He did not encourage his friends to treat life here as irrelevant.

Rather, Paul believed that we could choose to live in one of two directions. Either we align ourselves with this evil age and its rule and powers (the age which acknowledges nothing beyond the earthly), or else we identify with the age to come. The latter choice means basing our lives on the reality of who Jesus now is. If we chose to go this way, then Jesus calls us to express our heavenly life within our human-earthly structures such as marriage, family, friendship, work and the wider society (Colossians 3:5-4:6; 1 Thessalonians 5:1-11; 2 Peter 3:11-18).

Thus hope drives us on. We do not see all that waits for us, yet we trust our Lord to finish what he started. Our hope is in his return. So what is hope?

Hope is the evidence of the Spirit's striving within us to convince and comfort us with the reality of the future (Romans 5:1-5; 8:18-27). The Spirit reassures us that our future is guaranteed in Jesus' future since we will reflect and share in his glory (Colossians 3:4). Moreover, both futures were decided once for all in Jesus' past—his resurrection guarantees ours (1 Corinthians 15:20-23). We know that our lives now are anything but futile, and that one day Jesus will share his glory with us (verse 58).

Jesus' enemies: the judgement draws near

Back in chapter 6 of this book, we noted how a theme of warfare ran through Israel's history. The New Testament also used the theme as a way of understanding what Jesus did.

We also saw that this warfare began in Eden when the serpent deceived the woman, and God announced an on-going hostility between the woman's and serpent's respective offspring (Genesis 3:1-15). So who are these two groups?

The ancient drama   The seed of the woman are the people of God. They are the ones who look to the Lord in faith and who trust that ultimately he will triumph over their enemies. So this includes people such as Abel, Noah, Abraham, Moses, Samuel, David, the prophets and the many faithful Israelites. Finally, the promise, and the warfare, converged on one man, Jesus.

But the seed of the serpent are those who trust in their own strength and wisdom and who oppose God's people. This group includes people such as Cain, the people at Babel, Pharoah, the nations around the Israelites and, sadly, the many Israelites who resisted the Lord, including the religious leaders of Jesus' day.

The Bible also recognised that there were powers behind the scenes of human history and it used various symbolic characters to describe these powers. Sometimes these characters were historical figures who were pictured in terms that went beyond the historical. For example, the king of Babylon is seen attacking heaven (Isaiah 14:12-17), the king of Tyre is like a "super-Adam" who tries to make himself a god (Ezekiel 28:11-19)[5] and the king of Egypt is seen as the monster of the river Nile (Ezekiel 32:2-10). At other times, the Old Testament pictured God's enemies in purely symbolic and non-historical terms. Usually, it used images of beasts to do this, e.g., the great sea or river monster sometimes called Leviathan (see, e.g., Isaiah 27:1) and the strange beasts of Daniel's visions (e.g., Daniel 7:1-12). On yet other occasions, the prophets spoke of unknown nations as symbols of mankind's hostility (e.g., Ezekiel 38:1-6).

Jesus created a new people of God who no longer had a national identity. Now there were people from many nations all gathered around Christ. Thus it was totally inappropriate for the New Testament to speak of specific nations as the true enemies. Instead, the New Testament inherited the Old Testament use of symbolism and used it effectively to describe the enemies of Jesus and his people. Thus we find such figures as the man of lawlessness (2 Thessalonians 2:1-12), antichrist (1 John 2:18), the various beasts in Revelation, the harlot Babylon (Revelation 17-18) and the old Dragon himself (12:3; 20:2).

Our assurance   The point of these descriptions is not to precisely identify the roles, schemes and timetables of the characters. The New Testament used them for very practical purposes.

The imagery shows that we must learn to recognise the powers of darkness that are at work behind and through the events of history. The great danger lies not in isolated bizarre events or individuals, but in the diabolical way in which *every* society, culture and nation promotes the original lie that humans control their own destiny and can solve their own problems. In other words, the institutions, events and trends of *ordinary life* conspire to make us believe that we are gods.

The New Testament dramatised the warfare to reassure God's people of his justice. The Lord is not unconcerned about evil and injustice. At the present time, he continues to unleash his judgement through allowing sin to run its evil course (John 3:19; Romans 1:18-32); when he returns, he promises to judge every expression of sin (2 Thessalonians 1:5-10; Revelation 6:12-17; 20:11-15). But at that time, he will also wipe away every tear and quench every thirst of his people (Revelation 7:15-17).

UNRAVELLING REVELATION

How do you feel when you approach Revelation? Many people feel bewildered, intimidated and even scared. Of all the books in the Bible, with the possible exception of Ezekiel and Daniel which are akin to Revelation, the last book in the Bible is probably also the last one we would read. But why?

I'm convinced that we have made the book hard to read by ignoring three basic points:

1 It uses an unusual style of writing and we should read

it according to what we know about the style and
literary conventions of this sort of literature

2 It focuses on the gospel the same as any other New
Testament book

3 Its structure gives us some key insights into its message.

We will look at each of these points more closely.

The literary qualities of Revelation[6]

The value and power of imagery   Frequently, biblical writers
looked beyond the obvious and literal and drew on other
parts of life to describe something. Rather than bog down
in tedious, analytical descriptions, they lift us out of the scene
and into *another world* to force their original idea upon us
with unexpected power and colour. Consider these examples:

> The Lord is my Shepherd, I will lack nothing.
> He makes me lie down in green pastures,
> he leads me beside quiet waters (Psalm 23:1–2)

> In that day,
> the Lord will punish with his sword,
> his fierce, great and powerful sword,
> Leviathan the gliding serpent,
> Leviathan the coiling serpent;
> he will slay the monster of the sea (Isaiah 27:1)

> Put on the full armour of God so that you can take your
> stand against the devil's schemes (Ephesians 6:11)

> On each side of the river stood the tree of life, bearing
> twelve crops of fruit, yielding its fruit every month. And
> the leaves of the trees are for the healing of the nations
> (Revelation 22:2)

What can we say about interpreting passages like these?
Images are creative pictures, not literal descriptions. The
Lord isn't a shepherd, we don't get dressed in armour (either
seen or unseen!) and I doubt that we will dine on leaves in

the new earth! Yet each of these pictures plays an invaluable role. Imagine if David had simply said "the Lord looks after us"; if Paul only said "the gospel is our defence"; or if John ended his marvellous book without drawing on the earliest images of Genesis to show us that the story had finally reached its fulfilment.

We miss the creative point of an image if we try to dissect it and find some special meaning in every nook and cranny of it. For example, I doubt if we need to explore every possible feature of sheep farming to understand Psalm 23. The mind boggles at the thought of "spiritual footrot" caused by grazing in the still waters! Similarly, there's little point in trying to find subtle "spiritual" differences between the pastures and waters.

Some of the images may well have been borrowed. For example, the picture of Leviathan the sea monster was known in the mythology of the ancient Near East. I doubt that the Lord actually engaged in warfare with any large "fish". Nor is it necessary to read some "spiritual principle" into it by seeing it as a reference to Satan. Rather, Isaiah used the image to complete a section of prophecies (Isaiah 24-27) which emphasised the Lord's total kingship over the creation and his intention to judge the whole earth. From this perspective, Leviathan's death represents the Lord's supremacy over all his foes.

So how does this help us with Revelation?

The role of images in Revelation   There are two key and interrelated points to make. Firstly, everything I've said about images and metaphors, and about not trying to read passages "literally", applies to reading Revelation. Secondly, Jesus revealed himself to John with a message *for the believers of John's time* and in *the thought forms of John's time.*

The Old Testament prophets can guide us here. It was natural for them to explain their future hopes or the next stages of God's story in the images and patterns on which they and their audiences were raised—the patterns of creation, the covenants, Sinai, David, a renewed and rebuilt Jerusalem, and Israel.

When Jesus described himself as the new temple (John

2:19-21), he wasn't ignorant of the "literalness" of the Old
Testament hopes for the temple (Isaiah 2:2-3; Ezekiel 40-48).
Nor was he proposing an alternative "non-literal" plan.
Rather, he looked to the reality behind the Old Testament
symbol and proclaimed that it received its greatest expression
in his own life.

We should follow the lead of Jesus and look for the truths
of the kingdom of God within the images and visions of
Revelation. Instead of looking to the modern nation of Israel
as a key to understanding sections like the Jerusalem vision
of Revelation 21, we should build on the reshaping and
fulfilment of the symbol of Jersualem found in passages like
Galatians 4:26 and Hebrews 12:22-24.

One final remark about interpreting Revelation "literally".
No one consistently interprets the book literally. For example,
many people insist on a literal mark of "666" and on a literal
1000 year imprisonment of Satan following Jesus' return
(Revelation 13:18; 20:1-3). Yet these same people never think
of literal locusts or beasts. They do not think of bizarre
animals having the bodily features of different creatures
(9:7-11; 13:1-2, 11). But who decides which bits are literal
and which are not? We will get much further if we accept
that the book is highly symbolic, and then research the
possible Old Testament and Roman/Greek backgrounds to
its symbols.[7]

The gospel in Revelation

If you have read through *Days are Coming* it will not come
as a surprise to hear me say that the gospel is the key to
Revelation. At each stage of our studies, I have presumed
that Jesus is the climax of the Bible's story and that each
part only ultimately makes sense because of him. The Bible
is not a collection of isolated stories and good advice, but
the record of God's plan to exalt his Son over all and to create
a unique people through his death and resurrection.

We must always remember the key role of the letter to the
seven churches in the book of Revelation (Revelation 2-3).
The Lord gave John this revelation because his people ran
the risk of losing sight of who Jesus was and therefore of

forgetting their own identity and calling. The revelation showed them that there was far more behind the events of their own day than they had realised. it showed them that human history was the stage of an intense battle between God and his enemies. And it showed them that although this battle was as old as mankind, Jesus' death and resurrection had both brought a new intensity to the warfare and settled its final outcome for ever.

The central character of Revelation is undoubtedly Jesus. In several major sections (Revelation 1:5-18; 4:1-5:14; 7:9-17; 12:1-17; 19:1-16; 21:22-22:5) and in numerous smaller passages (e.g., 11:15; 14:1-5, 14-16; 21:6-7), John repeatedly emphasised that Jesus held all authority in heaven and earth because of his victory over death. This is the central thesis of Revelation. Jesus has overcome death and Hades and holds their power because he gave himself as a sacrifice for sin. Perhaps the most graphic expression of this is in 5:5-6 where John *hears* of the majestic and triumphant Lion of Judah, yet *sees* a bloodied lamb. In other words, Jesus calls his people to a deeper appreciation of who he is and what he has done for them; even as he brought them new life through his own death and resurrection, he is strong enough to lead them through their present trials to their final home.

John called his friends to persevere in their faith in the light of who Jesus was. He called them to look beyond what they saw on the surface of history. He called them to recognise that their Lord who gave his life for them was also now the great King of Kings and Lord of Lords who would vindicate his people and gather them into their inheritance.

Some perspectives on the structure of Revelation

Revelation shows the most remarkable structural phenomena. There seem to be many ways by which we can restructure its message. I will outline three of them and offer some ideas about how each structure helps us understand the book.

Ezekiel and Revelation used parallel structures　Ezekiel and Revelation share many features. Both were written to God's people at times when they had lost sight of his control over history and were tempted to give up. In Ezekiel's day, the Israelites had lost their land, temple and kings and lived as exiles in Babylon. In John's day, the believers watched the growing hostility of the Romans towards them and the Jews (with whom the Romans tended to lump them).

Both writers stressed the Lord's complete control over the affairs of men. Ezekiel recorded his visions of the Lord's majesty and power and described how he would judge the nations. John used his visions similarly and also painted vivid scenes of Jesus judging all his enemies. Both writers concluded with visions of restoration which picked up and recast themes they had used earlier in their prophecies to rebuke God's people.

And both writers used the same basic structure to get across their similar message. Their common outline is shown in diagram 18.

Revelation tells the same story from different angles   The desire to work out a neat chronology or explanation of every detail is perhaps the greatest obstacle to understanding Revelation. Such attempts blind us to the breadth of vision which Revelation provides by describing the same features of history from different perspectives.

Feature	Ezekiel	Revelation
Initial vision of the Lord in glory	1:1–28	1:9–20
Judgement on the people of God	2:1–24:27	2:1–3:22
Judgement on God's enemies (represented in general terms)	25:1–32:32	6:1–16:21
Promises of hope for God's people	39:1–37:28	4:1–5:14; 7:1–8:5; 11:15–12:17
Judgement on God's enemies (represented in terms of key symbolic figures involved in a final battle)	38:1–39:29	17:1–20:15
Final visions of restoration	40:1–48:35	21:1–22:17

Diagram 18: Parallels in the structures of the books of Ezekiel and Revelation

If we try to read Revelation as a calender of events we're bound to end up confused. For example, 6:17 (or 7:17) takes us to the Lord's return and the end of history as we know it. Yet 8:6 starts a whole new cycle of judgements. And if that doesn't upset our calender, consider that 12:1 takes us back to the birth of Jesus!

Revelation unfolds its story in a series of cycles. Each cycle covers essentially the same ground yet, progressively, they move closer to the Lord's return and what lies beyond it. The following diagram (diag. 19) shows the approximate extent of each cycle and the relationship of the events it describes to the Lord's return and life after that.

Introduction

Prologue (1:1–8)

The Present Scene (1:9–3:22)

Jesus'
Return

Main Section

Cycle 1: 7 Seals (4:1–8:1)

Cycle 2: 7 Trumpets (8:2–11:9)

Cycle 3: 7 Symbolic Histories (12:1–14:20)

Cycle 4: 7 Bowls (15:1–16:21)

Cycle 5: 7 Pronouncements on Babylon (17:1–19:10)

Cycle 6: White Horse Judgements (19:11–21)

Cycle 7: White Throne Judgements (20:1–21:8)

Final Act: New Jerusalem (21:9–22:5)

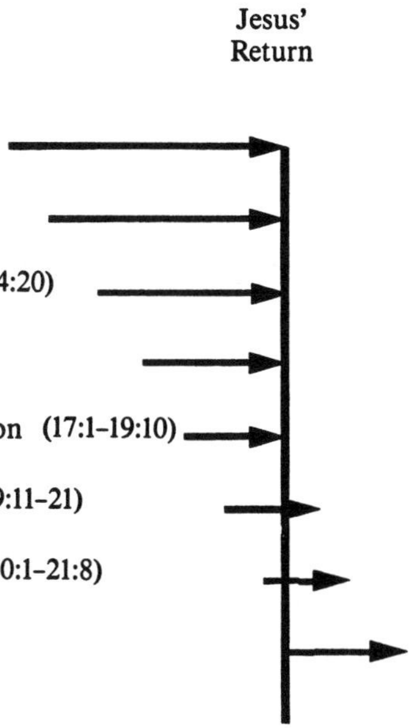

Conclusions

Final instructions and exhortations (22:6–21)

Diagram 19: The seven cycles of Revelation overlap each other while taking the reader progressively closer to the final events and reality

Later sections mirror earlier sections and this effect puts the focus on the central section Many people who study the book emphasise that there are broad similarities between earlier and later sections. Many of them also suggest that 12:1–14:20 (especially 12:1–13:18) is the climax of the book. It is possible that John used an ancient literary device to achieve this effect. The device is known as a chiasm and this is how it works. If we describe each major idea in a verse, chapter or book by a letter (A, B, C, etc.), then the sequence of ideas in a chiasm will be A1, B1, C, B2, A2 or A1, B1, D, C2, B2, A2 (etc). In other words, in each arrangement there is a central section and on either side of this central section the ideas mirror each other, although they are not identical—there are always new elements and emphases.[8] Diagram 20 shows how we might apply this to Revelation.

A[1] *Jesus and the 7 stars: chapters 1–5.* The throneroom visions of Jesus and his people providing the foundation for their hope.

   B[1] *The 7 seals: chapters 6–7.* The overall scene of the drama, including the central characters, events and outcomes.

      C[1] *The 7 trumpets: chapters 8–11.* A generalised picture of devastation on the earth and the battle against God and his people.

         D *The 7 symbolic histories: chapters 12–14.* Seven different portraits which represent the central figures in the drama.

      C[2] *The 7 bowls: chapters 15–16.* A generalised picture of devastation on the earth and the battle against God and his people.

   B[2] *Visions of final judgement: chapters 17–20.* The overall scene of the drama, including the central characters, events and outcomes, but focused on the key symbolic characters introduced in chapters 12–14.

A[2] *Jesus and his bride: chapters 21–22.* The throneroom visions of Jesus and his people enjoying the new heaven and earth.

Diagram 20: Revelation can be seen as two halves which mirror each other and which point to a central set of characters and events

DISCUSSION QUESTIONS

1 "Trying to relate bible prophecies to Israel, the Middle East, Russia and the USA distracts us from the Bible's real message for today. It makes current events more important than the gospel. And it leads to naive assumptions about 'good guys' (e.g., the USA) and 'bad guys' (e.g., Russia) even though the Bible warns us that all nations are corrupt." Discuss.

2 How should the fact that we know that Jesus will return influence personal ambitions and our involvement in society?

EXERCISES

1 It has been suggested that the key figures in Revelation relate to each other by way of a contrast between the true and the counterfeit, i.e., God the Father—the Dragon; Christ—the Beast from the sea; the Holy Spirit—the Beast from the land; the Bride of Christ—Babylon the Harlot. Basing your studies on chapter 13, explore the connections between the first three contrasting pairs. How does this help you understand the book as a whole?

2 Two major ideologies in the Western world are capitalism and marxism. Outline how *both* systems lead people away from Christ by seducing them to put their trust in the system itself.

3 Is there any sense in which *Christianity* has become merely another *ism* which also leads people away from Christ? How?

Notes

1 William Dumbrell (1985), *The End of the Beginning; Revelation 21-22 and the Old Testament*, Lancer/Baker. He begins with the visions of Revelation 21-22 and answers the questions, "How did the Bible's story lead to this conclusion?" and "Why is this such a fitting conclusion to the Bible's story?"

2 An example of this type of speculation is in Hal Lindsay (1970), *The Late Great Planet Earth*, Zondervan. For a balanced and gracious analysis of this approach, see Vern Poythress (1987), *Understanding Dispensationalists*, Zondervan.

3 This has already been covered in chapter 10.

4 Andrew Lincoln (1981), *Paradise Now and Not Yet*, Cambridge University, page 189.

5 Unfortunately the *King James Version* and the *New International Version* obscure this connection by mistranslating Ezekiel 28:14 and 16. They make it read as though Ezekiel identifies the king with the cherub (angel) which ignores the normal sense

of the Hebrew. They did so because they saw this passage (and Isaiah 14) as providing a possible explanation of Satan's origins. However, verse 14 should read, "I appointed you *with* a guardian cherub", and verse 16, "the guardian cherub expelled you".

6 If you wish to explore this further see Graeme Goldsworthy (1984), *The Gospel in Revelation*, Lancer/Paternoster, pages 13–17 and Tremper Longman (1987), *Literary Approaches to Biblical Interpretation*, Zondervan.

7 There are many other issues related to the literary characteristics of Revelation. As a generalisation, I believe that many people find the book difficult because they have little or no experience of literature like J.R.R. Tolkien's *The Lord of the Rings*, or Arthur Miller's play *The Crucible*, in which Miller used the Salem witch hunts of the 1600s to expose the prejudices and naivety of the McCarthy era in the USA in the 1950s. Newspapers, glossy magazines, educational and/or business documents are hardly a good preparation for reading an imaginative book like Revelation.

8 Several people have studied the frequency and significance of chiasms in stories and poetry within both the Old and New Testaments. Unfortunately, most of their work remains in relatively inaccessible academic journals. See Longman, *Literary Approaches*, page 146. If you do have access to journals, try Gordon Wenham (1978), "The Coherence of the Flood Narrative", *Vetus Testamentum*, 28, pages 336–348.

APPENDIX: AN OVERVIEW OF ISRAEL'S HISTORY FROM THE TIME OF THE KINGS

The ninth century (800s BC)

This period was characterised by conflict with near neighbours, particularly Damascus, Syria, Hamath, Moab, and Edom. Occasionally, Israel (the northern kingdom) joined with one of these nations against Judah (the southern kingdom, 1 Kings 15:25–16:7).[2]

Assyria was expanding but was not yet the power it would become in the late 700s.[3] Israel, Syria and a few smaller nations halted Assyria's drive towards them and Egypt at Qarqar in 853. But this alliance fell apart within ten years and soon each was paying tribute to Assyria.

Despite brief periods of security and prosperity, these were not golden years for Israel and Judah.

The eighth century (700s BC)

A great deal happened in this time:
1 Assyria came to prominence
2 Judah and Israel prospered until 721 when
3 Israel ceased to exist
4 The seeds of Judah's destruction were sown

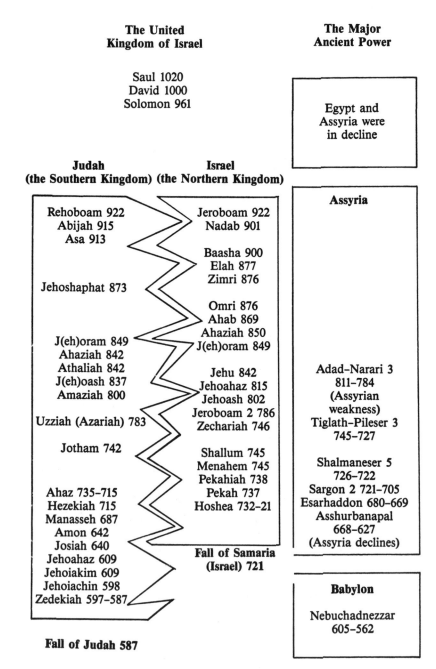

The United
Kingdom of Israel

The Major
Ancient Power

Saul 1020
David 1000
Solomon 961

Egypt and
Assyria were
in decline

Judah
(the Southern Kingdom)

Israel
(the Northern Kingdom)

Assyria

Rehoboam 922
Abijah 915
Asa 913

Jeroboam 922
Nadab 901

Baasha 900
Elah 877
Zimri 876

Jehoshaphat 873

Omri 876
Ahab 869
Ahaziah 850
J(eh)oram 849

J(eh)oram 849
Ahaziah 842
Athaliah 842
J(eh)oash 837
Amaziah 800

Jehu 842
Jehoahaz 815
Jehoash 802
Jeroboam 2 786
Zechariah 746

Adad-Narari 3
811-784
(Assyrian
weakness)
Tiglath-Pileser 3
745-727

Uzziah (Azariah) 783

Jotham 742

Shallum 745
Menahem 745
Pekahiah 738
Pekah 737
Hoshea 732-21

Shalmaneser 5
726-722
Sargon 2 721-705
Esarhaddon 680-669
Asshurbanapal
668-627
(Assyria declines)

Ahaz 735-715
Hezekiah 715
Manasseh 687
Amon 642
Josiah 640
Jehoahaz 609
Jehoiakim 609
Jehoiachin 598
Zedekiah 597-587

Fall of Samaria
(Israel) 721

Babylon

Nebuchadnezzar
605-562

Fall of Judah 587

*Diagram 21: The kings of Judah and Israel and the corresponding
rulers of the major world powers*

5 The prophets formed a hope which looked far beyond their present circumstances

Assyria (Adad–Nirari III, 811–784) crushed Damascus in 802. Israel, and possibly Judah, were forced to pay tribute to Assyria. However, the next three Assyrian kings (783–746) had too much trouble at home to bother with Israel and Judah.

Israel grew stronger under Jehoash (802–786), while Judah became somewhat weak under Amaziah (800–783). Judah tried to take on Israel. Israel didn't want to fight, but did. Judah was defeated but survived.

Under Jeroboam II, the king of Israel (786–746), and Uzziah, the king of Judah (783–742), Israel and Judah enjoyed their greatest power and prosperity since Solomon. But a large population, trade, luxury and military power together with injustice and exploitation were a bad mix. Israel had no reason to feel so optimistic and confident about its future. In this setting, Amos and Hosea prophesied against Israel.

Assyria (Tiglath–Pileser III, 745–27) began to march again. By 739 everyone in the region was paying him tribute. Hosea 7:9,14 reveals a fascinating but sad story of frantic and foolish political manoeuvres by Israel's kings at this time.

Israel (Pekah, 737–732) and Damascus (Rezin) formed an anti-Assyrian alliance and insisted on Judah (Jotham, 742–735 then Ahaz, 735–715) joining them. Judah refused. So Israel and Damascus attacked Judah in 735. This is called the "Syro-Ephraimitic War"—Damascus was now identified with Syria, and Ephraim was an older name for Israel.

During this time Judah (Ahaz) turned to Assyria (Tiglath-Pileser III) for help against Israel and Damascus, despite Isaiah's warning not to do so (Isaiah 7:1–8:18). Consequently, Judah paid a heavy toll to Assyria (2 Kings 16:7).

Assyria destroyed Israel and Damascus and made them into Assyrian provinces. Assyria would have annihilated Israel, but Pekah (Israel) was murdered and Hoshea (Israel) paid tribute (2 Kings 15:30).

But Hoshea didn't remain loyal to his treaty with Assyria. Instead, he rebelled against Assyria (Shalmaneser V, son of Tiglath-Pileser III) by appealing to Egypt for help. Unwittingly, Israel sealed its doom through this alliance.

Egypt was too weak to help. Assyria attacked and Israel fell with only the city of Samaria holding out (724–721). Shalmaneser V (Assyria) died but Sargon II (Assyria) finished his work by destroying Israel in 721.

Israel ceased to exist in 721. Assyria used the area as a resettlement zone for prisoners and refugees from other wars with other nations. These people intermarried with the few remaining Israelites and became the ancestors of the Samaritans of Jesus' day.

Judah survived the Assyrian onslaught but remained under the Assyrian thumb. There were even Assyrian deities in the temple of Jerusalem (Micah 5:12–14; Isaiah 2:6–8, 20; 2 Kings 16:3).

Micah and Isaiah (Judah) echoed the concerns of Hosea and Amos (Israel) as Judah repeated Israel's history. In the middle of this decline, Hezekiah (715–687) tried to reform Judah (2 Kings 18).

About this time Egypt rose to power again. Assyria was plagued by troubles at home, and Egypt sensed this was the opportune moment to strike. Looking to improve their chances against the formidable Assyrians, the Egyptians called on nearby nations including Judah to join them. However, when Ashdod (part of the old Philistine empire) did rebel against Assyria, Egypt did not help them. Obviously, Judah should have heeded this warning against trusting the Egyptians (Isaiah 20; cf. 28:14–22; 30:1–17).

Assyria seemed to lose power at this time as Sennacherib (705–681) followed Sargon. Judah (Hezekiah) tried to rebel against Assyria by refusing tribute (2 Kings 18:7), and once again Assyria had internal problems (2 Kings 20:12–19). Judah then joined in with Egypt, again despite Isaiah's warning (Isaiah 30:1–7; 31:1–3).

From the seventh century (600s BC) until the exile

Assyria moved on the western nations in 701. Tyre fell, while others paid tribute. Although Judah (Hezekiah) held out, they were humbled. Archaeological excavations relating to this time indicate that there was a massive slaughter in

Jerusalem and that Judah paid heavy tribute to Assyria. God ended the siege by sending a plague on Assyria (2 Kings 19:35). Isaiah, looking short-term, promised security for Jerusalem (Isaiah 37:21-35), while Micah, looking long term, promised destruction for Jerusalem (Micah 1:9-16).

Manasseh sealed Judah's doom (687-642) by taking Judah into its worst period of idolatry and immorality (2 Kings 21:1-16; 23; compare 2 Chronicles 33:1-20). His son, Amon (642-640), continued his father's sin.

After the death of Ashurbanipal (669-633), Assyria began to decline. While Jonah had not wanted to go to Nineveh, the great Assyrian city (probably in the 730s), Nahum prophesied in the 650s or later that Nineveh (Assyria) would fall. And it did—in 612—to the Babylonians.

Following Assyria's decline after 633, Josiah (640-609) led Judah in a religious reform (2 Kings 22-23, 2 Chronicles 34-35). This was perhaps partly a response to Jeremiah's and Zephaniah's calls for reform around 640/630.

As Babylon grew in power, Egypt feared for itself and sought to join its old enemy Assyria against Babylon. Josiah tried to stop Egypt's move through Judah but was killed at Megiddo in 609 (2 Kings 23:29-30). So Egypt seized control of Judah (2 Kings 23:31-33). Somewhere in this period (630s), Habakkuk prophesied that Babylon would continue to grow.

Babylon grew quickly and alarmingly. Judah's subjection to Egypt brought idolatry and immorality, which Jeremiah denounced. The prophet promised an end for Judah (Jeremiah 4:5-6:26), and Babylon (Nebuchadnezzar) began the process of fulfilling this word by defeating Egypt at Carchemish (605) and bringing Judah under Babylonian control.

In 601, Egypt managed a small win over Babylon. This encouraged Judah (Jehoiakim 609-598) to revolt against Babylon. But the Babylonians besieged Jerusalem in 598 and sent many of them into exile (2 Kings 23:34-24:6). Babylon then appointed Zedekiah as Judah's king (he was also called Mattaniah, 597-587, 2 Kings 24:17).

Zedekiah accepted Jeremiah's counsel to obey Babylon, but sympathisers with Egypt forced a rebellion in 589. So once again Babylon besieged Jerusalem (589-587) and eventually the city fell (587). Two more deportations in 587 ended Jerusalem. And so began the seventy years captivity prophesied by Jeremiah (Jeremiah 25:11-12).

THE TIME OF THE EXILE

The Babylonians divided up the territory of Judah. They included some of it in the northern province of Samaria and some was taken over by the Edomites (later called Idumeans) from the south-east side of the Dead Sea.

The Babylonians ravaged the countryside of Canaan and it took many years to recover. Many of Judah's fortified towns lay in ruins throughout the entire exile. Only a handful of Jews remained in Judah and Jerusalem; most migrated throughout the world, especially to Egypt.

However, life in Babylon was not all prison and hardship. There were opportunities to mingle and prosper and during this time the Jews involved themselves in intense literary activity. The beginnings of the rabbinical schools and written interpretations of the law probably date from this time. Since they had lost their temple and other institutions, the Jews turned to strict personal interpretation and practice of the law as a means of maintaining their purity. The origins of the local synagogues might also date from here.

AN OUTLINE OF THE HISTORY OF THE JEWS AFTER THE EXILE

Cyrus the Persian overthrew Babylon in 538 and permitted Jews to return under Sheshbazzar and a few years later under Zerubbabel. All the temple objects were returned and Persian funds used to rebuild (1 Chronicles 3:16-19; Ezra 1:2-11).

There was mixed reaction to the prospect of going home. Life in Babylon was good for many and those who returned had their own problems, particularly discouragement and intimidation, and occasionally violence from Samaria.

After an exchange of official letters with the Persians (Ezra 4), the rebuilding came to a halt for sixteen years. To counter this, the Lord raised up Haggai and Zechariah to urge the people not to commit the sins of their fathers, but to get on with the rebuilding (520). The temple was finished in 515.

In the mid-400s, Judea was still a puny province and once again had the same troubles. During this time there were several further returns from exile: one headed by Ezra in 458 which led to renewed festivals, an end to inter-marriage and a covenant renewal (Nehemiah 9); and two visits by Nehemiah (445-433) to urge the rebuilding of Jerusalem's walls.

Malachi prophesied somewhere in the time of Ezra and Nehemiah. The Book of Esther describes the troubles and triumphs of some of those who remained in Babylonia under Persian control.

Alexander the Great, the famous Greek military commander, conquered the Persians in 333. After Alexander's death in 323, his empire was divided between his four generals: the Ptolemies in Egypt and the Seleucids in the fertile crescent (the north-eastern areas of the old Hittites, Medes, Assyrians and Persians). These two groups opposed each other.

Judaea had the unfortunate position of lying between the warring Ptolemies and Seleucids. The Ptolemies ruled Palestine until 198 when the Seleucids defeated them.

A Seleucid, Antiochus Epiphanes IV caused the "abomination of desolation" in 168 by placing Greek idols in the Jerusalem temple as part of his campaign to make Greek culture predominate in the world (see Daniel 9:27b).

This act and the extravagances of some of the Judaean aristocrats led to the Maccabean revolt. From 143-76 this family (they came to be called "Hasmoneans") ruled Judaea and actually extended their territory towards the ancient boundaries of Israel. But from 76-63 their control grew weaker as the Roman (in the west) and Parthian empires (from the eastern lands of Persia, Babylonia) grew stronger.

Then in 63 BC the Romans overran Palestine and established an outsider, Herod the Great (an Idumaean, a descendant of Edom), as the ruler of Judaea (37-4). This is the king who rebuilt the Jerusalem temple, and who plotted to kill the young Jesus (Matthew 2:16).[4]

Notes

1 This diagram was adapted from H. Wendt (1984), *Crossways: A Survey Course of the Narrative and Major Themes of the Old and New Testaments*, Shekinah Foundation, page 180 (used with permission).

2 We need to recall that "Israel" existed as two related but distinct nations from the end of Solomon's reign (922 BC) until the Babylonian invasion of Jerusalem in 587 BC. The northern nation, known as Israel, ceased to exist in 721 BC. The southern nation, known as Judah (named after one of the tribes of the older *combined nation* of Israel), went into exile in Babylon in 587 BC. Although both nations were exiled, we usually refer to the time after 587 BC as *the exile*.

3 All dates are BC.

4 This is only the barest outline of the history of Israel after Solomon. It is vital to read more detailed accounts of Israel's history to understand the background of the Old and New Testaments. See the books by Kenneth Kitchen and John Bright in the section, "For Further Study".

FOR FURTHER STUDY

UNDERSTANDING THE BIBLE AS A WHOLE

Wendt, H. N. 1984. *Crossways: A Survey Course of the Narrative and Major Themes of the Old and New Testaments.* Shekinah Foundation.

METHODS FOR READING THE BIBLE AND
THINKING THEOLOGICALLY

Doriani, Daniel M. 1996. *Getting the Message: A Plan for Interpreting and Applying the Bible.* P&R.

Fee, Gordon D., and Douglas Stuart. 1993. *How to Read the Bible for All It's Worth: A Guide to Understanding the Bible.* 2d ed. Zondervan.

McCartney, Dan, and Charles Clayton. 2002. *Let the Reader Understand: A Guide to Interpreting and Applying the Bible.* 2d ed. P&R.

Nyquist, James, and Jack Kuhatschek. 1985. *Leading Bible Discussions.* 2d ed. IVP.

Poythress, Vern S. 1988. *Science and Hermeneutics: Implications of Scientific Method for Biblical Interpretation.* Academie (Zondervan).

_____. 2001. *Symphonic Theology: The Validity of Multiple Perspectives in Theology.* P&R.

BACKGROUND ABOUT THE BIBLE AND ITS TIMES

Bimson, J. J., and J. P. Kane. 1994. *New Bible Atlas.* 2d ed. IVP.

Bright, John. 1981. *The Kingdom of God: The Biblical Concept and Its Meaning for the Church.* 2d ed. Abingdon.

Bruce, F. F. 1982. *New Testament History.* 4th ed. Pickering & Inglis.

Douglas, J. D., and Norman Hillyer, eds. 1998. *The Illustrated Bible Dictionary.* 3 vols. IVP.

Kitchen, Kenneth A. 1977. *The Bible in Its World: The Bible and Archaeology Today.* Paternoster/IVP.

Robertson, O. Palmer. 1996. *Understanding the Land of the Bible: A Biblical-Theological Guide.* P&R.

Wright, Christopher J. H. 1984. *User's Guide to the Bible.* Lion.

THE LANGUAGE AND LITERATURE OF THE BIBLE

Longman, Tremper, III. 1987. *Literary Approaches to Biblical Interpretation.* Academie (Zondervan).

_____. 1988. *How to Read the Psalms.* IVP.

Pratt, Richard L., Jr. 1990. *He Gave Us Stories: The Bible Student's Guide to Interpreting Old Testament Narratives.* P&R.

Silva, Moises. 1994. *Biblical Words and Their Meaning: An Introduction to Lexical Semantics.* 2d ed. Zondervan.

Thiselton, Anthony. 1977. "Semantics and New Testament Interpretation." In I. Howard Marshall, ed. *New Testament Interpretation: Essays on Principles and Methods.* Paternoster/Eerdmans.

THE OLD TESTAMENT IN THE CONTEXT OF THE WHOLE BIBLE

Drew, Charles D. 2000. *The Ancient Love Song: Finding Christ in the Old Testament.* P&R.

Dumbrell, William J. 1993. *Covenant and Creation: A Theology of the Old Testament Covenants.* Baker.

Dyrness, William A. 1979. *Themes in Old Testament Theology.* IVP.

Goldsworthy, Graeme. 1987. *Gospel and Wisdom: Israel's Wisdom Literature in the Christian Life.* Paternoster.

_____. 1998. *Gospel and Kingdom: A Christian Interpretation of the Old Testament.* Paternoster.

Job, John B. 1984. *The Teaching of the Old Testament.* Scripture Union/Christian Literature Crusade.

Poythress, Vern S. 1991. *The Shadow of Christ in the Law of Moses.* P&R.

Van Gemeren, Willem. 1996. *The Progress of Redemption: The Story of Salvation from Creation to the New Jerusalem.* Baker.

Wright, Christopher J. H. 1995. *Walking in the Ways of the Lord: The Ethical Authority of the Old Testament.* IVP.

THE NEW TESTAMENT IN THE CONTEXT OF THE WHOLE BIBLE

Banks, Robert J. 1994. *Paul's Idea of Community.* 2d ed. Hendrickson.

Dumbrell, William J. 1985. *The End of the Beginning: Revelation 21–22 and the Old Testament.* Lancer/Baker.

Goldsworthy, Graeme. 1994. *The Gospel in Revelation: Gospel and Apocalypse.* Paternoster.

Ladd, George Eldon. 1959. *The Gospel of the Kingdom: Scriptural Studies in the Kingdom of God.* Eerdmans/Paternoster.

Morris, Leon. 1983. *The Atonement: Its Meaning and Significance.* IVP.

Ridderbos, Herman N. 1975. *Paul: An Outline of His Theology.* Translated by John Richard de Witt. Eerdmans.

APPLYING THE BIBLE TO LIFE

Banks, Robert J. 1987. *All the Business of Life.* Albatross/Lion.

Conn, Harvie M. 1982. *Evangelism: Doing Justice and Preaching Grace.* P&R.

Wright, Christopher J. H. 1995. *Walking in the Ways of the Lord: The Ethical Authority of the Old Testament.* IVP.

INDEX OF AUTHORS

INDEX OF BIBLICAL REFERENCES

This index contains passages which I have specifically discussed or have linked to a pattern which may shed new light on the passage. Often I have indexed the passage as a whole chapter or more though I may have only mentioned a few of the verses on some pages.

12—83-4
2 Samuel, 82-4
5-7—35, 82, 86-7, 97
7:1-16—36, 86, 96, 158, 202
1 Kings, 88-9
10—88
20:13-30—78, 115, 120
2 Kings, 88-9
1&2 Chronicles, 89-90, 146
Ezra, 140-4
Nehemiah, 140-4
Esther, 146-8
Job, 105-6
Psalms, 94-102
1—95-6
2—95-7, 158, 163, 202
8—91
18:9-15—78
22:1—178
23—264-5
51—97
68—241-2
110—188-9, 202
150—95-6
Proverbs, 106-7
1-9—109
1:7—104
8—104, 109
Ecclesiastes, 105
Song of Songs, 107
Isaiah, 117
1-12—171-2
1:10-17—64-5
2:2-4—88, 98, 242, 266
4:2-6—88, 98
5:1-7—56
6—115, 171-2
11—91, 108, 158
14:12-17—262
24-27—79, 120-1
27:1—262, 264-5
40:1-11—161
42:1-7—36, 56, 136, 160, 164, 208
49—36, 56
50:4-9—56
51—98, 177, 242

52:13-53:12—36, 56, 65, 91, 168, 186
56—243
60:1-3—100
61:1-4—91, 159
Jeremiah, 126-8
7—64-5, 98
25:15-38—177
31:31-34—36, 134-7, 176-7, 211
Ezekiel, 46, 120, 128-31, 267-8
1—129
8:1-11:25—129
16&23—46, 129, 177
28:1-19—262
32:2-10—262
38-39—79, 262
40-48—99, 126, 266
Daniel, 131-3
7:11-14—78-9, 91, 157, 168
Hosea, 117
6:6—64-5
Joel, 116
2—78, 152, 178, 208
Amos, 117
1-2—34, 87-8
5—64, 78
9—79
Obadiah, 119
Jonah, 116
Micah, 118
6:6-8—64-5
Nahum, 118
Habakkuk, 118
Zephaniah, 118, 120
Haggai, 141, 144
Zechariah, 90, 144-5
3—65
9:1-13—99, 158, 244
12-13—90, 177
14—90, 99
Malachi, 145
3:1-4—145, 161
4:1-6—145, 161
Matthew
1-7—46-7
1:18-23—159
2-4—160-4
8:32-39—243
12:28—159, 163, 167
13—171-3

16—244
23:37—164
27—178-9
Mark
8:27-31—164, 176
10—159, 176, 178
13—197-8
14-15—177-8
Luke
1—79, 91, 159-160
2-3—91, 161-2
4:16-21—28, 159
9:28-36—121
22-23—176-9
24—187-8
John
1—109, 121, 158, 189
2:12-22—100, 265-6
4—158, 222
8—100, 180
12:12-19—91
12:20-38—176, 244
13—91, 200-1
15:1-7—56
19:1-22—91, 178
Acts
Sermons—152
1:8—213
2—116, 122, 152, 208, 212-13
8—212-13
10—212-13
12—219
19—212-13
Romans
1:3-4—198-99
4—33, 180
5:1-11—181, 261
5:12-21—137, 229
6—191, 229-31, 261
8—180, 182, 211, 219, 231
16:25—122, 151
1 Corinthians
12—214, 251-52
15—189-92, 209, 229, 261
2 Corinthians
1—211, 231
3:7-18—53, 56, 210-11
12:7-10—71
Galatians, 68-9

3:6-4:7—37, 228, 249
4:25-27—247-49
Ephesians
1—151, 190, 211, 231, 250, 260
2:5-6—247-9
2:20—213
3:2-6—122, 151
4:11-16—249-50
6:10-18—264-65
Philippians
2:1-11—72, 91, 137, 199-201
3:19-21—122, 247-9
Colossians, 69-70, 233-4
1:9-14—233-4
1:15-20—29, 109, 234
1:26-27—122, 151
2:1-8—29, 109, 122, 151, 189, 234
2:16-23—29, 234
3:1-17—247-50
3:18-4:6—29, 234
1 Thessalonians
5:1-10—79
Hebrews, 67-8
1—91, 189, 201-2
2:10-18—100
4:14-5:10—100
6-10—66-7
8:7-13—137
9-10—179, 202
12:18-24—101, 202, 247-9
13:14—101
1 Peter
2:4-10—56
2 Peter
3—79, 153
Revelation, 263-70
1—203-4
2-3—266-7
5—267
12-14—270
13—258, 266
17-18—263
19:11-21—79
20—77, 258, 266
21-22—203-4
22:1-5—26, 264-5